CW01481276

# DECISION-MAKING IN GREAT BRITAIN
## DURING THE SUEZ CRISIS

# Decision-Making in Great Britain During the Suez Crisis

## Small Groups and a Persistent Leader

BERTJAN VERBEEK
*University of Nijmegen*

ASHGATE

Published by
Ashgate Publishing Limited
Gower House
Croft Road
Aldershot
Hants GU11 3HR
England

Ashgate Publishing Company
Suite 420
101 Cherry Street
Burlington, VT 05401-4405
USA

Ashgate website: http://www.ashgate.com

**British Library Cataloguing in Publication Data**
Verbeek, Bertjan, 1960-
    Decision-making in Great Britain during the Suez Crisis :
    small groups and a persistent leader
    1. Great Britain. Cabinet - Decision making 2. Group decision
    making - Great Britain - History - 20th century 3. Great
    Britain - Foreign relations - Egypt 4. Great Britain -
    Foreign relations - 1945-1964 5. Egypt - Foreign relations -
    Great Britain 6. Egypt - Foreign relations - 1952-1970
    7. Egypt - History - Intervention, 1956
    I. Title
    327.4'1'062

**Library of Congress Cataloging-in-Publication Data**
Verbeek, Bertjan, 1960-
    Decision-making in Great Britain during the Suez crisis : small groups and a persistent
    leader / Bertjan Verbeek.
        p. cm.
    Includes bibliographical references and index.
    ISBN 0-7546-3253-9
        1. Egypt--History--Intervention, 1956. 2. Great Britain--Foreign
    relations--1945-1964--Decision making. I. Title.

DT107.83.V47 2003
327.41062'09'045--dc21                                             2002041752

ISBN 0 7546 3253 9

Printed and bound in Great Britain by Biddles Ltd *www.biddles.co.uk*

# Contents

# List of Tables

# Preface

At least three compelling reasons exist for another book on Suez. First, a book-length application of a foreign policy analysis framework to British decision-making during Suez was still missing. Although many books on foreign policy analysis refer to the case, no full analysis has so far been conducted. This book thus offers something radically different compared to most studies of Suez, most of which are mainly historical analyses.

Second, this study offers a rather new interpretation of British decision-making on Suez. Many existing studies of Suez emphasize the role of Prime Minister Sir Anthony Eden and often focus on the matter of collusion with Israel. This study demonstrates that small group dynamics in the institutional context of cabinet decision-making in the British political system is much more important in explaining British decision-making than the personality and physical condition of the Prime Minister at the time. One of the few studies referring to the group aspect of decision-making as a major explanation of events is Robert Rhodes James's biography of Anthony Eden (James, 1986; cf. Louis, 1986). This book will show that individual factors related to the Prime Minister, notably his cognitive belief system and leadership style, mattered. However, contrary to many other books on Suez, this study argues that they were not as much related erratically to his temper or weak health, but systematically to the worldview he had built up in his early experience in politics. Moreover, the Prime Minister's impact was felt through the mechanism of the small groups he chaired.

Third, this book will be equally important to the (sub)disciplines of International Relations and Foreign Policy Analysis. The study will be of interest to scholars of International Relations because the empirical problem described above leaves the dominant explanation of international relations, neorealism, rather puzzled. This study thus offers the possibility of determining more precisely the interrelationship between systemic constraints on states' behaviour and the actual behaviour of states under such constraints. It thus adds 'second and first image' explanations to systemic ones. The book is also directed at foreign policy scholars because rather than merely pointing to the explanatory value of individual cognitive beliefs systems and small group dynamics it will demonstrate the extent to which these variables actually *explain* British foreign policy at the time. Many studies of cognitive belief systems, small groups dynamics as well as bureaucratic politics limit their analysis to describing the occurrence of such factors, yet fail to argue to what extent they really matter in explaining policies. This book will.

# Acknowledgements

This book would not have been possible without the criticism over the years of Agnes Akkerman, Jim Allen, Jean Blondel, Michael Doyle, Paul 't Hart, Charles F. Hermann, Hans Hermann Hoppe, Leo Huberts, Hans Keman, Kees van Kersbergen, Robert H. Lieshout, Mitya New, Michael Nicholson, Wim Noomen, Bob Reinalda, Steve Smith, Susan Strange, Douglas T. Stuart, Bengt Sundelius, Eric Stern, Sjaak Toonen, Anna van der Vleuten, and D.C. Watt.

I am especially grateful to the hospitality of Laurence Morel and Kevin and Sarah Woodfield who gave me a real home during the archival research. At the Public Record Office Michelle Ann Lewis was an inestimable help. I am indebted to the staff at Ashgate for their prompt and accurate advice.

I wish to express my gratitude to SAGE Publications Ltd. for permission, on behalf of copyright holder © NISA: Nordic International Studies Association, to re-use the following material: Bertjan Verbeek, 'Do Individual and Group Beliefs Matter? British Decision-Making during the 1956 Suez Crisis', *Cooperation and Conflict. Nordic Journal of International Studies*, Vol. 29, 1994, pp. 307-32. The theme that images shared by the foreign policy elite may affect the contents of decisions taken by small groups suffering from Groupthink found its first formulation in that article. In that same publication tables 6.1 and 6.5 appeared as tables 1 and 2 (on pages 317 and 320, respectively).

Chapter 1

# Introduction: The Puzzle of Suez

## Introduction

This book puts forward three major claims. First, decision-making in Great Britain during the Suez crisis of 1956 was concentrated in the hands of a small group of policy-makers, who met in different organizational settings. Throughout the crisis the group would sometimes meet as part of the full Cabinet. At different instances, it would gather as the so-called Egypt Committee. On other occasions different members of the group would convene informally. Second, the deliberations of this small group of policy-makers failed to meet important procedural criteria of high quality decision-making. This failure contributed to what in the literature generally is considered a policy fiasco: the Anglo-French bombing of Egypt and invasion of the area of the Suez Canal in October-November 1956. Small group dynamics, including the leadership style of Prime Minister Sir Anthony Eden, constitute the major explanation of the group's poor performance. Moreover, parts of the contents of the group's decisions are related to its common perspective on Anglo-American relations regarding the Middle East and to the Prime Minister's individual beliefs regarding the conduct of international affairs. Third, the institutional setting of the British political system is conducive to promoting the impact of small groups and their leader on decision-making, especially in crisis situations. The hierarchy between Prime Minister, Senior Ministers, Junior Ministers, and backbenchers threatens the quality of decision-making, within the full Cabinet as well as in special bodies like the Egypt Committee.

The development of this threefold claim is prompted by the next section's description of Britain's failure to meet important procedural criteria of high quality decision-making and of their consequences for its foreign policy during the Suez crisis. This will result in the formulation of an empirical puzzle of Suez. The following section takes stock of the existing literature on Suez, both in history and in political science, in order to assess existing resolutions to this empirical puzzle. This will give rise to a theoretical puzzle of Suez, followed by an overview of the way in which the book's subsequent chapters will resolve both puzzles of British decision-making during the Suez crisis. This introductory chapter will be concluded with a short chronology of the events leading up to the Suez crisis, the crisis itself as well as its aftermath.

## The Empirical Puzzle

For Great Britain the Suez crisis is usually portrayed as a major foreign policy fiasco. In the short run, Great Britain failed to reach its, as we will see, implicit and contradictory, immediate objectives. The Anglo-French military intervention did not undo Egypt's nationalization of the Suez Canal Company of 26 July 1956 or result in the downfall of its President Gamal Abdul Nasser. It also soured the 'special relationship' between Great Britain and the United States as well as Britain's standing among the international community. Moreover, Great Britain suffered economically. Supporting Sterling had cost the country a large portion of its financial reserves. Sunken ships blocked passage through the Suez Canal. Cargo had to sail pass Cape of Good Hope instead, thus increasing the price of many goods, including oil. In the long run, the Suez crisis ended Great Britain's influential position in the Middle East, although it would engage in limited military action in the region for at least four times between 1957 and 1963 (Wilkie, 1984). More generally, Suez implied the reduction of Great Britain, together with France, to the rank of secondary power. After Suez, Prime Ministers Macmillan, Home, and Wilson tried to maintain major power status for Great Britain. However, Great Britain no longer had the financial means to sustain this claim. In 1968, the Wilson government recognized the impossibility of conducting a major power's foreign policy and decided to abandon British military presence 'east of Suez' by 1971. Domestically, the Suez crisis produced a rift in the country. British citizens remained highly divided on the issue of military intervention. Even today, people over 60 still harbour very strong sentiments regarding the conduct of Great Britain and its Prime Minister at the time. Of course, for him, Sir Anthony Eden, the crisis resulted in a personal defeat with his resignation on 9 January 1957. Arguably this was not directly prompted by the aborted intervention itself, but by his poor health (James, 1986) or his absence from Whitehall at the end of 1956, which prevented him from affecting the decisions taken by the top of the Conservative Party (Carlton, 1981).

Interestingly, throughout the crisis British decision-makers had anticipated several of these negative consequences. Senior Ministers, such as Harold Macmillan, had made it clear that failure to undo Egypt's nationalization of the Suez Canal Company, if necessary by force, would reduce Great Britain's international status to that of Denmark. Members of the Cabinet and the Egypt Committee regularly warned that British weakness would inevitably lead to the end of its influential position in the Middle East. It is thus reasonable to assume that in the autumn of 1956 British decision-makers must have been convinced that the Anglo-French intervention was going to be a success. In that light it becomes all the more puzzling why on 6 November 1956 they decided to halt the advance of their troops, scarcely 36 hours after the invasion. Their troops had captured Port Said and were almost halfway along the isthmus that would bring them to Suez, so close to accomplishing their operational objectives. The reasons for stopping military operations reveal the fundamental puzzle of British decision-making during the Suez crisis. Why did British policy-makers fail to anticipate the lack of American support?

Lack of American support was the main reason why the Cabinet decided to halt the invasion. Throughout the crisis until the Cabinet meeting on 6 November had British policy-makers counted on the United States to deter the Soviet Union from interfering, as well as to provide diplomatic and financial support. It the end the United States was helpful on the first count only. Diplomatically, the United States actively worked against France and Great Britain at the United Nations during the week between the sailing of the Anglo-French Armada from Gibraltar, Oran, Malta, and Cyprus on 30 October and the actual assault on Port Said on 5 November. France and Great Britain's legal fig leaf had been to separate Egyptian and Israeli troops fighting near the Suez Canal in order to protect international shipping and had co-ordinated their plans with Israel to that effect. One day after the agreed-upon Israeli attack on Egypt, the United States, however, introduced a resolution in the Security Council calling for Israeli withdrawal, thus removing the basis for Anglo-French intervention. On 30 October France and Great Britain had to use their veto in the Security Council for the first time ever. Later that night, the United States lent crucial support to a Yugoslavia-sponsored Uniting for Peace Resolution, calling for an emergency session of the General Assembly on 1 November.[1] Over the next five days the United States tried to muster enough international support to isolate Great Britain and France diplomatically.

The final blow, however, was dealt on 6 November. In the middle of the Cabinet meeting, Chancellor of the Exchequer Harold Macmillan was informed that the United States would use their veto power at the International Monetary Fund to ensure that the procedure for a British request for a loan could not be started. From mid-September the position of Sterling had weakened. In several internal memoranda that month, Sir Edward Bridges, Permanent Secretary to the Treasury, had pointed out to Macmillan that Sterling would only survive a military adventure in the case of American support 'and a fairly united Commonwealth'. If Great Britain and France decided to go it alone, 'we can expect little or nothing' to support the currency.[2] Until mid-October Sterling still seemed strong enough. Shortly before the start of hostilities, however, on 26 October Sir Leslie Rowan, a high Treasury official, warned Macmillan that towards the end of the year gold and dollar reserves would be below $2,000 million, 'which has always been regarded as a rather crucial dividing line'.[3] Nevertheless, on 30 October, two days into the crisis, a party of Macmillan, Rowan, and Sir Roger Makins, the new Under-Secretary at the Treasury,[4] decided not yet to turn to the IMF for help.[5] As a matter of fact, during the Cabinet meeting that morning, when the decision was formally taken to issue an 'urgent communication' to Egypt and Israel to withdraw from the Canal zone within 24 hours, American financial assistance was discussed. The cabinet expected it to be forthcoming if the United States were not alienated 'more than was absolutely necessary'.[6] Even mounting American opposition at the United Nations did not particularly worry them. Indeed, an IMF loan was not asked for until 5 November. The fact that Great Britain waited for a whole week despite the rapid weakening of Sterling (cf. Kunz, 1989; Kyle, 1991), and despite clear signals of American opposition to Anglo-French policies, suggests that British decision-makers counted on American support until the very last moment. This is all the more puzzling because from the outset of the crisis American policy-makers had given at best very mixed signals about American support. At no point, however, did the United States promise explicit support for a military solution to the crisis. As a matter of fact, the British Embassy in Washington persistently sent warnings to London not to count on American support for the use of force.

The persistent belief that American support would be forthcoming played a crucial role in British decision-making. As a matter of fact it served as the basis for several implicit and explicit choices that would contribute to the outcome of the crisis. These choices ensured that British decision-making failed to meet at least three criteria of high quality decision-making. In the decision-making literature criteria have been developed to judge the procedural quality of decision-making. Their application makes it possible to investigate the relationship between the quality of decision-making and specific outcomes of the policy eventually chosen. Such an analytical focus prevents the scholar from inadvertently pronouncing a verdict on a specific policy. Indeed, what constitutes a policy fiasco is never obvious, but rather the product of a variety of political and social factors (Bovens and 't Hart, 1996). Table 1.1 presents the seven procedural criteria of high quality decision-making that are commonly distinguished in the literature (cf. Herek et al., 1987).[7]

### Table 1.1 Procedural Criteria of High Quality Decision-Making

1.  Survey of objectives
2.  Survey of alternatives
3.  Search for information
4.  Assimilate and process new information
5.  Reconsider originally rejected alternatives
6.  Evaluate the costs, risks, and implications of the preferred choice
7.  Develop implementation, monitoring, and contingency plans

*Source:* Adapted from Janis (1989, p. 91) and Haney (1997, p. 48).

The British decision to go ahead with the so-called Challe-plan failed to meet at least three such criteria, all of which were related to the crucial assumption that American support for the use of force would be forthcoming. This plan, put forward by the French General Maurice Challe, envisaged an Anglo-British 'policing action' to separate Egyptian and Israeli forces in order to protect the free flow of traffic through the canal. It was originally presented to British policy-makers as a contingency plan in case Israel was to attack Egypt. Later on, British policy-makers became aware that collaboration between French and Israeli officials already existed and grudgingly had to engage into detailed planning with Israel themselves (cf. Challe, 1968).

*No Explicit Identification and Ranking of Objectives*

From the outset of the crisis British policy-makers had been caught in a dilemma regarding their objectives. Officially, they had declared the restoration of international control of the canal as their official aim. At the same time, they wanted the downfall of Nasser and the end of Egypt's meddling with British policies in the Middle East. Of course, this was never officially proclaimed. Neither the Arab world nor the United States would ever agree to an occupation of a large proportion of Egyptian territory. However, military action that would remain confined to the canal area might not be sufficient to provoke Nasser's removal from power. This dilemma was more acute, once on 12 October the so-called Challe-plan had been adopted. This plan drew its justification from protecting the free flow of traffic through an international waterway rather than from toppling a 'dictator'. The only way out of the dilemma was not to raise the possible incompatibility of the official and non-official objectives, to limit any occupation to the area of the canal and believe that Nasser's regime would fall immediately after the start of military operations.

*Lack of Contingency Plans*

By consequence, British policy-makers were not prepared to face the various contingencies of such a move. First, they were very reluctant to consider the possibility that Anglo-French troops might have to stay longer in Egypt than envisaged in order to protect a new, presumably anglophile, government. Indeed, the Chiefs of Staff warned that this might require the occupation of Cairo and possibly Alexandria.[8] Second, the assumption that quick and successful military operations would provoke the fall of Nasser,[9] prevented British policy-makers from examining the contingencies of the military time table. At no point was there any discussion of the dangers of the lack of speed of the Anglo-French Armada. They never considered the possibility that international (and domestic) public opinion might turn against France and Great Britain with the ships at sea and aircraft bombing targets in Egypt. British policy-makers assumed that procedures at the United Nations would amount to going through the motions. Instead, they must have felt entrapped in their operational plans. The only way out was the decision to advance the drop of paratroopers as much as possible in order to present the world with a *fait accompli*.

*Limited Search for, and Selective Processing of, Information*

The adoption of the Challe-plan was a way out of a crucial dilemma as will be argued in chapter five (see pp. 108 ff.). It provided a legalistic justification for a military intervention in the canal area. British policy-makers feverishly looked for justifications of the plan in international law, convinced that international public opinion and, especially, American officials would be persuaded as well. On 29 October, the Lord Chancellor presented such an international legal argument to the Cabinet in a memorandum entitled 'The Right of Intervention'.[10] Advice from the

Law Officers at the Foreign Office that the arguments used were invalid under international law were ignored (Johnman, 2000). More importantly, as will be shown in Chapter five, British senior policy-makers ignored or misread incoming information on 30 and 31 October that the Americans would not support military intervention, not even remain neutral, but would actually work hard against French and British plans.

All in all then, the Challe-plan seemed to offer a justification of the use of force in Egypt without the risk of alienating the actor whose support was deemed essential for the success of the operation, the United States. At the same time, the adoption of the plan implied that one had to stick to that justification. By consequence, it implied that Anglo-French troops could not march to Cairo, in order to put an end to General Nasser's grip on Egypt and on British influence in the Middle East. It thus put at risk an important, possibly the most important, yet implicit, British (and French) objective.[11]

Almost 50 years later, one remains puzzled by British decision-making. Why did policy-makers ignore the signals that the United States would not support the use of force? Throughout the crisis American foreign policy had been directed at discouraging France and Great Britain from military intervention. The principal American strategy was to invent diplomatic moves in order to let French and British feelings cool down and create a situation that would not justify the use of force. The two international diplomatic conferences in London as well as talks at the United Nations in New York during the autumn of 1956 served that particular purpose. At the same time, in their messages and conversations American policy-makers, such as President Eisenhower and Secretary of State John Foster Dulles, persistently tried to dissuade the British and French policy-makers from military intervention. At many instances, British civil servants, such as British Ambassador to the United States Sir Roger Makins, warned their superiors that American support would not be forthcoming in the event of war. If British decision-makers were persistently faced during that summer, with so many indications, from various sources, that American support, at the very least, was not a guarantee, how then to explain the way they treated these pieces of unwelcome information? How to explain their eventual decision to embark on a plan that constituted the thinnest veil of legal justification, that would offer opponents the opportunity to mobilize support with the ships at sea for almost a week, and that would not even guarantee the main prize, the end of the Nasser regime? This book seeks to solve that puzzle.

**The Theoretical Puzzle**

Historians and political scientists have formulated various answers to the empirical puzzle of Suez. As a matter of fact, the Suez crisis has been the subject of many studies in both disciplines. Within that collection British, and to lesser extent American, foreign policy has been the most popular theme, no doubt in part due to the availability of official sources.[12] What explanations of British decision-making have been put forward so far?[13] Roughly, four different sources of explanations can be distinguished: the international political system; the domestic political system; the British foreign policy elite; and, finally, the Prime Minister himself.[14]

## The International Political System

The international environment in which the Suez crisis occurred was characterized by change. Globally, during the 1950s the world had increasingly developed into a bipolar system. The United States and the Soviet Union, each dominating an alliance, were each other's global adversaries. The growth of this bipolar world had taken place at the expense of traditional great powers such as France and Great Britain. At the same time, the world had witnessed the growth of Third World nationalism and a subsequent increase in major decolonization struggles, including in the Middle East.

Within the political science discipline, neorealist systemic theories of international relations (e.g., Waltz, 1979) consider the Suez crisis as exemplary (see Waltz, 1988). The United States brought the Anglo-French intervention to a standstill because it did not serve the American national interest. From the United States' perspective, the massive use of force by the two traditional colonial powers in the region ran the risk of driving genuine Middle East nationalism into the hands of the Soviet Union, thus upsetting the regional and global balance of power. Given the distribution of power, British and French national interests were subordinate to those of the United States. This account is often confirmed by historical studies that adopt an international perspective (e.g., Neff, 1981; Carlton, 1988). Neorealist theories of the international political system certainly account for the outcome of crisis. They have more difficulty in explaining why Great Britain went to war, itself having recognized the importance of American support, while many signs pointed to its unlikelihood. Neorealism allows for the possibility that states fall prey to misperception and miscalculation, which may account for their inability to assess accurately the distribution of power and the stakes involved (Waltz, 1979). Yet, it does not claim to provide an explanation of misperceptions and miscalculations. Therefore, although neorealism provides an explanation for the British decision to stop the invasion on 6 November, it cannot account for British decision-making prior to that date.

In one respect, however, does neorealist theory contribute significantly to British decision-making during Suez, and international crisis decision-making in general. Neorealist theory is deduced from the central notion of international anarchy, the absence of an overriding central authority in international relations. Anarchy implies, amongst other things, that states can never be certain of the intentions of other states (cf. Schelling, 1966). One of diplomacy's functions therefore is to attempt to obtain as much relevant information as possible on the intentions of other states. From that perspective, the British misperception or miscalculation of American intention is not exceptional. At no point did the United States government literally announce that it would oppose the use of force by France and Great Britain under all circumstances. The logic of anarchy explains why. Such an announcement would have given free way to Egypt to ignore every demand regarding the issue of the Suez Canal Company and the canal itself. It might also have given the wrong signal the Soviet Union. Despite the fact that uncertainty is a normal condition under anarchy, also during the Suez crisis, it remains puzzling why British policy-makers did not show more care in assessing the American attitude and took, from a neorealist perspective, the wrong decision.

Constructivist theories of international relations emphasize the emergence of international norms and their impact on the behaviour of states. They argue that states are not motivated exclusively by the implications of international anarchy, but may also develop and respect specific codes of conduct (e.g., Klotz, 1995). Starting from this framework, Risse interprets British (and American) policies over Suez as the consequence of the British failure to abide with the norm developed among western allies to keep each other informed and consult each other timely on major foreign policy decisions (Risse, 1995). It is certainly true that during the month before the Anglo-French invasion it was official British policy not to inform the United States of developments. This situation was worsened by the absence of a British Ambassador in Washington during that period. Risse, however, does not provide a satisfying explanation for the British attitude. This study will argue that the explanation can be found in the individual cognitive belief system of Sir Anthony Eden.

*Domestic Politics*

British domestic politics often figures in analyses of British decision-making during the Suez crisis (e.g., Epstein, 1964; Thomas, 1986). Some studies pay attention to the government's struggle to maintain its majority in the House of Commons. The main conclusion is that the Suez crisis occasioned the first instance that Great Britain entered a major, armed conflict without a bipartisan consensus. The government therefore had to keep its own ranks disciplined. Occasionally, this implied walking a thin line between hawks and doves within the Conservative Party. Party politics certainly added to the pressure in early October when the annual Conservative Party conference at Llandudno took a very hawkish stand on Suez at a moment when the use of force seemed very unlikely (cf. Epstein, 1960). Yet, relatively little is known of the exact effect of domestic British politics on actual decision-making. Some analyses are available of public opinion and of the attitude of British newspapers (Parmentier, 1980; Negrine, 1982). However, their precise impact on decision-making remains unclear. Similarly, although various accounts exist of the military side of Suez, the precise impact of military planning on political decision-making remains under-explored (with the possible exception of Grove and Rohan, 2000).

Political scientists, mainly Epstein, have been correct in pointing to the impact of party politics on Cabinet decision-making. At the same time, however, they have neglected how domestic institutions, especially the formal and informal rules of Cabinet decision-making in Great Britain, mediate between the majority party in the House of Commons and the Cabinet. These rules favour the position of so-called Senior Ministers. This study will show that these decision rules contributed to the centralization of decision-making into the hands of a small group of ministers and thus facilitated its control over the party in the House of Commons.

*The Political Elite*

Several studies point to the attitude of the British political elite in explaining Great Britain's foreign policy during the Suez conflict. To the extent that they focus on the elite's attitude towards the United States, they tend to emphasize the risks of long term co-operation, such as between Great Britain and the United States. Long-standing allies tend to take too much for granted. In particular, successful co-operation in the past may enhance the occurrence of two types of problems. First, it may create the false impression that both allies think they know how the other operates. It makes policy-makers insensitive to signals of the opposite, thinking they know better. Accounts of Suez often suggest that Eisenhower, Eden and Macmillan misread each other assuming that their intensive collaboration during the Second World War would ensure consensus. Second, successful past co-operation may produce the incorrect expectation that both continue to have common interests. It blinds policy-makers to the possibility that interests may diverge in a new situation. Analyses of Suez point to the British failure to see that American interests might not lie with continued British influence in the Middle East, despite common Anglo-American Cold War objectives.

These stories of misperception by the political elite in both countries figure in studies from political science (e.g., Neustadt, 1970; Jervis, 1976; Jönsson, 1990; Risse, 1995) as well as history (e.g., Watt, 1965; Neff, 1981; Watt, 1984). Although they point to relevant mechanisms that mediate between elite perception and policy-making, they suffer from two deficiencies. First, they give an overall portrait of the British policy elite without stipulating which members of the elite were influential at specific instances during the crisis (with the possible exception of Neustadt, 1970). Second, they offer only a general account of the roots of British perceptions (with the exception of Watt, 1984). This book offers a reconstruction of the structure of decision-making in Great Britain during the Suez crisis (see Appendix 2). It therefore traces the influence of individual members of the political elite. It can thus establish with more certainty how and why misperceptions occurred. In addition, this study argues that during the Suez crisis several unrealistic expectations of British policy-makers regarding American support were rooted in their specific experiences with Anglo-American co-operation in the Middle East in the 1950s.

*The Prime Minister*

Several studies focus on the political drama of Prime Minister Sir Anthony Eden. Many authors have been puzzled by a man, who had generally been considered as an excellent Foreign Secretary, who in 1954 had lived his *annus mirabilis*, but only two years later had to end his political career during a crisis which should have been his expertise (Carlton, 1981; James, 1986). Eden's dominant role is often invoked to explain British policy-making. Much has been made of his unwillingness to grant his foreign secretaries (Macmillan in 1955; Lloyd in 1956) leeway to develop their own course and his tendency to dominate foreign policy-making. Similarly, such accounts seldom fail to stress that Eden fought a personal battle with Nasser, sometimes to the point of calling the Suez intervention 'Eden's war'. Explanations are usually sought in Eden's personality and his poor health. Eden's personality was a strange combination of a man who was convinced of being a 'prima donna' in politics, yet who suffered from low self-confidence at the same time. This combination resulted in a need to be liked and a tendency to rage if his immediate environment failed to live up to his expectations. His health had suffered from a badly executed bile-conduct operation in 1953. Eden would occasionally suffer from sudden fevers accompanied by anger, irritability, and anxiety. He took medicine to suppress these side effects, but these may have had their own effect on his physical conditions. Some authors claim that Eden's personality combined with his health seriously impaired his judgement during the Suez crisis, also because of his use of amphetamines to cope with his lack of sleep. This is true for political scientists (Roberts, 1988; Post and Robins 1993), historians (Lamb, 1987; Adamthwaite, 1988), as well as people close to the Prime Minister during the crisis. Eden's Press Secretary William Clark noted in his diary: 'it seems to me that the PM is mad, literally mad'.[15]

Although the impact of personality and health under stressful conditions such as a major international crisis cannot be ruled out (see Appendix 3), this study takes a different course. It argues that the behaviour of the Prime Minister should be analyzed from two angles. First, his worldview (or cognitive belief system) should provide a clue to the specific substance of his preferred policies. This should make it possible to assess to which extent Eden pursued a normal type of policy, or erratically rode the storm of his fevers and tempers. Second, the Prime Minister should be investigated as the leader of a group of decision-makers, be that the full Cabinet or the Egypt Committee. Because the full Cabinet agreed to going to war with Egypt, Eden's personality or health does not provide a sufficient explanation (see Appendix 2). An approach that assesses Eden's role as small group leader seems to bear more fruits.

## Plan of the Book

Existing explanations of Suez thus fall short of giving a comprehensive account of British misperceptions and miscalculations during the Suez crisis, especially of the failure to assess the American position correctly. This book argues that an adequate focus should be on those policy-makers who constituted a small group that convened formally as (part of) the Cabinet and the Egypt Committee and informally in various compositions. The Egypt Committee was an official committee composed of Cabinet Ministers that was installed on 27 July to deal with the situation. Prime Minister Sir Anthony Eden was, and therefore should be analyzed as, the leader of that group. Groupthink theory offers a relevant tool to assess the performance of the group and its leader. Groupthink explains the failure of small groups to meet the standards of high quality decision-making in terms of characteristics of the group, its leader as well as the context in which it operates. In order to explain specific substantive choices, however, it is necessary to determine the worldview of both the group and its leader. The worldview of Sir Anthony

Eden is determined by composing his so-called Operational Code. The outlook of the members of the small group is ascertained by the assessment of the images of Anglo-American relations between 1951 and 1956 held by British policy-makers. At the same time, this study takes domestic politics and organizational processes into account as the context in which the small group had to operate. Domestic politics refers, in a narrow sense, to the formal and informal rules of cabinet decision-making in Great Britain, and, in a wider sense, to maintaining a majority in the House of Commons. Organizational processes refer to the impact of military planning, both in substance and in timing, on political decision-making. All in all then, the interplay between four factors (small group dynamics, leadership, domestic politics, and organizational context) will resolve the puzzle of Suez guiding this book: how to account for British misperceptions and miscalculations during the Suez crisis, especially regarding American support?

Chapter two provides a theoretical argument of the interplay between small groups, leaders, and the organizational and domestic context in which they have to operate. It will also offer a methodological section on analyzing crisis decision-making in the specific case of the Suez crisis. Chapter three gives an overview of the dominant perspective of British policy-makers on Anglo-American relations in the early 1950s. Chapter four will present the worldview of Sir Anthony Eden in terms of his so-called Operational Code. Chapter five provides an analysis of British decision-making during the Suez crisis from the theoretical angle developed in chapter three. It will demonstrate that decision-making in Great Britain during the Suez crisis was concentrated in the hands of a small group of policy-makers under the leadership of the Prime Minister. The next chapter resolves the puzzle of Suez that has been developed in this introduction. The final chapter compares the results of this study with other works on British decision-making during the Suez crisis and explores the implications for the future analysis of comparable cases and for the study of Foreign Policy Analysis. Before all that, however, the next section provides a short history of the Suez crisis.

## A Short History of the Suez Crisis

The Suez Crisis was prompted by Egypt's nationalization on 26 July 1956 of the Suez Canal Company, which organized traffic through the Canal and collected the shipping fees. It escalated into a war between Egypt and three nations, France, Great Britain and Israel, resulting in Anglo-French landings at Port Said and Israeli occupation of the Sinai. The fighting ended on 6 November because of strong international, especially American pressure. The conflict can be divided into four phases: the prelude to nationalization; diplomatic efforts to avoid armed conflict; the war itself; and its aftermath.

### Prelude to Nationalization

The Suez crisis unfolded against the background of the Cold War, Third World nationalism, the Arab-Israeli conflict and the related shifting regional balance of power in the Middle East. Nationalist parties and organizations in the Middle East and North Africa had long been campaigning for the end of the formal and informal influence of European powers, especially Great Britain and France, in the Middle East. In North Africa France faced independence movements in Algeria, Morocco, and Tunisia. France's problems were particularly complicated in Algeria, which housed a large number of French colonialists who often had lived there for three generations. They often held a more privileged position than the Arab and Berber indigenous population. The French brutally suppressed a nationalist rising in 1945, but had been unable to re-install full control. Resistance movements were active in many areas in the Atlas Mountains. In 1954 Algerian nationalist organizations put aside their differences and started a battle for independence that would last until 1962. In the Middle East nationalism was directed at informal rather than formal forms of rule. Because of its many military basis in the Middle East Great Britain held the key to politics in formally independent countries such as Iraq, Jordan, Oman, Persia, as well as Egypt. In Persia and Egypt strong nationalist movements had existed since long, but remained unable to stop the British policy of playing off national parties against each other. This changed in the early 1950s when nationalist movements in Egypt and Persia dealt significant blows to British prestige in the area. In 1950 the Persian government of Mussadiq nationalized the Anglo-Iranian Oil Company. After a war of nerves that lasted almost a year Great Britain decided not to intervene militarily to restore its pivotal position. This sent a clear signal throughout the area. In Egypt, one year later, a group of army officers led by Generals Neguib and Nasser disposed King Faruk and installed a nationalist government.

Meanwhile, the Middle East was the scene of a violent conflict between Arabs, Jews, and Palestinians. After the British withdrawal from Palestine in 1947 and the failure of the United Nations to reach consensus between Palestinians and Jews on a partition of Cisjordania, Jewish nationalists had declared the independent state of Israel, thus triggering a war with its Arab neighbours. In the early 1950s Egypt, Jordan, and Syria were still formally at war with Israel. Although no major armed conflict occurred between 1948 and 1956, Egyptian-sponsored guerrillas, the *fedayeen*, regularly attacked Israeli villages across the border. Nevertheless, successful secret international diplomacy led by Great Britain and the United States, called plan-Alpha, brought Israel and its neighbours close to a diplomatic settlement of their dispute in the mid-1950s.

Middle East nationalism and the Arab-Israeli conflict took place against the background of the Cold War. Arab countries often tried to avoid becoming entangled in Cold War differences. Egypt actually was one of the leaders of the Movement of Non-Aligned Countries, founded at the conference of Bandung in 1955. Great Britain had a different assessment of Middle East nationalism. The British preferred to portray nationalist movements as forerunners of communism. This helped them in persuading the United States that British predominance over the Middle East was the best guarantee of avoiding the growth of communism in the area. This strategy, combined with the British habit of exploiting differences between local political parties, blurred the British perspective on nationalist movements.

The waning of British prestige due to events in Egypt and Persia combined with the Arab-Israeli conflict, and the rise of Arab and North African nationalism resulted in changes in the regional balance of power in the Middle East. Several larger states in the area, especially Iraq and Egypt, jockeyed for regional leadership. Egypt in the 1950s campaigned against English influence in the area by supporting nationalist movements, not only in the Middle East, but also in Algeria. These developments threatened the position of Great Britain, traditionally the holder of the balance in the area. At the same time, Egypt built up its military power in order to resume the war against Israel in the near future, stirring unrest in the new state. When in September 1955 Egypt announced the purchase of weapons from communist Czechoslovakia, Great Britain and the United States feared growing influence of the Soviet Union, while Israel started preparing a pre-emptive war against Egypt.

At the beginning of 1956, therefore, for the later key actors of the Suez crisis a lot was at stake. France was involved in a violent war of independence in Algeria. Egypt actively supported France's main adversary, the *Front de Libération Nationale*. Israel anticipated a war with Egypt before the summer and had started preparations for a pre-emptive strike, aimed at ending the *fedayeen*-attacks, safeguarding its harbour at Eilat, and diminishing the strength of the Egyptian army. Egyptian leaders aimed at the leadership of the Arab world and at strengthening the domestic position of the regime with various development projects. Great Britain tried to protect its dominant position in the Middle East. This was essential to its international status as a major power as well to the supply of Middle Eastern oil through the Suez Canal. The aims of the United States were the prevention of the spread of communism in the area and the securing of oil from the region.

With these stakes involved the region bordered on the edges of a major conflict. Egypt's nationalization of the Suez Canal on 26 July 1956 set off the conflict. Egypt had been negotiating with Great Britain, the United States, and the World Bank a loan for the construction of a high dam at Aswan, an important element in the Egyptian government's development programme. Under pressure from a variety of domestic interest groups, such as Southern cotton producers and pro Israel organizations, American Secretary of State John Foster Dulles withdrew from financing the Aswan High Dam on 19 July. Egypt responded with nationalizing the Suez Canal Company in the hope of financing the dam partly with the revenues of the shipping dues.

*International Diplomacy*

During the first days of the crisis British and French policy-makers hoped they could undo nationalization by threatening the immediate use of force. This would deal a decisive blow to Egypt's prestige in the Middle East and thus strengthen Britain's position. At the same time it would weaken support for the FLN in Algeria. Within three days, however, the British Chiefs of Staff ruled out the possibility of an immediate occupation of the Canal Zone and recommended a carefully prepared operation. Meanwhile, in the United States the Eisenhower

Administration had grown worried about the rumours of war that could be heard in London and Paris. On 31 July Dulles arrived in London for talks with British and French policy-makers. The purpose of American foreign policy throughout the summer and autumn was to prolong international diplomacy as long as possible in order to have the feelings of crisis dissipate until the window of opportunity for the use of force would have closed. By that time, joint Anglo-French military planning had resulted in a proposal to land near Alexandria, called *Musketeer*.

The American strategy resulted in a conference in London between 16 and 23 August of the signatory states to the 1888 Treaty of Constantinople, which had established the Suez Canal as an international waterway. Eighteen of the 22 countries present at the conference endorsed a proposal of Dulles that invited Egypt to open negotiations on the instalment of an international supervisory board and agreed to send a mission headed by Australian Prime Minister Menzies to Cairo. While France and Great Britain expected Egypt to reject forthwith these proposals and continued military preparations, the United States looked for further possibilities to win time. Five days before Egypt's formal rejection of the 18 countries' proposals on 9 September, Dulles sounded out Great Britain about the possibility of an association of users of the Suez Canal. Around that time British policy-makers were again facing a change of military plans. The Chiefs of Staff judged landings near Alexandria too risky and preferred to return to the original landing site, Port Said. This new plan, *Musketeer Revise*, caused another delay in the readiness of the Anglo-French forces. Under these circumstances Great Britain agreed to Dulles's idea of a users' organization. In Britain's view, the organization should collect the shipping dues, which could then be used as a tool of leverage over Egypt. The British, however, had great difficulties in persuading the French to go along. French policy-makers mistrusted American intentions and considered the users' association as an attempt to postpone force indefinitely.

A second conference, held in London between 19 and 21 September, established the Suez Canal Users Association (S.C.U.A.). Two days later France and Great Britain referred the dispute to the Security Council of the United Nations. During the following days the United States proved reluctant to commit itself to a users' association that could be used as a stick against Egypt. The already wary French started secret talks with Israel about their possible involvement. An Israeli attack on Egypt would offer an opportunity for France and Great Britain to intervene in the Canal Zone. Initially, the French put the issue to British as a problem of contingency planning. However, because Israel demanded certain measures of military protection, it was necessary to obtain formal British co-operation with the plan. In early October, British policy-makers had become dissatisfied with the American attitude to S.C.U.A. At the same time, the British Chiefs of Staff issued the so-called Winter-plan, which foresaw further relaxation of the state of readiness of the forces. Under these circumstances they were open to the plan presented by French General Maurice Challe on 14 October, which proposed the intervention of France and Great Britain to safeguard the Suez Canal in case of an Israeli attack on Egypt. Ironically, on 10 October the negotiations, conducted at the United Nations between the Foreign Ministers of Egypt, France, and Great Britain, had resulted in an agreement on six principles for the international management of the Suez Canal. France and Great Britain, however, continued their secret negotiations with Israel on the details of the Challe-plan, resulting on 24 October in the so-called secret Sèvres-protocol, signed by representatives of the three governments.

## The War and its Aftermath

On 29 October Israel attacked Egypt. The next day the British and French government issued ultimatums to Egypt and Israel asking them to withdraw ten miles either side of the Canal in order to allow Anglo-French occupation of the Canal Zone. At the United Nations France and Great Britain used their veto twice to defeat American and Russian resolutions calling for a cease-fire. That same day the Anglo-French force set sail for Port Said, followed by Anglo-French air raids on Egyptian airfields on 31 October. On 1 November the Security Council called for an emergency meeting of the General Assembly, which adopted a cease-fire resolution the next day. In Great Britain large protests were raised in the streets of London as well as in the House of Commons. Internationally, the United States strongly opposed the Anglo-French intervention. In order to save Britain's international face, Canada floated the idea of a United Nations intervention force. Great Britain was prepared to accept such a force provided the Anglo-French forces would be part of it. On 4 November, the Soviet Union, itself involved in crushing the Hungarian uprising, threatened a nuclear attack on London and Paris. Time was now running out fast. Great Britain and France decided to advance the landing of paratroops at Port Said to 5 November. On 6 November the main landing force disembarked at Port Said and started its advance to Suez. That day the position of the Pound became critical, when the United States refused to support financial assistance from the International Monetary Fund unless a cease-fire was announced. That evening the Anglo-French advance halted 23 miles down the Suez Canal from Port Said.

It would take until 22 December before the withdrawal of the Anglo-French intervention force would be complete. France and Great Britain hoped to be part of the United Nations Emergency Force. This proved in vain, because of persistent American resistance to support Great Britain financially before a complete withdrawal from the area. On 23 November, Prime Minister Anthony Eden had left for Jamaica to recover from the strain. He returned on 14 December to find out that he had lost his power position in the Conservative Party. On 9 January 1957 Eden resigned and was succeeded by Harold Macmillan. The Suez Canal, which had been blocked because ships sunk by Egypt during the war, re-opened on 24 April. Egypt accepted a settlement to the dispute based on the six principles negotiated in the previous October.

**Notes**

[1]   Invoking a Uniting for Peace Resolution at the Security Council is a procedural matter, the adoption of which requires seven votes in favour. American abstention would have been enough to reject the proposal.

[2]   T 236/4188, Bridges to Macmillan, 7 September 1956; T 236/4188, Bridges to Macmillan, 11 September 1956.

[3]   T 236/4188, Rowan to Macmillan, 26 October 1956.

[4]   Makins had been British Ambassador to the United States until September 1956 and had taken up his appointment at the Treasury in October.

[5]   T 236/4188, Note for the Record, record of a discussion between Macmillan, Makins, and Rowan, on 30 October 1956 at 5 p.m.

[6]   CM(56)75, 30 October 1956.

[7]   These criteria themselves closely resemble the ideal type of comprehensive rational decision-making. Indeed, they serve as measuring rod, first, to determine the extent to which decision-makers deviate from the ideal type, next as a start to explaining such a deviation.

[8]   PREM 11/1103, Memorandum of the Chiefs of Staff, EC memorandum EC(56)63, 25 October 1956.

[9]   The Cabinet agreed on this analysis when they had to consider implementing the Challe-plan, CM(56)73, 24 October 1956.

[10]  The full text is reproduced in Marston (1988, pp. 800-1).

[11]  France wanted to bring about the downfall of Nasser in the assumption that this would put an end to Egypt's support for the Algerian independence movement FLN (Ferro, 1982).

[12]  France's Suez policy surfaces in the memoirs of quite some former participants (Challe, 1968; Beaufre, 1969; Ely, 1969; Pineau, 1976), but in only a few historical studies (Bromberger and Bromberger, 1957; Neff, 1981; Ferro, 1986; Vaisse, 1989).

[13]  When I use decision-making I refer to political decision-making rather than military planning and operations.

[14]  The following overview of the literature does not discuss general historical works on the Suez crisis that do not put forward explicit explanations of British foreign policy, such as Love (1969), Robertson (1964), Fullick and Powell (1979) and Kyle (1991).

[15]  Clark, 'Whitehall Diary', entry 4-5 November 1956, p. 158. It is important to keep in mind for many former participants in the decision-making process it was later convenient to describe Eden as mentally weak, because it removed part of their own burden of responsibility. This, of course, is not the case for Clark, who was more of an inside observer.

Chapter 2

# Theory: Crisis Decision-Making

## Introduction

The occurrence of a crisis-like situation has important consequences for the way individuals take decisions. This is the case in both their personal and their political life (Janis and Mann, 1977). It is true for domestic politics as well as international politics. This chapter argues that the occurrence of a foreign policy crisis is likely to lead to centralization of decision-making because of the threat that is posed to a country's basic values. Often, decision-making is concentrated in the hands of a small group of policy-makers, sometimes even one individual. A foreign policy crisis therefore tends to reinforce the impact of individuals and small groups on decision-making. It does not necessarily nullify the impact of bureaucratic organizations, interest groups or public opinion, but it is likely to alter the nature of that impact. Foreign policy crises often coincide with high levels of stress experienced by decision-makers. This may cause individuals and small groups to perform worse than they would have under normal conditions. This chapter therefore investigates theoretical approaches to analyzing the performance of individuals and small groups in times of crisis. Its innovative theoretical claim is that the formal and informal rules of a country's political system set the institutional boundaries within which individuals and small groups have to operate.

This chapter identifies two specific theoretical approaches that will be used to analyze British decision-making during the Suez crisis. Groupthink theory will be utilized to assess the performance of small groups. The so-called Operational Code technique will be applied to studying the behaviour of a small group's leader. The informal and formal rules of parliamentary democracy in Great Britain provide the institutional constraints within which small groups and leaders have to operate. The chapter concludes with a methodological section in which specific choices are explained that are necessary to conduct the empirical research. These choices relate in particular to the ascertaining of the occurrence of crisis and stress during the Suez crisis as well as to the choice of primary and secondary sources.

**Crisis Decision-Making**

*Foreign Policy Crises and their Effect on Decision-Making*

*The concept of foreign policy crisis*   First of all, a distinction should be made between an international crisis and a foreign policy crisis (Brecher and Wilkenfeld, 2000). The former refers to a disruption of the normal interaction between two or more states, which destabilizes their relationship and challenges the structure of the international system. The term foreign policy crisis points to a crisis for an individual state, which may or may not have serious consequences for the international system. One should also differentiate between objectivistic and subjectivistic approaches to analyzing crises (Hermann, 1969; Holsti, 1979; Roberts, 1988). The former considers a crisis to be a type of situation that can be defined by the analyst from the outside. The latter conceive of crisis as a situation that is perceived as such by decision-makers themselves.   An objectivistic approach to an international crisis investigates those international situations that demonstrate a disruption of (part of) the international system or a sudden change in one or more systemic variables. Such a focus would approach the Suez crisis as a conflict that upset the regional balance of power in the Middle East, created serious tension between the two superpowers and, because of divisions among Western countries, threatened the cohesion of the Western alliance. Objectivistic studies of a foreign policy crisis focus on individual units in that system and look for a significant change in the 'quantity, quality of intensity of interactions among nations' (Holsti, 1979, p. 101).   From this angle, the Suez crisis is investigated as a conflict between different (pairs of) states: Great Britain and France versus Egypt or Israel versus Egypt.

This study adopts a subjectivistic approach to foreign policy crises because of its principal interest in explaining British misperception and miscalculation during the Suez crisis. Within the subjectivistic approach to foreign policy crises, scholars tend to agree on two defining characteristics (Hermann, 1969; Brecher and Wilkenfeld, 2000). First, the decision-makers' perception of a threat to their country's important values. These core values usually include territorial integrity, economic survival, or a state's standing in the world (Roberts, 1988). Second, their perception of a clear restriction of time available to reach a decision. This element of time constraint is difficult to confine. Sometimes, as in the case of an ultimatum, there is no doubt about how much time is left to reach a decision. Ultimatums, however, are not issued frequently. It may be a handicap to restrict crisis to short time decision-making, 'a few days at the most' (Hermann and Mason, 1980, p. 193). Crises often seem to last weeks, or even months, rather than hours or days. 'Finite time' rather than 'short time' may thus be a better definitional element (Brecher and Wilkenfeld, 2000). In addition, it should be recognized that time restrictions in crises are often self-imposed, because decision-makers feel they should reply within a limited amount of time.

A third element of existing definitions of crisis, perceived surprise, is much disputed. In principle, however, it could be argued that an actor that is caught by surprise would be relatively unprepared. Such a situation might then affect the quality of the decision-making process, resulting, for instance, in a frantic search for alternative courses of action. Surprise may thus add to a policy-maker's perception of time constraints, but it implies that perception of time is the more important variable. Surprise may affect the start of a crisis, as well as the challenged actor's initial handling of the situation, but it is not a necessary element of a definition of crisis.[1] Brecher and Wilkenfeld argue that the decision-makers' expectation that the involvement of military hostilities will be likely should be part of a crisis definition rather than surprise (Brecher and Wilkenfeld, 2000). They identify the start of a crisis with a sharp increase of policy-makers' perceptions that, first, basic values are under threat, second, relatively little time is available to take decisions, and, third, military hostilities are highly probable. This choice has a clear methodological advantage, because it makes it easier to mark out the crisis period. It becomes possible to distinguish a crisis period from a so-called pre-crisis period. The latter is characterized by a specific event that triggers an increase in threat perception, but not in perceptions of restricted time or probable hostilities. A drop in the perceptions of all three elements marks the end of a crisis (Brecher and Wilkenfeld, 2000).

*The consequences of crisis for decision-making* A foreign policy crisis, defined as a perception of threat and limited time coupled with a perceived increased likelihood of hostilities, has significant consequences for both the locus and the process of decision-making (Cohen, 1979; Jervis, 1985). The locus of decision-making is likely is to shift from the departmental agencies to key decision-makers at the political level. Precisely because of the perceived lack of time and high stakes involved, policy-makers want to keep matters in their own hands and avoid the lengthy process of routine policy-making of governmental departments. Very often, governments constitute specific ad hoc committees to deal with the newly arisen situation. However, the advent of a crisis need not always result in centralization of decision-making. Overload at the central level of government may invite informal decentralization of decision-making. Similarly, time constraints at the operational level may cause a downward shift in the locus of decision-making ('t Hart et al, 1993).

The impact of centralization of decision-making on the decision-making process can be positive as well as negative. On the one hand, it may reduce the weight of parochial interests, simply because less actors will be involved. Bureaucratic conflicts may thus be circumvented, or, indeed suddenly be resolved by decision from above (Vertzberger, 1990). From this point of view, a higher quality of decision-making can be expected (George and Holsti, 1975). On the other hand, emotional stress aroused by a foreign policy crisis may seriously hamper the performance of the central decision-makers. Experimental evidence shows that, although medium levels of emotional stress may actually be beneficial to an individual's cognitive performance, high levels of stress tend to reduce the ability of both individuals and groups to process information accurately. This may eventually cause the failure of decision-makers to meet the criteria of procedurally high quality decision-making (see chapter 1) (Holsti, 1972; Janis and Mann, 1977; Holsti, 1979; Janis 1989; Vertzberger, 1990).

The challenge for an analysis of Suez thus will be to ascertain that British policy-makers perceived a foreign policy crisis and experienced high levels of emotional stress. Centralization of decision-making is the prediction that follows from the presence of those conditions. Moreover, the smaller the decision unit the more likely it is that individual and small group factors affect British decision-making during the crisis. Identifying the proper British decision unit during the Suez crisis will thus be the first objective of the empirical analysis (cf. Hermann and Hermann, 1989).

## *Small Group Dynamics: Groupthink*

The occurrence of a foreign policy crisis is likely to concentrate decision-making in the hands of a limited number of key decision-makers. Frequently, these individuals meet on a regular basis in a small group. Insight from social psychology suggests that small group dynamics have specific effects on decision-making, compared to individual or organizational decision-making, both under normal conditions and under stressful circumstances. On the one hand, these effects may be beneficial. As a member of a group an individual is more easily exposed to new information than alone. Groups also tend to use more resources to assess information than individuals. Such effects may contribute to higher quality decision-making (Vertzberger, 1990). On the other hand, group effects can be detrimental to decision-making quality. The larger the size of a group, the smaller the number of individuals actually contributing to group deliberations (Burnstein and Berbaum, 1983). Moreover, the perceptions that group members already share before they meet as a group tend to carry more weight than the actual contents of new information discussed by the group (Bettenhausen and Murnigan, 1985).

Many of these insights are based on experimental research designs, which allows for control of crucial variables. In foreign policy studies such neat designs are very difficult, if not almost impossible, to accomplish (cf. George, 1980). Systematic application of small group theories to analyzing foreign policy crises has been limited mainly to the so-called Groupthink-syndrome (Janis, 1982), because its framework explicitly links social psychology with public policy. Groupthink refers to the possibility that small groups reach consensus too quickly and fail to meet the criteria of procedural high quality decision-making. Application of the Groupthink-framework to British decision-making during the Suez crisis requires first an overview of the substantive body of literature on Groupthink, in particular with respect to its usefulness for analyzing foreign policy crises. This study will argue that, despite its applicability to analyzing British decision-making during the Suez crisis, the Groupthink literature neglects three important issues that may play a role in this case. First, the impact of leaders within the group requires that attention be paid to the leader's individual cognitive belief system. Second, the weight of cognitive beliefs that group members already share before they meet as a group requires that attention be paid to the impact of such shared beliefs. Third, the institutional constraints set by the formal and informal rules of the political system may explain part of the working of group norms.

*Small groups, decision-making quality, and policy outcomes*  Groupthink explains the failure of small decision units to meet the criteria of procedural high quality decision-making by their tendency, under certain conditions, to reach a decision too early. This is called premature concurrence-seeking, or Groupthink. The term premature implies that the group reaches agreement before it has taken into account all relevant criteria of a high quality decision-making procedure. Failure to meet these criteria increases the likelihood of a disastrous policy outcome.[2] As was argued in Chapter 1, British neglect of these criteria resulted in a foreign policy that led to a situation that no one in Great Britain had wanted. The Suez Canal Company still in Egyptian hands, General Nasser still in power, a serious conflict with the United States, and loathing from international public opinion. Comparative analysis of 19 American foreign policy crises suggests a relationship between decision-making quality and policy outcome. The lower the quality of decision-making, the less successfui the policy outcome for the United States (Herek et al., 1987). A recent study of 33 foreign policy crises involving, not only the United States, but also France, Great Britain, and Israel, found a significant relationship between notably the way small groups process information and policy outcome. The poorer the search for, and processing of, information, the worse the outcome in terms of a country's national interest (Schafer and Crichlow, 2002). Clearly, then, a decision unit should heed the quality of its decision process.

*Two explanations*  Groupthink-theory claims that premature concurrence-seeking, or Groupthink, increases the likelihood of low decision-making quality. Two types of explanations of this relationship surface in the literature. On the one hand, social psychologists emphasize the emotional need for an individual group member to be held in esteem by the other members of the group. On the other hand, scholars from public administration and political science point to the individual group member's assessment of the usefulness of his or her support for specific policies proposed in the small group. The difference between these perspectives is rooted in the fundamental question whether small groups inside government differ fundamentally from small groups outside. To Irving Janis, an individual group member's wish to become and remain a valued member of the group in the eyes of the other group members accounts for the individual's tendency to suppress his or her doubts and criticism regarding the group's course. Collectively, therefore, members of the group attach more value to the unity of the group than to a systematic resolution of the problem facing them. Concurrence-seeking is the result (Janis, 1982). In his reformulation of Janis's theory for small groups in government, Paul 't Hart argues that in government small groups composed of largely the same individuals are not that frequent. Indeed, small groups sometimes meet only once or twice in an ad hoc fashion. The emotional pressure on an individual to preserve group unity may thus not be comparable to small groups outside government. Indeed, individual members of a group within government are often held accountable outside rather than inside the group ('t Hart, 1990/1994). In government, therefore, individual members tend to calculate their behaviour on the basis of their expectation of the likely outcome of the group's decision. If policy failure is anticipated, he or she will not want to be associated with the decision. If success is expected, joining the group's consensus is likely, because he or she will be eager to share the fame. This study takes the position that members of small groups in government will be subject to both types of pressures. Groupthink may thus be the product of varying combinations of emotional attachment and political calculation.[3] Applying Groupthink to British decision-making during the Suez crisis thus requires an assessment of both elements.

*How to identify Groupthink?* Janis's original framework singled out eight indicators, or symptoms, of premature concurrence-seeking, which could be grouped under three categories (Janis, 1982, pp. 174-5). The first category referred to tendency of a group to overestimate itself. Overestimation can be observed in two symptoms. First, the illusion of invulnerability. This refers to the feeling among group members that they can handle any kind of trouble. Second, a belief in the inherent morality of the group, or the absence of any doubt that its motives and actions might not be principled or justifiable. The second category is symptomatic of the group's closed-mindedness. This transpires in two symptoms. Collective rationalizations that result in discounting information that might contradict the group's analysis of the situation, and the development of stereotyped views of outgroups, which facilitates the discrediting of their communications. The third category consists of forms of pressures toward uniformity. This is the case if the following phenomena can be observed. Self-censorship by individual group-members. This occurs if each member tends to minimize the importance of personal doubts and counter-arguments. A shared illusion of unanimity. Direct pressure on those members who express doubt and who formulate strong arguments against the overall consensus. Finally, the emergence of self-appointed mindguards. These are group members who withhold adverse information from the group.

These eight symptoms basically constitute Janis's operational definition of Groupthink. They allowed Janis to conduct six in depth case analyses of Groupthink in American foreign policy.[4] On the basis of his operational definitions he concluded that Groupthink characterized four of them (Pearl Harbor in 1941, the decision to pursue North Korean troops into North Korea in 1950, the 1961 Bay of Pigs fiasco, and the series of decisions of the Johnson Administration to escalate the Vietnam War), while two cases displayed no indication of Groupthink (the devising of the Marshall Plan in 1947 and the 1962 Cuban missile crisis). On the basis of a technique to quantify and compare expert assessments of group dynamics, it was subsequently established that Janis's operational definitions had allowed a correct detection of Groupthink in his original cases (Tetlock et al., 1992). They thus provide an important tool for comparative research. As a matter of fact, Groupthink has been identified in various other foreign policy crises. Some of them regard instances of American foreign policy, such as the 1980 Iran hostage crisis (Smith, 1984) and the 1985-6 Iran-Contra affair ('t Hart 1990/1994). Other studies examined non-American examples of foreign policy crises, such as British decision-making during the 1982 Falklands War (Heller, 1983) and the foreign policy of the Netherlands towards its conflict with Indonesia over West New Guinea in 1961-1962 (Metselaar and Verbeek, 1997).[5]

Despite its proven usefulness for empirical research, the operational definition of Groupthink in terms of eight symptoms entails three important problems. First, are all symptoms equally important? At some point Janis suggested that nearly all symptoms should be observed in order to be able to speak of Groupthink (Janis, 1985). This study distinguishes between several degrees of Groupthink, depending on the number of different symptoms that can be observed and their frequency (see Chapter 6). A second problem regards the question whether all symptoms distinguished by Janis can be considered actual manifestations of concurrence-seeking? It has been argued that the illusions of invulnerability and unanimity are indicative of a phase that precedes concurrence-seeking (Longley and Pruitt, 1980). Similarly, a belief in the group's inherent morality and the stereotyping of outgroups may be unrelated to concurrence-seeking as such. They can be themes on which concurrence is sought, but are not part of the process of concurrence-seeking (ibid.). By consequence, four symptoms (collective rationalizations, self-censorship, direct pressure on dissenters, and self-appointed mindguards) would qualify as Groupthink's most relevant indicators. The fundamental problem underlying these two problems is the impossibility to observe Groupthink directly. Indeed, it cannot be excluded that a group that does not display a single symptom may still suffer from Groupthink (George, 1997).

*Causes of Groupthink*    The three causes of Groupthink that Janis originally distinguished (high group cohesiveness, structural faults of the organization, and a provocative situational context) have been the subject of much debate. High group cohesiveness has often been considered the core of Janis's argument because cohesion goes to the heart of the explanation of an individual member's behaviour. Members of cohesive groups are likely to suppress doubts about the proposed policy in order to preserve the respect and friendship they receive from other group members. Groupthink symptoms are indicative of that phenomenon. Collective rationalizations and a shared illusion of invulnerability serve to suppress feelings of personal inadequacy. A belief in the group's moral cause as well as its stereotyped view of opponents help its members to overcome value conflicts, especially when military action is seriously considered. The forms of pressure toward uniformity and the resulting illusion of unanimity are devices to improve individual confidence and self-esteem, which have become dependent on group unity (Janis, 1982). It has also been argued that cohesion may not be detrimental to group decision-making at all ('t Hart, 1990/1994). Laboratory experiments failed to find any direct relationship between group cohesion and Groupthink (Flowers, 1977). However, such experiments are often considered not to resemble the type of decision-making situations Janis had in mind (Fuller and Aldag, 1997). Indeed, a comparative analysis of group decision-making in 19 Cold War crises demonstrated the frequent occurrence of group cohesion (Schafer and Crichlow, 1996).[6] On the other hand, a different case survey of ten foreign policy crises found no relationship between cohesion and the occurrence of Groupthink (Tetlock et al., 1992).

Structural faults of the organization form the second major cause of Groupthink. This refers to four elements. First, the insulation of the group from direct contact with persons in the organization who are not members of the group. Second, a tradition of directive leadership. This is a situation where the group's leader promotes personal views. Third, a lack of established norms that set methodical procedures of decision-making. Fourth, homogeneity of group members in social background and ideology is expected to promote Groupthink. Several case surveys of foreign policy decision-making by small groups confirm that group insulation, directive leadership and lack of methodical procedures are negatively associated with the quality of decision-making (Tetlock et al., 1992; Schafer and Crichlow, 1996, 2002). Similarly, laboratory experiments suggests that the decision rules that groups adopt have an impact on the occurrence of Groupthink. The unanimity rule, unlike the majority rule, is likely to promote Groupthink (Kameda and Sugimori, 1993).

A provocative situational context makes up the third cause of Groupthink. Small groups are usually installed in order to cope with a newly arisen threatening situation. The higher the level of stress generated by such a threat, the more probable it is that early concurrence seeking will occur. Second, group members may be suffering from low self-esteem that has developed before the group confronts the new threat. This may have been provoked by recent failures, excessive difficulties at resolving other, contemporary, policy problems, or by moral dilemmas. The impact of stress has been inconclusive from the outset. Even in Janis's original cases Groupthink occurred despite the absence of stress (Pearl Harbor) or was absent despite the condition of high stress (Cuban Missile Crisis). The existing evidence on small group decision-making in about two dozen foreign policy cases suggests that the occurrence of Groupthink is unrelated to stress or the group's recent failures (Tetlock et al., 1992; Schafer and Crichlow, 1996). Rather, stress seems to have contributed to higher quality decision-making (Schafer and Crichlow, 1996). All in all, therefore, structural faults in the organization, rather than cohesion or situational variables, seem to account for the occurrence of Groupthink.

*Groupthink in this study*    This study builds on recent Groupthink-research emphasizing the political-administrative context in which small groups involved in public policy-making have to operate ('t Hart, 1990/1994; 't Hart et al., 1997). As explained above, the point of departure is that small groups in government often do not display high cohesion. As a matter of fact, this may explain the finding in the larger case surveys of foreign policy crises that cohesion cannot account for the occurrence of Groupthink. At the same time, these surveys demonstrate the salience of directive leadership and the lack of methodical procedures in explaining the occurrence of Groupthink. Hierarchical power relations usually characterize small groups in government. This is true for civil service committees as well as for political decision-making bodies such as cabinets. Recent studies of American foreign policy suggest that Groupthink may be related to the specific manner in which American Presidents structure their policy advisory process and solicit frank advice (Preston, 2001; Kowert, 2002). This recognition of the weight of leadership has two important consequences. First, it implies that impact of leadership is likely to vary with political and administrative systems. The impact of the American president on small group decisions is likely to be different from a Prime Minister's in a parliamentary democracy. An analysis of Groupthink in Great Britain during the Suez crisis thus will have to take into account how power relations in the British political system affect small group decision-making. Second, the persistent empirical finding that leadership matters to small group decision-making implies that a leader's worldview, or cognitive belief system, may become relevant in explaining a small group's deliberations. However, leadership implies followership (Blondel, 1987). Leaders and followers are likely to share several basic assumptions regarding the world around them. If this were not the case, a leader would not be able to persuade his followers to follow. Studies of Groupthink have so far neglected the possibility that the specific contents of a group's chosen policy may be rooted in beliefs held in common by a majority of group members (Verbeek, 1994).[7] This despite the fact that laboratory experiments suggest that the beliefs group members already share before they meet as a group tend to carry more weight than the actual contents of new information discussed by the group (Bettenhausen and Murnigan, 1985).

Applying Groupthink-theory to British decision-making during the Suez crisis thus requires an appraisal of images shared by most decision-makers as well as an assessment of the worldview, or the cognitive belief system, of Prime Minister Sir Anthony Eden. This calls for an overview of the literature on individual belief systems.

## *The Role of Individual Belief Systems*

The advent of a foreign policy crisis is likely to result in centralization of decision-making. This increases the likelihood that small groups are assigned to deal with the new situation. Existing research on the performance of small groups during foreign policy crises emphasizes the effects of leadership. Leadership can have detrimental effects on group performance. One reason can be the leader's detailed interference with the group's deliberations in order to impose his or her own private view and policy preference (directive leadership). A second reason can be the specific fashion in which a leader organizes his or her advisory system and makes use of it. It is thus important to investigate further the role of individual leaders. Studies that recognize this need often focus on the specific style a leader develops in order to explain his or her relationship to the group (e.g., Haney, 1997). Other studies attempt to explain variation in leadership style by differences in personality characteristics between leaders. Differences in leadership styles appear related to differences in the motivational structure displayed by different leaders (Hermann and Preston, 1994; Preston, 2001). Undoubtedly it is important to establish precise connection between personality characteristics, leadership styles and group processes. At the same time it is equally important to explain why policy-makers take one decision rather than another. This requires that attention should be paid not only to policy style but also to policy contents. This demands taking into account the worldview of policy-makers. This study argues that the worldview of a group's leader as well as the images broadly held by a country's foreign policy elite will contribute to explaining the extent to which a group meets the procedural criteria of high quality decision-making.

*Cognitive belief systems as information filters*   The term cognitive belief system refers to an individual's more or less coherent whole of descriptive and normative opinions about his or her environment. Belief system theory argues that individuals cannot absorb all environmental stimuli they encounter, because if they were, they would no longer be able to make choices and act. Individuals therefore have to develop mechanism that helps them regulate the influx of stimuli. This mechanism helps them decide which stimuli to note and ignore, and how to interpret them. These interpretations subsequently serve as a basis for action. A cognitive belief system is such a filtering mechanism. Foreign policy decision-makers are also expected to note and interpret information on the basis of belief systems that may to a smaller or greater degree be related specifically to international politics (Holsti, 1976a; Vertzberger, 1990; Rosati, 1995).

Within the social psychological literature on the role of beliefs two major, not necessarily incompatible, approaches can be distinguished. On the one hand, the cognitive consistency approach argues that individuals are driven by a need to maintain consistency in their beliefs (Larson, 1985; Rosati, 1995). On the other hand, the 'naive scientist' approach rejects this premise. Cognitive consistency theory emphasizes the close link between cognitive beliefs and deeper-lying psychological needs or drives. The belief system serves an individual's personality (cf. Walker and Falkowski, 1984). Discrepancies between incoming information and an individual's belief system thus pose a serious threat to the individual. This premise has given rise to cognitive dissonance reduction theory (Festinger, 1957) which predicts that an individual will eliminate these discrepancies. Cognitive consistency theory in principle allows for changing the belief system as well as adjusting or ignoring the unwelcome piece of information. In practice, however, most research in this tradition has pointed to the rigidity of belief systems and the individual's tendency to invent all sorts of cognitive tricks to make unwelcome information fit the belief system. In foreign policy analysis, the most popular example is the cognitive belief system of American Secretary of State John Foster Dulles. He solved all discrepancies between the Soviet Union's actual foreign policy and his belief of the Soviet Union as an inherently expansionist state by explaining away seemingly co-operative Soviet policies (Holsti, 1970).

Other studies play down the idea that belief systems are steered by psychological needs. They prefer to portray the individual as a 'problem solver' or 'naive scientist' implying that an individual is not the victim of a rigid belief system but maintains a fairly open mind to problematic situations. Within this approach two major currents exist: attribution theory and schema theory (George, 1980a, Larson, 1985). Attribution theory claims that beliefs are based on an individual's genuine effort to explain other people's behaviour each time they are facing a puzzling situation. This allows for more flexibility in assessing new information and suggests that beliefs are more easily adjusted to discrepant information instead of the discrepant information to the belief system. Schema theory, however, discards the idea of attribution theory that individuals have this open, quasi-scientific mind when it comes to problematic situations. Rather, individuals make 'snap judgements' (Larson, 1985, p. 50) about the situation, with the help of heuristic devices, so-called *schemata*. In particular, they employ metaphors and analogies. Again, schema theory rejects the rigidity of cognitive consistency theory and suggests that beliefs can be adjusted because individuals apply different schemata to different situations. Attribution and schemata are not without dangers, however. The so-called Fundamental Attribution error points to the tendency of individuals to explain other people's behaviour in terms of their personal characteristics ('He does not want to change that habit') while explaining their own behaviour in terms of their situational circumstances ('My work does not allow me to change that habit'). The Arab-Israeli conflict has been analyzed from this perspective (Heradstveit, 1981). Schemata may be very helpful to cope with unfamiliar situations, but may be based on erroneous assumptions. Studies of foreign policy often point to the potentially disastrous consequences of policy-makers deciding on the basis of incorrect historical analogies (Neustadt and May, 1986).

The differences between cognitive consistency theory and the 'naive scientist' approach are substantial, yet not incompatible. Both agree that beliefs do matter and that man's cognitive mechanisms may have serious drawbacks, be they complete cognitive rigidity, false attributions, or erroneous *schemata*. All theories recognize the effects of a crisis situation. A crisis situation is likely to increase the amount of information that reaches the individual as well as the individual's need to make sense of the situation. Added to that, the emotional stress provoked by the threats the crisis poses to important values as well as by the perception of limited amount of time available will make an individual rely on his or her belief system. These circumstances may reinforce the potential negative consequences both approaches distinguish.

The cognitive consistency and 'naive scientist' approaches, however, dispute the extent to which belief systems are open to change. This study, however, is not concerned with the relative openness to change. Rather, it aims at an assessment of the impact of a leader's cognitive belief system on both the process and outcome of small group decision-making during a foreign policy crisis. The belief system sort of predicts what type of information the leader is likely to see and how he or she will interpret it. This requires first the selection of a technique to ascertain the cognitive belief system of the leader of a group.

*Techniques for determining belief systems*  Over the past four decades scholars interested in the cognitive dimension of foreign policy have developed several concepts to determine the cognitive belief systems of foreign policy leaders. Some of these concepts have been developed into sophisticated tools of analysis, notably the Operational Code and the Cognitive Map techniques (cf. Little and Smith, 1988; Rosati, 1995). One major strand of research builds on the notion of images. Policy-makers are expected to hold stereotypical views of other countries. Moreover, negative images of adversaries are usually mirrored by positive self-images (Boulding, 1956). Image plays an important role in the comparative design of the *International Crisis Behavior Project* led by Michael Brecher (Brecher et al., 1969). The notion of image is of only limited help in determining an individual's belief system. Although images clearly are a component of an individual's belief system, they should be supplemented with other elements, such as an individual's ideas about history and international politics in general as well as about foreign policy instruments and their timely application.[8]

A second strand of research developed out of cognitive consistency theory. Cognitive consistency theory assumes that an individual's belief system constitutes a coherent whole in which some beliefs are more important than others. Indeed, it holds that the most important, or master, beliefs determine to a large extent the specific fashion in which individuals adjust discrepant information to their belief system. Scholars who work in the 'naive scientist' tradition also acknowledge the relevance of these master beliefs. They suggest that master beliefs are the most difficult to change in the face of contradictory information. Two major techniques have been developed to measure an individual's cognitive beliefs system and to determine its most important, or master, belief. They are the Operational Code and the Cognitive Map.

The Cognitive Map is an inductive technique. Beforehand, no assumptions are made about the possible relevance of beliefs for foreign policy-making. Rather, the researcher investigates a relevant text, for instance, the minutes of a meeting, a public speech, or a memorandum, and assesses which concepts in the text are inter-linked. It thus becomes possible to induce from the text an individual's cognitive belief system. Once all relevant concepts and their interrelationship have been identified a schematic overview is drawn up, a so-called Cognitive Map. The Cognitive Map recognizes a concept as a master belief if it is connected with the highest number of other concepts displayed by the individual (Axelrod, 1976). The Operational Code on the other hand consists of a set of questions that have been determined beforehand to be likely relevant beliefs regarding foreign policy-making. A relevant text is subsequently analyzed by answering the questions involved. The Operational Code defines that belief to be of central importance that remains stable over time and from which other cognitive beliefs can be logically deduced (George, 1969; Holsti, 1976b). Both approaches have developed into sophisticated tools of analysis (Axelrod, 1976; Holsti, 1977; Walker et al., 1998). Both techniques, but the Operational Code in particular, have been used to measure the cognitive belief systems of individuals engaged in foreign policy.[9] Far fewer analyses, however, exist of the impact of an individual cognitive belief system on a country's foreign policy.[10] That is the objective of this study.

Both Operational Code and Cognitive Map have their advantages and drawbacks. The Cognitive Map has one major disadvantage, related to its method in determining the master belief in a cognitive belief system. In a Cognitive Map, the belief that has the largest number of connections to other beliefs is defined as the master belief. The frequency criterion, however, may yield implausible master beliefs. This is due to the tendency of Cognitive Maps to display predominantly so-called instrumental beliefs, that is, beliefs related to practical issues. Indeed, Cognitive Maps often fail to bring out the objectives that steer instrumental considerations. A Cognitive Map is thus likely to reflect considerations of policy implementation, but seems less able to reproduce considerations that help explain choices in tradeoffs between different conflicting objectives.[11] The Operational Code on the other hand offers the possibility of identifying choices between conflicting values and objectives because its subjects, especially the so-called philosophical questions, explicitly refer to these items. Table 2.1 gives an overview of the items under research during the construction of an Operational Code.

## Table 2.1 Operational Code Categories

A  Philosophical beliefs
1.       The fundamental nature of politics and political conflict, and the image of the opponent.
         1.1      What is the 'essential' nature of the political universe?
         1.2      What is the fundamental character of one's political opponents and of other significant political actors?
         1.3      What is the nature of the contemporary international system? Is conflict a permanent or a temporary feature? Is conflict caused by characteristics of man, nation-states, or the international political system?
2.       What are the prospects for the eventual realization of one's fundamental political values and aspirations? Can one be optimistic, or must one be pessimistic on this score?
3.       Is the political future predictable? In what sense and to what extent? What is the role of chance in human affairs and history?
4.       How much 'control' or 'mastery' can one have over historical development? What is one's role in 'moving' and 'shaping' history in the desired direction?
5.       What is the role of 'chance' in human affairs and in historical development?

B  Instrumental beliefs
1.       What is the best approach for selecting goals or objectives of political action?
2.       How are the goals of political action pursued most effectively?
3.       How are the risks of political action calculated, controlled, and accepted?
4.       What is the best 'timing' of action to advance one's interests?
5.       What is the utility of different means for advancing one's interests? What resources can one draw upon in the effort to advance one's interests?

*Source:* Holsti (1977, pp. xii-xiv).

The Operational Code, however, has serious disadvantages of its own. A major problem involves the determination of a master belief. Master beliefs are detected by looking for an individual's most persistent beliefs over time. A comparative analysis of existing Operational Code studies showed that two types of Operational Codes exist, each organized around a different master belief. One type of belief system is based on a policy-maker's view of his principal opponent in world politics; a second group is structured around a policy-maker's ideas about the nature of international politics (Holsti, 1977). However, it could well be the case that someone's belief system changes over time, if only because learning takes place permanently during an individual's lifetime: either gradually, because of an accumulation of experiences, or suddenly after a dramatic event. Studies of Secretary of State Dean Acheson and Senator Frank Church demonstrate that cognitive belief systems can change in the course of a political career (McLellan, 1971; Johnston, 1977). Within the concept of the Operational Code this is not a real problem as long as a change of master beliefs is followed by a consistent change of other beliefs. Nevertheless, the explanatory value of the Operational Code may be severely limited when in principle the possibility exists that during the foreign policy crisis, which the Operational Code is supposed to help understand, a policy-maker radically changes his or her belief system. This study will nevertheless opt for an application of the Operational Code, primarily because of the greater likelihood that master beliefs can be captured. For the problem of changes in the belief system adequate methodological solutions are available (see Chapter 4).

*The Operational Code and British decision-making during the Suez crisis*  This study will present the Operational Code of British Prime Minister Sir Anthony Eden (Chapter 4). It is assumed that Eden's worldview at the moment of the start of the crisis, as measured by his Operational Code, will form the filter which will help choose to accept incoming pieces of information and will provide clues to their interpretation. In addition, it is expected that his worldview will contribute to explaining in which fashion Eden exercised his leadership of the various decision-making groups, such as the Cabinet and the so-called Egypt Committee. It is hypothesized that the circumstances of a foreign policy crisis will have an effect on the impact of Eden's worldview. Threats combined with time pressure and an increased likelihood of hostilities are likely to increase the amount of emotional stress. Stress is likely to make individuals rely on their core beliefs in order to appreciate the new situation quickly. Under conditions of stress, therefore, master beliefs in particular are expected to be of influence on decision-making (George and Holsti, 1975).[12]

### The Impact of Domestic Political Institutions

Decision-makers do not operate in a political vacuum, even in the event of a foreign policy crisis. On a general level, one might argue that foreign policy will reflect sets of tradeoffs by policy-makers between the mobilization and maintenance of domestic support, the effective and efficient use of resources, and the need for high quality decisions (George, 1980; Janis, 1989). Some even go as far as claiming that no foreign policy is acceptable that is not also accepted by domestic constituents (Putnam, 1988). Thus study takes the position that different political systems display different institutional mechanisms through which domestic politics can have an impact on foreign policy. Political institutions, or the formal and informal rules regulating political life, provide constraints and opportunities to mobilize support or protest (March and Olsen, 1989; Peters 1998). A study of British foreign policy thus requires an assessment of such British institutional mechanisms and how they are likely to affect decision-making during a foreign policy crisis (cf. Steiner, 1987).

*The political system of Great Britain*  The principal institutional setting is Britain's majoritarian electoral system. Since the end of the Second World War this has tended to produce clear-cut parliamentary one-party-majorities. Second, its government is characterized as a so-called Prime Ministerial system. The Prime Minister has a strong position as he or she has the authority to hire and fire new Cabinet members as well as to determine (within margins) the precise moment of the next general election. These characteristics of the British political system point to two import fashions of how British politics affects foreign policy-making in small groups such as the Cabinet: through the power of the Prime Minister and through the group's accountability to Parliament.

The Prime Minister has some quite formal powers. (S)he can hire and fire individual Ministers. In addition, (s)he can decide for a formal Cabinet reshuffle. This usually occurs in September (just before the parties' congressional season in autumn) and provides an opportunity to give new individuals a ministerial post, promote some, and punish others. In terms of small group decision-making this power to remove someone from office or send him to another Department (for instance to faraway Scotland or Ulster) affects the position many members of the Cabinet may take, or of smaller groups such as Inner Cabinets. Indeed, Margaret Thatcher used the reshuffles of her first two years as Prime Minister to 'exile' dissenters to distant Departments, as she did not yet have the authority to simply sack them. Another important element is the Prime Minister's discretion to decide (within margins) when to call an election. On the other hand these powers are balanced by several factors. First, most Prime Ministers face political heavyweights in their parties. Although sometimes they are defeated in formal attempts to challenge the Prime Minister's leadership over the Party, most of the time the heavyweights are co-opted into the Cabinet. Within the Cabinet, however, they tend to exert a restraining influence on the Prime Minister's powers. This implies that the Prime Minister's impact on decision-making is limited by the opinion of so-called Senior Ministers. It also implies that the jockeying for power positions with an eye on a possible leadership change is a permanent feature of the Cabinet. Narrow career calculations may thus affect a Senior Minister's stand during small group decision-making. What exactly constitutes a Senior Minister is a bit of a mystery. Its prestige is based on a combination of inner party status, the status of the department a minister is leading (esp. Foreign Office, Treasury, Chancellery, Defence, Home Office) and an individual's seniority. Together these Senior Ministers are, as Anthony King calls them, the 'big beasts of the jungle' (King, 1994: p. 219).

Their existence has important implications for small group decision-making in British Cabinets. A Prime Minister cannot simply impose his or her will on the Cabinet unless consensus exists between the Prime Minister and the Senior Ministers. This implies that criticism within the Cabinet is less relevant as long as so-called Junior Ministers express it. As soon as one Senior Minister indicates doubts about the current course of action, it becomes clear to the Junior Ministers that a change of policy becomes possible.

The circumstance that majoritarian electoral systems often produce stable one-party-governments has important implications for the relations between a small group and its wider political environment. The first implication is that domestic public opinion is much less a concern than one would expect in a democracy. British Cabinets win or lose their battles in Parliament, that is, the House of

Commons. This implies first of all maintaining the support of the Party. Domestic public opinion therefore matters only to the extent that a faction of the party forming the government expects its constituents to send them home at the next election. On the whole, however, the Government is likely to obtain the support of the party. This is guaranteed first by the fact that in Great Britain about one third of the winning party's members of parliament are given a governmental position. In addition, the office of the Whips ensures that those without a government job (backbenchers) stay in line. Indeed, British Cabinets worry about their political environment to the extent that they risk losing the support of backbenchers. That is why Labour governments closely monitor the so-called *PLP* (Parliamentary Labour Party) and Conservative governments intimately watch the so-called *1922 Committee*. Both are the formal institutions of the two parties' respective backbenchers. Again, backbenchers smell blood if Senior Ministers are seen to defect from the government's consensus. If a governmental majority is so narrow that it risks losing important votes of censure, a government will pay even more attention to the position of its backbenchers.

*British domestic politics and analyzing the Suez crisis*  The specific institutional features of British domestic politics have important implications for an analysis of British decision-making during the Suez crisis. First, it is to be expected that public opinion will not affect decision-making directly. Its impact is felt through the parliamentary institutions of the majority party. Second, party politics is expected to be of heavier consequence than public opinion throughout the nation. The smaller the government's majority, the larger the impact of its backbenchers. Third, decision-making is affected by the position of Senior Ministers because of their capacity to legitimize and strengthen opposition to the Government's official course. It is expected that criticism within the Cabinet will not be effective unless one or more Senior Ministers underwrite it. By consequence, it is to be expected that Prime Ministers who want to persuade the Cabinet of a certain policy will ensure consensus among Senior Ministers beforehand. In sum, the Prime Minister's power and the counterweight of Senior Ministers, as well as their permanent battle for (future) party leadership will ensure that any cohesion of small groups members engaged in foreign policy crisis decision-making will be mixed with the politics of British political institutions (cf. 't Hart et al., 1997).

*The Organizational Context of Decision-Making*

The occurrence of a foreign policy crisis is likely to lead to the concentration of decision-making into the hands of a few key policy-makers, often meeting in ad hoc decision-making bodies. It was explained above that the circumvention of patterns of routine-like organizational policy-making could be one of the potentially beneficial effects of centralization (cf. Vertzberger, 1990). On the other hand even the smallest group of decision-makers remains dependent on the departmental organizations around it. Governmental organizations still provide much of the information that decision-makers need to reach a decision. Moreover, governmental organizations will have to implement such a decision. Obviously then, even if governmental organizations are an unlikely *locus of decision* during a foreign policy crisis, they can still affect the actual decision-making body.

*Bureaucratic politics and standard operation procedures*   The impact of governmental organizations on foreign policy is usually assessed by applying two theoretical notions, bureaucratic politics and standard operation procedures. The theory of bureaucratic politics explains a state's foreign policy as a compromise between mutually dependent governmental organizations. Governmental organizations develop their own definition of the national interest. This can be based on material considerations (expansion of budget, or tasks, or number of personnel employed) or on substantive policy considerations. Governmental organizations often are dependent on each other for actual policy-making. Very frequently, issues of foreign policy regard the Foreign Office as well as the Ministry of Defence or the Treasury. Individual civil servants and politicians heading these bureaucracies are assumed to be spokespersons of the organizational interest ('Where you stand depends on where you sit'). By consequence, decision-making turns into a struggle between departments. The outcome will be a compromise reflecting the power relations between the departments involved. Moreover, these conflicts recur at the implementation stage. Because governmental organizations are responsible for policy-implementation, and because, again, they are regularly mutually dependent on each other, similar types of conflict are likely to occur (Allison, 1971; Halperin, 1974; Allison and Zelikow, 1999). The theory of bureaucratic politics conceives of an organization as an actor defending an interest in a political arena. The theory of standard operation procedures, however, considers an organization as a social system adjusting to its environment in order to survive. Social systems develop routine-like solutions to problems that recur on a regular basis. These routine solutions are codified in so-called standard operation procedures. Foreign policy is thus explained as the product of governmental organizations that apply standard solutions to standard problems (Allison, 1971; Welch, 1992; Allison and Zelikow, 1999).

The explanatory value of both theories has been severely questioned over the years (see, for an overview, Stern and Verbeek, 1998). Both approaches figure prominently in foreign policy analysis giving weight to the suggestion that organizational conflicts are paramount. Yet, very few actual empirical tests of their theoretical propositions have been conducted. Indeed, the problem may well be that it is relatively easy to show the presence of organizational conflict in the policy-making process. It is much more difficult to assess its impact on decision-making. Both approaches have also been criticized for several theoretical flaws. First of all, the theory of bureaucratic politics suggests that governmental organizations operate in a political vacuum. Yet, political leaders can have a significant impact on the occurrence and nature of bureaucratic politics (Krasner, 1972; Preston and 't Hart, 1999). Second, it is very difficult to ascertain the policy preference of a governmental organization. Protection of its budget and tasks may mark the boundaries within which a bureaucratic agency operates. However, these limits give no easy prediction of what an agency's policy position in specific situations will be. Third, no a priori reason exists why a bureaucratic struggle would necessarily result in a compromise rather than other types of outcomes, such as a stalemate between conflicting parties

(Preston and 't Hart, 1999). Despite these shortcomings, both theories point to a potentially important aspect of decision-making. How then to take it into account?

*Is the organizational context relevant for analyzing crisis decision-making?* The theories of bureaucratic politics and of standard operation procedures are both usually considered relevant for the analysis of foreign policy under 'normal' conditions. In the absence of crisis situations or of issues that are thought to be politically highly salient, standard procedures may explain the outcome of day-to-day policy-making at the Foreign Office. Similarly, as long as no outsider intervenes in the daily struggles between governmental agencies, foreign policy may indeed resemble a compromise between them. Yet, it can be argued that even under the conditions of a foreign policy crisis the impact of governmental organizations can be felt. First, before coming to a decision key policy-makers depend for their information to a large extent on governmental departments. This may affect both the substance and the timing of their decisions. The range of alternatives under policy-makers' scrutiny and their estimation of the feasibility of each may thus be heavily influenced by bureaucratic organizations. The nature of the information the latter provide may itself be the product of bureaucratic conflict or of standard operation procedure. Also, these organizational processes may affect the timing of decisions by key policy-makers. The moment at which information, deemed crucial, becomes available from the governmental agencies may alter assessments of feasibility and desirability. For example, the precise timing of the Cuban missile crisis in 1962 (the discovery of missile sites on photographs taken by the U2 spy plane) was in large measure determined by the end of the bureaucratic stalemate between the CIA and the Pentagon over the U2 reconnaissance flights over Cuba (Allison 1971; Allison and Zelikow, 1999). These patterns of organizational influence are more likely when policy-makers lack the technical expertise to assess the kind of information they invite in order to make a sound decision. Second, organizational processes may surface during the stage of implementation. Decision-making that meets the criteria of procedural high quality decision-making may still fail because of organizational politics. For example, the discovery of Soviet missile sites on Cuba was in large part caused by the Soviet agency responsible for their construction. The agency applied its standard operation procedure of constructing missile sites in the open (Allison, 1971; Allison and Zelikow, 1999). Third, organizational interests may have an impact on key policy-makers if individual ministers assume policy preferences that are a direct translation of the interest of the organization they head. For instance, in 1947 the Dutch Minister of Finance spoke up in the Cabinet in favour of a military intervention in Indonesia because tax revenue from Dutch-owned plantations on Java and Sumatra were deemed crucial for the balance-of-payments position of the Netherlands (Fennema, 1994). An analysis of British decision-making during the Suez crisis should take into account these three possible patterns of organizational influence.

*Organizational context and British decision-making during the Suez crisis* This study takes as its point of departure that bureaucratic organizations will not be the locus of decision during the Suez crisis. Centralization of decision-making into the hands of a relatively small group of decision-makers is expected to take place. This will not lead, however, to a complete immunization of policy-makers from their organizational surroundings. In general, the more policy-makers lack specific expertise, the more influential departmental organizations are likely to be. In the case of considering and preparing massive military intervention, as in the case of Suez, experts from the armed forces at the Ministry of Defence and from the international legal divisions at the Foreign Office are expected to affect both the contents and timing of decision-making by key policy-makers. The organizational context can also be expected to have an impact during the phase of policy implementation. This study, however, as explained in Chapter 1, aims at resolving the puzzles related to the British decision to intervene militarily despite the slim chance that American support would be forthcoming. It will not investigate the implementation of the use of force. Implementation processes are thus confined to the planning and preparation stages.

## Methodological Considerations

The basic theoretical propositions guiding the analysis of British decision-making during the Suez crisis have now been put forward. The occurrence of a foreign policy crisis situation and the emotional stress aroused by it are expected to have important consequences for the decision-making performance of a small group of key policy-makers and their leader. This requires several important methodological decisions regarding the measurement of the period of crisis and the circumstance of emotional stress. In addition, it demands an assessment of the validity of available data on British decision-making during the Suez crisis.

### How to Measure a Crisis and Emotional Stress?

*Four phases*  In order to measure the start of a foreign policy crisis it is useful make a distinction between four phases: the pre-crisis, the crisis, the end of crisis and the post-crisis (Brecher and Wilkenfeld, 2000). The pre-crisis phase only involves one element of the crisis definition adapted above, namely a sharp increase in a perceived threat to important values, often provoked by a symbolic act of the adversary. The crisis phase is characterized by the presence of all three defining elements, that is, high threat to values, restricted time for responding, and the perceived likelihood of military hostilities. The end of crisis phase displays a decline in threat perception, time pressure and military hostilities. The post-crisis phase sets in when all three defining elements of crisis are no longer present. Different levels of emotional stress experienced by policy-makers are expected to accompany these four phases, with the crisis phase displaying the most intense stress levels.

From the perspective of Great Britain the pre-crisis set in on 1 March 1956 with the dismissal by Jordan's King Hussein of Sir John Glubb, Commander of the Arab Legion, allegedly at the instigation of Egypt's President Nasser. The Glubb-affair contains only one aspect of crisis, an increase in threat perception. No increase in the perception of time constraints or the likelihood of military hostilities can be observed. Although the Cabinet decided to change its policies towards Egypt, this was not conceived in terms of an immediate response. Rather, the British Government decided to intensify Anglo-American co-ordination of Middle East policy (see chapter 3). The evening of 26 July 1956 marks the start of the crisis phase, when President Nasser nationalized the Suez Canal Company in response to the Anglo-American decision to withdraw an offer to lend Egypt money to construct the Aswan high dam. All three elements of crisis seem present. Nasser's move was considered a serious threat to British interests and assets in the Middle East. Moreover, the British Cabinet perceived a limited amount of time available for a response, because a 'failure to hold the Suez Canal would lead inevitably to the loss one by one of all our interests and assets in the Middle East'. Third, it was recognized that only the threat with, and even use of, force might hold the Suez Canal.[13] The sense of crisis may have been aggravated by the considerable surprise of British policy-makers at Nasser's move. The end of the crisis started with the Cabinet's decision of 6 November to accept the United Nations resolution that called for a cease-fire. The likelihood of military hostilities had thus been sharply reduced. It ended with the Cabinet's decision on 3 December to agree to a withdrawal of British troops in order to obtain American financial assistance. This marks the start of the post-crisis phase.

For the purpose of this study, the solving of the puzzles presented in the Introduction, the Suez crisis can be defined as the period between 26 July and 6 November 1956. This confinement is of considerable methodological importance, because a crisis period is expected to manifest a sharp increase in the level of emotional stress, which may in turn influence the quality and outcome of the decision-making process.

*The interrelationship between crisis, stress and decision-making*  In practice, it is very difficult to separate symptoms of crisis and stress. The literature on cognitive psychology shows that time pressure does indeed generate emotional stress, but it is equally true that aroused stress itself causes a sense of time constraints (George and Holsti, 1975). Measuring the occurrence of a crisis situation by looking for perceptions of time pressure is thus methodologically risky, especially if the subject of investigation is a presumed relationship between an increase in levels of emotional stress and the decision-making process. It is tempting, yet methodologically unsound, to present changes in the decision-making process or judgements about its quality as evidence of high levels of stress.

Ideally, stress generated by perceptions of crisis should be measured independently from the consequences it may have on the decision-making process. Two solutions to this problem have been suggested. One solution is to measure to what extent policy-makers suffer from high stress. Next, these data should be confronted with, on the one hand, data on perceptions of threat and time pressure, and, on the other hand, symptoms of defective decision-making, a solution proposed by Margaret Hermann (1979). She developed several verbal and non-verbal indicators of the presence of aroused stress among decision-makers, such as flustered speech, increased speech tempo, body tension, irritability, signs of distress on the individual's face, hyper-vigilance, and changes in the quality of the individual's voice. The use of verbal and non-verbal indicators is problematical because most such data are derived from public statements by foreign policy-makers. During foreign policy crises these are usually made when decision-makers have already made up their minds about the nature of the threat, and often have already taken a decision. Very crucial elements of an analysis of decision-making, like the definition of the problem, the identification of objectives and alternatives, etc., are unlikely to be captured. This makes it difficult to relate indicators of high stress to the decision-making- process itself.

A second remedy is to measure the existence of a crisis situation in an indirect manner. One example is Holsti's study of the outbreak of the First World War (Holsti, 1972). Holsti used on the one hand the level and intensity of communications between actors in a crisis and on the other hand the actors' perception of international hostility. He found that in a situation of increasing stress actors tend to perceive their range of alternatives to be shrinking and those of their opponents to be expanding. They thus perceive themselves to be reacting to their opponent's behaviour as if under conditions of necessity, while they perceived their opponent to have alternative courses of action, which might avoid further escalation. Holsti's analysis suggests that changes in the intensity of communications can serve as an indirect indicator of levels of crisis and stress, which can then be related to the decision-making process. It may thus be possible to separate the measurement of stress from the measurement of its consequences after all.

As a matter of fact, the intensity of communications between actors during the Suez crisis has been analyzed in a quantitative study of hostile signals between Egypt and the United Kingdom (Azar, 1972). Employing data from the so-called Conflict and Peace Data Bank, Azar coded 169 signals about Egypt that were communicated by the United Kingdom between 26 July 1956 and 11 January 1957[14] making use of a 13-points scale with categories ranging from very friendly to very hostile. These utterances of hostility could serve as evidence of variations in levels of stress. However, a comparison of the level of hostility with evidence from primary sources about what seem to have been crucial decision moments, suggests that these hardly coincide with an increase in hostility.[15] For instance, no hostile signals were sent from Britain to Egypt between 15 and 25 August 1956. At first sight, this seems relatively easy to explain because, in that period, a diplomatic solution was sought at the first London Conference. However, primary sources show that the British Cabinet was facing a pressing dilemma towards 23 and 24 August, insecure whether it would be justified to go to war after a possibly unsatisfactory outcome of the Conference. It decided to temporarily play down its hostile attitude towards Egypt for the sake of domestic and international public opinion. The period between 14 and 23 October poses another problem. No hostility signals are coded for this period, although in those days, with the visit of General Maurice Challe to Eden at Chequers and meetings of the inner circle of the British Cabinet, the foundations were laid for Israeli involvement in an Anglo-French policing operation. In both instances British decision-makers experienced considerable time pressure (see chapter 5). Indirect indicators of crisis, such as hostility signals between states, may therefore not be adequate to suggest stress among decision-makers.

This study takes the position that the concept of *decisional conflict* (or *crucial decision* or *hot cognition*) offers a solution to the problem. Decisional conflicts are characterized by a high risk of suffering serious losses, no matter which course of action is selected, as perceived by the decision-maker (Janis, 1959; Janis and Mann, 1977). These loss-loss situations are expected to produce high levels of emotional stress, simply because any course of action entails the loss of a highly valued item. In this study it is assumed that during the Suez crisis emotional stress is generated by the occurrence of a decisional conflict, defined as those situations producing the perception of a serious dilemma, that is, a choice between alternatives each of which would entail important losses.

*Decisional Conflicts in Great Britain during the Suez Crisis*

Six decisional conflicts can be distinguished during British decision-making over Suez. Decision 1 (26 July-2 August). British policy-makers faced the dilemma of how to respond vigorously to the Egyptian challenge of nationalizing the Suez Canal Company without alienating the United States and endangering Britain's long term interests in the Middle East. An immediate military attack was considered, either with airborne troops or with bombardments. Another important plan involved the invasion of Egypt by British troops in eastern Libya. On 2 August it was agreed to call for a Conference of the original signatories of the 1888 Constantinople Conference that had established the international character of the Suez Canal Company.

Decision 2 (2 August-22 August, 2 a.m.). British policy-makers had to determine what they would consider a satisfactory outcome of the London Conference. Could they accept an outcome that would not declare them outright winners? In the early morning of 22 August, at the request of Eden, Dulles, and Foreign Secretary Lloyd, the Australian Prime Minister, Sir Robert Menzies, accepted to head a delegation to Egypt.

Decision 3 (2 August, 2 a.m.-11 September). British policy-makers had to respond to a possible failure of the Menzies mission. Should they refer the matter to United Nations, despite American reluctance to such a move or should they agree to Dulles's proposal for a Users' Conference? On 11 September the British Cabinet accepted the S.C.U.A. proposal. That same day the Suez Canal Company recalled its pilots from Egypt.

Decision 4 (19 September-23 September). British policy-makers had to find a response to a possibly unsatisfactory outcome of the S.C.U.A. Conference. On 23 September the British Government decided to refer the case to the Security Council of the United Nations, despite American opposition.

Decision 5 (23 September-25 October). British policy-makers were facing three dangerous developments. First, a possibly unsatisfactory outcome of negotiations between France, Egypt and the United Kingdom at the United Nations. Second, the Winter-plan presented by the Chiefs of Staff, which relaxed military preparations until the spring of 1957 and thus weakened British leverage on Egypt. Third, the likelihood that the United States would not be prepared to use S.C.U.A. as a tool for putting pressure on Egypt. On 24 October the British Cabinet accepted to intervene in the event of an Israeli attack on Egypt that threatened the flow of traffic in the Suez Canal.

Decision 6 (25 October-4 November). British decision-makers had to face mounting pressure of international public opinion calling for a cease-fire, especially at the General Assembly of the United Nations, including the United States. Moreover, Israel (temporarily) complied with the United Nations' call for a cease-fire, thus depriving Great Britain and France of their pretext to occupy the Canal Zone. To stop the operations would imply the abandonment of one of its principal goals, the toppling of Nasser. On 4 November, the Cabinet decided to go on with the operations, and, as a matter of fact, to drop airborne troops one day earlier than planned.

These six decisions mark six phases that will be analyzed separately in the next chapter. For each phase the impact of Groupthink, cognitive beliefs, domestic political institutions and the organizational context on British decision-making will be assessed. The six decisions eventually culminate in the British Cabinet's awareness on 6 November 1956 that American diplomatic and financial opposition to the Anglo-French invasion made continuation of the operation impossible.[16] Methodologically, this study applies the methods of process tracing (George 1979a) and structured-focused comparison (George, 1979b). It involves identifying and analyzing the steps and tasks performed by policy-makers in six separate phases leading to six distinct decisions. It comprises structured-focused comparison, because each decision will be analyzed in terms of Groupthink, cognitive beliefs, domestic political institutions, and the organizational context. Together, these six decisions should add up to resolving the puzzles of Suez.

## A Reflection on Primary Sources

Process tracing implies the reconstruction of the decision-making process. For that purpose this study has made extensive use of primary and secondary sources on the Suez crisis. The reconstruction of the decision-making process is summarized in Appendix 2 at the end of this study. The official Cabinet documents allow for a fair reconstruction of meetings of formal committees. This was much more difficult for the reconstruction of informal meetings between policy-makers. Although extensive crosschecks across primary and secondary sources have been performed and are reported on in chapter 6, their reconstruction relies on two primary sources in particular. First Foreign Secretary Selwyn Lloyd's personal diary of engagements between July and November 1956, filed at the Public Record Office under FO 800/713-717. Second the original diary of Eden's Press Secretary William Clark, the 'Whitehall diary', guarded at the Bodleian Library at Oxford.

Primary sources should, of course, be handled with care. This is particularly true for documents that seem genuine accounts of men and events, such as the diaries of William Clark and Evelyn Shuckburgh. Both worked closely with Anthony Eden and used their diaries to gain some relief from the pressures at work. As to Shuckburgh's account, it should be kept in mind that his judgement of Eden and his policies changed substantially after his appointment as Under-Secretary at the Foreign Office dealing with Middle Eastern Affairs in May 1954. Part of this changed attitude can certainly be attributed to identification with a new role. As Under-Secretary

Shuckburgh was responsible for the secret 'Alpha'-Project that aimed at a settlement between Israel and her neighbours. Part of Shuckburgh's statements thus reflects his interests as Under-Secretary, which differed from those he had as Eden's Principal Private Secretary. Most books on Suez rely on Clark's memoirs *From Three Worlds* (London, 1986). However, it is better to rely on the original diary (although it may have been edited later as well). It should be kept in mind, however, that towards the end of the crisis Clark's account is becoming blurred by his outrage over the Challe-plan. Clark's account, however, is an important source for the reconstruction of the decision-making process, and for inside information on important meetings because of Clark's regular lunches with Minister of Defence Sir Walter Monckton and Secretary to Cabinet Sir Norman Brook.

## Conclusions

This chapter has outlined the theoretical expectations that constitute the basis for an analysis of British decision-making during the Suez crisis. First of all, it is expected that the occurrence of a foreign policy crisis will lead to the centralization of decision-making into the hands of a small number of key decision-makers. If the start of the Suez crisis can be identified with Egypt's nationalization of the Suez Canal Company on 26 July 1956 centralization of decision-making is expected to take place soon afterwards and to last throughout the crisis phase that ends on 6 November 1956. Second, the circumstance of crisis is expected to raise the levels of emotional stress. High levels of stress are expected to affect the quality of decision-making by increasing the chance that Groupthink will occur. Moreover, stress is expected to make individuals rely more on their so-called central beliefs. With respect to the puzzle of Suez this implies that British policy-makers in general are expected to seek guidance for their policies in their shared images of Anglo-American relations. Third, centralization of decision-making is likely to increase the weight of leadership. For this study this suggests that Prime Minister Anthony Eden's behaviour is of particular importance. In addition, the presence of high levels of stress is likely to make the leader rely on his central cognitive beliefs. The so-called Operational Code construct has been selected to assess his cognitive belief system and to investigate the extent to which it has affected his handling of decision-making. Fourth, decision-making is expected to be regulated by political institutions, that is, formal and informal rules. In the case of Great Britain, it is expected that the delicate balance between Prime Minister, Senior Ministers, and backbenchers will affect the possibility of raising criticism during policy deliberations. Finally, policy-makers operate within an organizational context. In general, centralization of decision-making is likely to reduce the impact of governmental organizations. Nevertheless, the more policy-makers are dependent on expertise from governmental organizations, the more likely it is that these will affect both the timing and the contents of decision-making.

Chapter 5 will present a reconstruction of the decision-making process in Great Britain during the crisis phase. Chapter 6 will answer the question whether the empirical material will fit the expectations formulated above and will resolve the puzzle of Suez that was formulated in the Introduction. First, however, it is necessary to describe the ideas with which British policy-makers entered the crisis. Chapter 3 portrays the development of the images of Anglo-American relations that were widely shared by British policy-makers between 1945 and 1956. Chapter 4 presents the worldview of Sir Anthony Eden at the moment the crisis started unfolding. These shared images as well as Eden's individual worldview are expected to be important clues to resolving the puzzle of Suez.

## Notes

[1]  Surprise was part of Hermann's original definition (1969, p. 414). Hermann and Mason (1980) recognized its problems and took surprise out of the definition of crisis.

[2]  However, even the failure to meet all criteria of high quality decision-making is not a recipe for disaster. Fortune may still be on the policy-makers' side (Janis, 1989).

[3]  't Hart argues that these motivational differences lead to two distinct types of Groupthink, collective avoidance and collective optimism ('t Hart, 1990/1994, pp. 181-93, 201-03). However, the calculated silence of some group members, or collective avoidance, still presumes premature consensus by the rest of the group who do believe in wisdom of the proposed policies (collective optimism). They cannot exist independently from each other, except in the highly unlikely case that all group members remain silent after one group member has suggested a course of action.

[4]  As a matter of fact, a seventh case Janis analyzed concerned domestic politics (the inner circle around President Nixon during Watergate).

[5]  Groupthink has also been applied outside the domain of foreign policy crises to policy failure in many different policy areas and organizations as well as in experimental laboratory settings. See, for a recent overview, Kowert (2002).

[6]  It occurred in eleven out of 19 cases. Unfortunately, Schafer and Crichlow correlated cohesion with decision-making quality, but not with symptoms of Groupthink.

[7]  The importance of beliefs widely shared among government officials has since long been an element of the analytical framework for studying foreign policy crises developed by Michael Brecher and others in the *International Crisis Behavior Project* (Brecher et al., 1969).

[8]  Other scholars refined the concept of images into so-called national role conceptions, a term that refers to the foreign policy elite's view of their country's place in world politics (Walker, 1987). Although an improvement on the general notion of images, role conceptions are a property of elites or even the whole population, not of an individual leader.

[9]  Cognitive Maps have been drawn up of Latin American policy-makers (Hart, 1977), British decision-makers on nuclear policy (Hamwee et al., 1990), and British foreign policy-makers in 1938-9 (Walker and Watson, 1992). Operational Codes have been composed of many, although mainly American, foreign policy-makers, including Dean Acheson, Jimmy Carter, Frank Church, John Foster Dulles, Lyndon B. Johnson, John F. Kennedy, Henry Kissinger. See, for an overview, Walker (1990). A recent addition involves Bill Clinton (Schafer and Crichlow, 2000).

[10]  An example with the use of a Cognitive Map is Japan's 1941 decision to go to war (Levi and Tetlock, 1980). A study applying the Operational Code is Henry Kissinger's policy towards Vietnam (Walker, 1977).

[11]  This is the case at least for several applications of the Cognitive Map technique in Axelrod's seminal volume (1976).

[12] However, see Astorino-Courtois (2000) for contradictory evidence from laboratory experiments.

[13] CAB 128/30, CM(56)54, 27 July 1956.

[14] The day when all occupying forces had withdrawn or were about to withdraw from Egypt.

[15] The following is based on Azar (1972, p. 191, table 3; p. 192, figure 1).

[16] As such this study of British foreign policy can be called a study of sequential decision-making (Billings and Hermann, 1998).

# Chapter 3

# Images Held by the British Political Elite

## Introduction

Misperception and miscalculation are inherent to the foreign policy of states, because of the basic insecurity that characterizes the international political system. Sustained patterns of co-operation and norms shared between states may reduce the amount of insecurity between them, but will not eliminate it completely. An incorrect sense of security may occur, if on the surface co-operation between states continues and the same time norms continue to be professed, while underneath the distribution of power between them is changing and their interests are no longer identical. The discrepancy between new diverging interests and past converging mutual images can be a major source of misperception and miscalculation on both sides. This chapter argues that between 1945 and 1956 the British political elite appreciated the changing power relations between Great Britain and the United States, but failed to deduce a subsequently growing divergence of interests, in particular regarding the Middle East. This perception was widely shared among those in the Government involved in foreign policy, both in the post-war Labour government (1945-51) and in the Conservative government that succeeded it (1951-5). Their experience furthered a very precise interpretation of Anglo-American common interests and the best way of obtaining American support for British foreign policy. In a nutshell they amounted to two basic convictions. First that the United States acknowledged Great Britain's position as a major power with exclusive interests in the Middle East. Second that the United States could always be persuaded eventually to defend British interests as long as British diplomacy persisted in its efforts to convince Washington. These two ideas prevented the British political elite from discerning substantive changes in Anglo-American relations. At the start of the Suez crisis, major players in Whitehall, such as Anthony Eden, Harold Macmillan, Lord Salisbury, and John Selwyn Lloyd, would bring these images to the meetings of the Cabinet and the Egypt Committee. This chapter recounts the development of these ideas, which would prove erroneous in the summer of 1956. The following section will examine their foundations, which can be traced to the foreign policy of the post-war Labour government. The next section will demonstrate that these ideas were particularly powerful regarding the foreign policy towards the Middle East of the Conservative government under Sir Winston Churchill.

**Laying the Foundations: the Labour Government 1945-51**

Three elements constituted the core of Anglo-American relations during the two Labour governments under Clement Attlee. First, a weak economy made Great Britain heavily dependent on support from the United States. Second, this weakness did not lead to complete American domination because of important British military-strategic assets. These assets constituted the basis for various British diplomatic successes, which in turn created the impression that the United States considered Great Britain still as a major power with certain privileges, especially in the Middle East.

*Economic Weakness*

Economically, post-war Britain was in a deplorable state. Its war debts and shortage of dollars made her dependent on American financial support, trade with the Commonwealth, and simple barter trade. The United States thus had quite some economic leverage over Great Britain. However, the United States could not convert this source of power into instant British compliance with American demands. Although in some instances, notably oil production, the United States succeeded in making Great Britain adjust to American interests, this was not the case in other important areas. This is demonstrated by failed American attempts to abolish the preferential trading system of the Commonwealth and British barter trade with Communist countries.

*Weakness* During almost the entire period up until Suez Great Britain faced gigantic financial debts. In order to finance its war efforts, it had liquidated over 1 billion pounds of overseas investments and had increased its foreign debts to 3 billion at the same time. Britain owed large sums to notably India (1.1 billion), Egypt (400 million), and Iraq (70 million) (Louis, 1984). The abrupt termination in August 1945 by the United States of the Lend-Lease Act, which had basically allowed Great Britain to buy now and pay later, caused acute liquidity problems. The British government had to ask for a loan of 3.75 billion dollars, to which the United States agreed only on the condition that the Pound would be made convertible one year after ratification of the loan, which eventually meant July 1947. British officials had expected other countries to write off some of the British debt in order to help with Britain's economic recovery, but apart from the United States, which cancelled the Lend-Lease debt, no sterling creditor in Asia or the Middle East was willing to follow. This set the economic stage for Britain's withdrawal from Greece, Turkey and Palestine in 1947, simply because limitless British money seemed to be wasted there, while at home bread, dairy products, sugar, meat and petrol were under restriction, and holidays abroad were forbidden. The United States made an attempt to exploit British financial dependence and reach three important objectives of American foreign policy: the end of the preferential sterling trading area, the end of barter trade with communist nations, and the weakening of British oil interests in the Middle East.

*Preferential trading* From the moment they entered the Second World War the United States made attempts to dismantle the Imperial Preferential Trading System that connected the United Kingdom with its colonies and dominions. The Americans made use of the Lend-Lease Act to undermine the British position, especially in the Middle East, by setting up a non-military assistance programme, formally meant to improve the stability of Middle Eastern regimes (Herring, 1965). Already during the Lend-Lease negotiations in 1941, the United States tried to tie Lend-Lease to the removal of discriminatory British trade policies and to commit the United Kingdom to liberal multilateral trade principles. Another attempt was made during the 1944 Bretton Woods negotiations on post-war monetary arrangements. But both in trade and money the United Kingdom managed to resist a liberal regime by emphasizing the need for national control over economic and monetary policies or the purpose of post-war recovery.

The end of Lend-Lease, and the subsequent British need for an immediate 3.75 billion dollar loan offered the United States another opportunity. Great Britain, because of its economic weakness, had to accept the conditions of the loan. As a first step to embracing a liberal, multilateral world order, the British agreed to make Sterling convertible in 1947. The implementation of this measure, however, was halted only six weeks after its initiation, because of the massive drain on British reserves (Ikenberry, 1989). The United States, however, was unable to impose its design of a world order of free trade. European economic weakness prevented this, and, by consequence, made the British resistant to change their own preferential trading system. The United States did not want to become directly involved in administrating Europe, and therefore, in its implementation of the Marshall Plan, conceived of a relatively independent, economically integrated Europe as a third force between the Soviet Union and itself. The British, however, wanted to retain their own Imperial system and to keep their special position in between the United States and Europe, and therefore resisted those American efforts (Lundestad, 1998). Great Britain, France and the emerging Federal Republic of Germany tried to persuade the Americans to remain politically and militarily committed to Europe by underlining the communist threat. This led the United States to modify its multilateral trade ideas to the point of accepting a watered-down version of the original plans, which allowed for Western Europe's Keynesian macro-economic policies and welfare state arrangements (Ikenberry, 1989). In sum, extreme British economic weakness was not sufficient to provide the United States with sufficient political leverage to end British preferential trading.

*Trade with communist countries* Between 1947 and 1954 the United States made an effort to persuade Western Europe to cut off trade with the Soviet Bloc. The traditional view is that, by adopting the 1948 European Co-operation Act, the United States linked economic and military aid to Western Europe's trade policies. However, no aid to Western European countries was ever cut off, because the United States accepted their allies' trade policies, even to the point of granting formal exemptions, especially in order to accommodate urgent Western European needs for raw materials from the Soviet Bloc (Mastanduno, 1988). Great Britain in particular had a strong interest in trading with communist countries. The exchange of industrial products for raw materials was an important means to save dollars. In 1948, however, the United States started to confer with Great Britain about the question of how to impose export controls on Western Europe (incidentally confirming British perceptions that they functioned as a go-between). The British successfully resisted American pressure to stop the export of industrial products (products on so-called List 1-B). The British Cabinet accepted an embargo on strategic goods (List 1-A), as a means of keeping a source of influence on the Americans in order to prevent them from imposing a complete embargo on trade with the Soviet Bloc. The Korean War, however, brought new American pressure. The United States linked military aid for Western Europe's re-armament programme with trade policies. The Battle Act of October 1951 forced Western Europe to cut off trade with the Soviet Bloc. During the Korean War the United States coerced Britain and the rest of Western Europe to accept economic warfare against the Soviets by threatening to reduce military aid and to cut off the exports of those American goods that Western Europe could subsequently process into export goods for Eastern Europe. Later, however, Britain and the rest of Western Europe managed to resist all new initiatives to extend trade controls and managed to persuade the Americans to dismantle controls after 1954 (Sørensen, 1989).

*Oil production*   The United States was able to reach its objective to end British dominance in Middle East oil production. The original plan to establish an Anglo-American cartel with an International Petroleum Commission was never realized because of domestic pressure in the United States against such an arrangement. The agreement that eventually secured American oil interests was implemented through private companies rather than governmental agencies. The arrangement involved the dissolution of the so-called Red-Line agreement of 1928 that had set sharp restrictions on American access to oil production on the Arab peninsula. The position of the United Kingdom, severely weakened by the end of the Red-Line agreement and by the foundation of Saudi-American *Aramco*, was not completely annihilated, because the United States had agreed to the continued existence of the Sterling area. This ensured that British oil prices were set in Sterling, rather than (scarce) dollars.

By 1949 the British Government was able to persuade those countries that were short on dollars, such as the Scandinavian countries, to buy sterling oil. Because over-production characterized the oil sector, British companies effectively sold at the expense of their American competitors. Further protective measures by the Attlee Government in December 1950 caused American oil companies to lobby the Truman Administration to end British protectionism. Despite an attempt to cut off all Economic Co-operation Administration (ECA) assistance to Britain, it only led to the suspension of ECA-aid for those projects that sustained the British oil industry. Eventually, the Korean War ended the period of overproduction of oil (Keohane, 1984). Nevertheless, although the United States succeeded in breaking the British dominant position in Middle Eastern oil production, it could not simply impose its own terms and had to take into account the oil interests of Great Britain.

*Strategic Advantage*

Dramatic events, such as the British withdrawal from Greece and Turkey, the retreat from India, and the giving up of the Palestinian mandate, showed that Great Britain lacked the economic resources to maintain the strategic-geopolitical positions of its pre-war Empire. At the same time it retained strong spheres of influence that would prove a source of influence on the United States in certain diplomatic conflicts.

*Weakness* The deplorable state of the British economy forced the United Kingdom to withdraw its troops from Greece and Palestine, and to stop its financial assistance to Turkey. In 1946 the British had 40,000 troops in Greece and paid for most of the Greek government's army, which fought against the armed branch of the Greek communist party K.K.E. in the north of Greece. British troops in Palestine numbered about 100,000 men. In Palestine Great Britain feared that the large wave of Jewish immigrants, which caused serious tensions with the Palestinian and Arab population, would jeopardize the friendship with Arab rulers needed to keep its informal empire in the Middle East intact. The maintenance of this force cost between 30,000,000 and 40,000,000 pounds a year (Louis, 1984). Moreover, Britain supported Turkey financially and diplomatically in its effort to resist Russian claims on Turkey's North Eastern provinces and demands for a naval base near the Dardanelles. Turkey's stability and independence were seen as crucial for the protection of British interests in the Middle East (Thomas, 1987).

*Strength* Abroad, the reduction of its overseas commitments was perceived as the beginnings of the final dissolution of the British Empire. British policy-makers at the time considered it only a reduction of their financial burden in order to be better able to maintain an influential position throughout the Empire. Indeed, the foreign policy of the Attlee Government was an attempt to transform Britain's formal rule over most of the Middle East into an informal empire in which Britain's military and economic necessities would be safeguarded by offering development to modern Arab nationalists (Louis, 1984). From the British perspective the retreat from Greece and Turkey implied an understanding with the United States that the Middle East was a British region of influence. Interestingly, the United States shared this view. In talks with the British in late 1947, the United States recognized that 'the security of the Eastern Mediterranean and of the Middle East is vital to the security of the United States', and that this required that Great Britain keep its strong strategic, political and economic position in those areas. An internal memorandum acknowledged British 'primary responsibility' for the areas, which implied 'that the British should have mutually satisfactory political and economic relations of a long-term nature with the countries in the area, as a foundation for their military position'.[1]

An example of how Great Britain managed to expand its sphere of influence in the Middle East is their success at turning the former Italian colony of Libya into a British client state. By 1949 Great Britain argued that, in order to defend the Middle East from a Soviet attack, strong military bases in weak Libya were required. The United States agreed to setting up a weak federal Libyan state. Great Britain would dominate the eastern province of Cyrenaica, in order to avoid Egyptian dominance over her neighbour. The United States even agreed, albeit reluctantly, to Libya joining the sterling area (Louis, 1985).

How to explain American acquiescence to British geopolitical dominance over the Middle East? The United States was unable, well into the 1950s, to effectuate a global policy of containment without British co-operation. In case of Soviet aggression the United States would have to rely on its medium range bombers to counter such a move. By the end of 1950, the United States possessed only a small number of intercontinental bombers (38 B-36s) and had to rely on its large number of medium range bombers (477). The United States, however, lacked route rights as well as landing rights for refuelling at bases located strategically along trunk routes. Only Britain could grant those rights because of its extensive overseas colonies and Commonwealth connections (Jönsson, 1987; Strange, 1988). This very lack of landing and fuelling rights points to America's inability to implement a strategy of containment from 1947 on without British co-operation. The 1948-1949 Berlin Blockade crisis and the first months of the Korean War had demonstrated the importance of British bases to the Americans (Shlaim, 1983; Foot, 1988/1989). The relevance of British bases in the Middle East was their vicinity to important Russian industrial centres (Edmonds, 1986).

*Diplomatic Success*

Great Britain was well aware of its strategic leverage over the United States and used it to its advantage. In early 1951 Sir William Strang, Permanent Under-Secretary at the Foreign Office, thought it possible to extract concessions from the United States because it was 'equally true that the Americans cannot do without us. Though the Americans often behave as though our views and interests were of little regard to them, in the last resort, they know they must rely on us. This strengthens our position in dealing with them'.[2] This British strategic and geopolitical advantage could be an asset only if the United Kingdom and its Commonwealth and Empire were perceived to be essential for the defence of the free world against communist aggression. Here Great Britain possibly accomplished its most precious aim. Much of British diplomacy during and immediately after World War Two had been directed at persuading the United States that communism was threatening the West, and that Great Britain and its Empire were an essential element of Western defence.

*World War Two*  The future of the British Empire and Commonwealth had regularly strained wartime relations between the United States and Great Britain. On various occasions, the Americans had made it clear that they were not fighting the war for the preservation and restoration of the British Empire. In the American press the colonial issue was a regular topic of discussion, usually in the context of the establishment of a postwar international society, in which nations that were still under colonial rule would be granted eventual independence. British diplomacy therefore made an attempt to 'educate' the Americans on the merits of the British Empire for American security needs (Sbrega, 1983; Ryan, 1987). In reality, American anti-colonialism was strongly balanced with security needs. During the war the United States had not supported the 'Quit India now' movement because it deemed British predominance in

India essential for the struggle against Japan. Similarly, it had accepted an effective British protectorate in Libya in 1949, because it recognized British presence in the Middle East as crucial in the battle against communism. During the founding negotiations of the United Nations Organization, Great Britain succeeded in preventing the United States from equating the U.N.O.-principle of self-determination with the end of colonialism. Furthermore, Great Britain made the United States engage in a form of colonial tutelage itself, namely the responsibility of administrating certain trust territories themselves (Louis, 1984). The decision not to include existing colonial empires in the U.N.O. Trusteeship system, and to reserve this agency for former mandates of the League of Nations and for colonies of the Axis-powers, should therefore be considered a success of British diplomacy. Great Britain had been very anxious for the trusteeship-system not to harm its Empire. In January 1945 Eden reassured Churchill that 'there is not the slightest question of liquidating the British Empire', and judged the trusteeship system a useful way of convincing the Americans that they should accept colonial responsibility themselves (quoted by Sbrega, 1983, pp. 126-7).

*The Labour Government* The Attlee Government did not consider the retreat from Empire, as evidenced in India, Burma, and Palestine, as a first step toward its total dissolution, but as a way out of a precarious economic situation. Great Britain's objective was to keep the rest of the Empire intact, although governed by informal rather than formal rule. As a matter of fact, the Empire and its sterling trading area were considered a necessary condition of economic recovery. The attempts of the Attlee Government at involving the Americans in Western security served therefore two essential aims: first, to ease the financial burden of Britain's worldwide commitments; second, to make the Truman Administration recognize British predominance in the Middle East and Africa. Both aims required playing the communist card.

The communist danger should make the Americans realize that they should not withdraw in isolation, but assume responsibility for the defence of Western Europe. At the same time, it would bring home to the United States that the strategic assets of the British Empire were necessary for this defence (Folly, 1988). The explicit American recognition of the British position in the Middle East in 1947 when the United States took over British responsibilities over Greece and Turkey should therefore be considered as a British diplomatic success. In this context a welcome side effect of American participation in Western security through NATO was that the United States, in paying for Western security, indirectly paid for the continuation of the British Empire.[3] At the same time, it was not the case that Great Britain's principal aim was to make the United States pay for Britain's recovery as a world power. The Foreign Office at that time clearly perceived the Soviet Union to be a real threat, and therefore not just a handy bogeyman to obtain guarantees of American assistance. Nevertheless it was a convenient and deliberately sought side-effect (Boyle, 1979; Anstey, 1984).

*Conclusion* When in 1951 the Churchill Government replaced the Attlee Government, British policy-makers shared an optimistic view of Britain's position in the world. In July 1950 Sir Oliver Franks, Permanent Under-Secretary at the Foreign Office, wrote to Prime Minister Attlee that only two years before Britain had been one of many European countries. It had now acquired new vigour and strength thanks to the Commonwealth and the stronger currency, and held an improved overseas payment position: 'we are out of the queue, one of two world powers outside Russia. This has been recognized by the recent exchange of messages' (quoted by Edmonds, 1986, p. 229). The acceptance by the United States of Britain's position in the Middle East was crucial to this perception. Foreign Secretary Ernest Bevin thought that loss of the Middle East would lead the United States 'to write us off as a first class power' (quoted by Weiler, 1987, p. 67). The incoming Conservative government was not to adopt a different perspective.

## Knowing the Americans: The Churchill Government and the Middle East

Churchill's Indian Summer, as it has been called, coincided with a further weakening of the United Kingdom's position vis-à-vis the United States. Economically, Great Britain had become dependent on the United States more than ever. It still possessed some important strategic assets, and its preponderance over the Middle East was still recognized by the United States, but it was becoming increasingly difficult to convert that strategic currency into diplomatic successes. British policy-makers, however, continued to believe that the Americans would leave them a free hand in the area. Moreover, they were convinced that they could use the United States as a bogeyman in order to extract concessions from countries such as Egypt. This will be shown by examining three key issues of British Middle East policies in the early 1950s: British oil interests in Persia, strengthening the Baghdad Pact, and the British military base in the Suez canal area.

### Increasing Dependence on the United States

What remained of Sir Oliver Franks's optimistic vision, once Sir Winston Churchill had returned to 10 Downing Street in October 1951, accompanied by Sir Anthony Eden, who had become Foreign Secretary for the third time in his career? The economic position of the United Kingdom in the early 1950s continued to be weak, despite Whitehall's prudent optimism of 1950. Part of the deterioration was caused by American pressure to rearm in the wake of the outbreak of the Korean War. Great Britain had set her hopes for recovery on the development of a free trade area between Commonwealth and Empire nations in which Sterling would be the central currency. However, the important problem of earning dollars in order to pay for essential imports could not be resolved by the creation of a Sterling trade area. R.A Butler, the Chancellor of the Exchequer, travelled to the United States several times, hoping to obtain important tariff reductions from the Americans for the export of British products, but his efforts were to no avail. Shortage of dollars led to a balance of payments crisis in 1952, and Butler had to beg for swift American financial assistance. The Americans, however, were willing to provide only one third of the 900 million dollars that were needed (Boyle, 1988).

The major British strategic advantage was still intact. During the first three years of the Korean War the United States continued to need British bases for their strategic bomber force against the Soviet Union (Edmonds, 1986). The United States re-confirmed the need for continued British predominance over the Middle East. In 1953 the American National Security Council observed that 'even though British and French influence in the Near East has declined, the United Kingdom retains substantial interests, experience, and security positions so that the United States will need to act in concert with the United Kingdom to the greatest extent possible'.[4] Yet, the N.S.C. ominously added that the United States should reserve 'the right to act with others ... or alone'. The United States increasingly recognized that it would not always be prudent to rely on Great Britain if it wanted to safeguard its interests. 'It is important to the settlement of outstanding political disputes that the U.S. convince the Arab states that it is capable of acting independently of other Western states and of Israel'.[5] Here lies a source of British and American misunderstanding, as will soon become clear. For some time, Great Britain had been developing a second strategic asset. In October 1952 it had exploded an atomic bomb and with the development of its Venom-bombers it had acquired a substantial deterrent of its own (Edmonds, 1986). The joy over this newly found source of strength did not last very long. That same year the United States exploded a hydrogen bomb, one year later followed by the Soviet Union. Britain would not catch up until 1957. Moreover, the development of thermonuclear technology was to have a dramatic impact on the British assessment of the importance of Egypt and the Suez Canal Zone, serving as a catalyst of the British withdrawal from the area.

It proved increasingly difficult, however to convert these strategic assets into diplomatic successes. The Churchill Government suffered a number of diplomatic defeats against the United States. Churchill's numerous attempts after Stalin's death in March 1953 to organize a conference of the Heads of States of the United States, the Soviet Union, and the United Kingdom constituted the most symbolic of such defeats. Churchill feared that the United States would exclude Great Britain (and him personally) from a summit with the new Soviet leadership. A British absence would poignantly underline the country's decline as a world power. Churchill therefore launched a proposal on 11 May 1953 before the Americans would seize the initiative. However, Eisenhower consistently turned down this and the other proposals he put forward throughout the rest of 1953 (Fish, 1986; Shuckburgh, 1986).

*The Middle East 1951-5: Diverging Interests and Perceptions*

Great Britain continued to perceive the Middle East as its private sphere of influence, and remained convinced that the United States sanctioned this situation. Great Britain therefore persisted in its usual game. It used the United States as a bogeyman in its relations with Arab countries and it played on American fears that communism would spread in the region. Several consequences followed from this attitude. First, British policy-makers were unable to learn from Anglo-American discord over Iran between 1951 and 1953. They failed to appreciate that American interests and policies might conflict with British interests. Despite warning signals that the United States might be developing a Middle East policy of its own, British policy-makers continued to rely on their traditional tactics. Second, British policy-makers interpreted two important diplomatic outcomes, the conclusion of the Suez Canal Treaty with Egypt in 1954, and the foundation of the Baghdad Pact in the same year, as two more successes. They were convinced to have cajoled the Americans into accepting arrangements that were favourable to the interests of the United Kingdom, and remained unaware of the possibility that the United States might have interpreted these events in a radically different way. Third, this inability to assess the American attitude towards the Middle East reinforced the dominant British interpretation of Arab nationalism. Traditionally, British policy-makers held the view that almost any Arab regime that became hostile to British interests could be easily substituted for another.

*Iranian oil 1951-1953*   The Anglo-Iranian Oil Company (A.I.O.C.) was 100% owned by British interests, and operated from the south-western Iranian island of Abadan, which hosted the world's largest oil refinery. In 1951 it produced the largest share of Middle East oil. It thus was an important source of income for the British Government, who in 1950 received 40 million pounds from taxes alone. Its significance for the British economy became more evident after Iran nationalized the A.I.O.C. in 1951. Great Britain had to buy its oil elsewhere, and worse, had to pay for it in dollars, of which she possessed so few: this cost the United Kingdom about 40 million pounds a month (Leitner, 1985).

Anglo-American co-operation over Iran between 1951-1953 demonstrated that the United States would be insensitive to British concerns if its own interests were at stake. After the nationalization of AIOC the Labour Government tried to rally American support behind the British case, arguing that the nationalist government of Mohammed Mussadiq was driving Iran right into arms of the Soviet Union. They failed to obtain American support, because British oil interests in Iran did not bother the United States, which rather wanted to break the British monopoly over Iranian oil. Moreover, the United States had a considerably different appreciation of Mussadiq's nationalist government. It felt that the genuine nationalism of the organizations around Mussadiq would form an effective counterweight to the influence of the communist Tudeh party. The United States dissuaded Great Britain from using military force to defend British oil interests. Instead, the United States offered to co-ordinate policies with Great Britain in order to reach a settlement with Mussadiq's government. British policy-makers certainly perceived this as a major success. Churchill's Private Secretary noted in his diary: 'it is the first time since 1945 that the Americans have joined with us in taking overt joint action against a third power. Fear of ganging up has hitherto prevented them' (Colville, 1987, p. 310).

However, in 1952, the resumed negotiations failed and diplomatic relations between Great Britain and Iran were broken off. Mussadiq, after having been accused of being an American agent, had decided to withdraw from bargaining. At that moment, American and British interests temporarily coincided: the Americans no longer saw Mussadiq as an effective agent against communism, and agreed to co-ordinate his downfall with the British. Nevertheless, the temporary character of Anglo-American understanding became evident as soon as the new regime under

General Zahedi had been put into power, and negotiations about the nationalization of A.O.I.C. were resumed. The United States forced Great Britain to accept an agreement far worse than it could have obtained in 1950 when a 50/50 distribution of net profits had been proposed. The new settlement of September 1954 provided for 40% of Iranian oil to be produced by American oil companies, leaving only 40% to British Petroleum, thus breaking the British monopoly on Iranian oil and opening up the market to American companies (Keohane, 1984; Cottam, 1988).

The events in Iran between 1951 and 1954 could have taught Great Britain some important lessons. First, American and British interests need not coincide in the Middle East. Second, the United States would be prepared to exert strong pressure on Great Britain not to act unilaterally, such as over Abadan. Third, the United States might hold a different view of Middle East nationalism than Great Britain. Fourth, by consequence, the card of a Communist threat, displayed in nationalist movements, might not always be helpful in attracting American support for British interests. Nevertheless, British foreign policy-makers looked the other way, and continued believing that the United States recognized their privileges in the Middle East.

*The concluding of the 1954 Suez Canal Treaty* In early 1953 Great Britain and Egypt were renegotiating the Suez Canal Treaty, which regulated the presence of British troops in the Suez Canal area. British policy-makers put pressure on the United States to help them persuade Egypt to accept an agreement on British terms. Drawing a parallel to events in Iran, Eden and Churchill were anxious not to allow the Egyptian leader, General Neguib, to play the same game as Mussadiq had played in their perception, playing off the United States against Britain (Aronson, 1986). Great Britain wanted the United States to join the negotiations. This would make the United States look less like a mediator and more like Britain's major ally who would put pressure on Egypt, if it showed intransigence. The United States had to be persuaded to make economic and military assistance to Egypt dependent on Egyptian acceptance of the new treaty on British terms. In January 1953 Great Britain prevented the United States from delivering arms to Egypt. By March, however, the Americans had grown impatient with the British attitude, not in the least because Churchill, in a letter to Eisenhower, had threatened to go it alone and to simply stay in the Canal Zone, stating: 'We are not afraid of Neguib'.[6] By the Autumn of 1953 the United States seemed prepared to give economic aid to Egypt. When the Bermuda summit in December failed to bring Anglo-American consensus, Churchill increased the pressure. He warned Eisenhower that if the United States were to give assistance to Egypt 'we cannot help you any longer over the Far East [Korea, BV] in the face of general feeling of indignation throughout the country'.[7]

British policy-makers persisted in their belief that the Middle East, and certainly Egypt, was an exclusive British zone of influence that merited American support. Moreover, they used all leverage they could obtain from the American dependence on Great Britain for the implementation of its containment strategy. In the end, not until after the conclusion of the Anglo-Egyptian negotiations in July 1954, did the United States announce its willingness to provide 40 million dollars in military and economic assistance to Egypt. British policy-makers perceived the conclusion of the Treaty as an important success by all measures. It had seemed as if, in the end, resisting American pressure had produced the necessary American attitude to persuade Egypt to sign a treaty favourable to the United Kingdom. British policy-makers failed to appreciate that since 1953 the United States had been developing an attitude towards the Middle East that was increasingly insensitive to British interests. The United States perceived the Anglo-Egyptian treaty as a major achievement of its cold war diplomacy. From the American perspective, Anglo-Egyptian difficulties should be resolved before these would make Egypt dissociate from the West (Aronson, 1986). Washington and London thus interpreted the treaty in a completely opposite fashion. While British policy-makers thought they had been able to make use of United States' pressure on Egypt in concluding a treaty they found acceptable, the United States considered the negotiations the result of their pressure on both Great Britain and Egypt to reach a settlement.

*An anti-communist Middle Eastern alliance*     Before 1953 the United States had attempted to draw Egypt into a multilateral security agreement for the Middle East, the so-called Middle East Command. This military structure deliberately aimed at preserving British predominance in the area.[8] The events of Black Saturday (26 January 1952) when Egyptian crowds attacked and killed British citizens after British soldiers had killed 43 Egyptians, marked the beginning of a redefinition of American policy towards Egypt. The United States judged a communist revolution possible and considered the British practice of playing off different Egyptian factions against each other counterproductive. After the Free Officers coup against King Faruk in July 1952, the United States contacted Neguib and Nasser in order find a stable Egyptian regime that was safely linked with the West. The Americans hoped and expected that Neguib and his Free Officers could act like Atatürk in Turkey and worked to that effect by promising economic assistance to the new rulers (Aronson, 1986). Great Britain, however, continued to believe that Neguib's government was like any other Egyptian government. Eden thought they played the 'usual tactic of every Egyptian Government to represent themselves as the last bulwark between us and mob disorders'.[9]

     Although the Truman and Eisenhower Administrations judged Egyptian nationalism on its own merits, they preferred to define it as a tool in constructing an anticommunist alliance in the Middle East. Great Britain continued to ignore Arab nationalism altogether, and thought it could continue influencing Arab politics as before, by maintaining client regimes in Iraq and Jordan, and by playing off different factions against each other in Egypt and, apart from the 1951-1953 Mossadiq interlude, in Iran. British policy-makers thus remained blind to American worries about British foreign policy towards the Middle East in general, and Egypt in particular. In 1953 Secretary of State John Foster Dulles was growing impatient with British stubbornness over the Canal Zone and its consequences for security in the Middle East. He preferred a security arrangement that would comprise those states in the Near East that bordered the Soviet Union. American interests in the Middle East thus slowly started to conflict with Britain's dominant position in the area. Nevertheless, the United States involved Great Britain in its security policies, thus giving the British the impression that they could hold on to that position.

The first results of Dulles's attempts to create a 'Northern Tier' were the Pact between Turkey and Pakistan of 19 February 1954 and the supply of American arms to Iraq in April that year. At the same time, the United States stepped up pressure on Great Britain to reach an agreement with Egypt. British policy-makers grew worried, but remained convinced that they could make the Americans support them over Egypt. The British refused to consider the possibility that the United States could decide on Middle Eastern matters without Great Britain. United States officials thought that they could persuade Egypt to conclude a defence treaty with Pakistan, and to agree to Iraqi adherence to such a Pact. They remained insensitive to Egyptian objections that this would actually strengthen the position of one of Egypt's major rivals for leadership in the Arab world. Neguib and Nasser had been disappointed by the American decision to grant arms to Iraq while military assistance to Egypt was still conditional on Egyptian agreement to participate in some form of security arrangement in the Middle East (Rubin, 1982). On top of that, Iraq and Turkey announced the imminent signing of a defence treaty on 11 January 1955 (the so-called Baghdad Pact), agreed upon in February 1954 after an Egyptian attempt had failed to rally Arab states behind a revival of the collective security arrangements of the Arab League.

American foreign policy assumed that all Arab and Islamic states could be unified against the threats of communism. The United States chose not to be a formal partner of the security arrangement because of Egypt's opposition against a cluster of treaties that reinforced Iraq's position in the area. Great Britain, however, had joined the Turk-Iraqi treaty in April 1955 in order to preserve its influence in Iraq. The 1930 Anglo-Iraqi treaty, allowing for British military bases, was due to expire, and joining the Turk-Iraqi treaty seemed an easy way to maintain the British position. The United States preferred to remain unidentified with the Pact as long as Egypt, its model of Arab nationalism, remained opposed to it. The United States, however, co-operated with the pact, by appointing Loy Henderson as a formal observer. Dulles's objective of creating an anticommunist alliance in the Northern Tier had been achieved, even more so after Iran and Pakistan joined the Pact in the late Summer of 1955. The events did not alter the British perception of the role they and the United States played in the Middle East. Harold Macmillan, who had become Foreign Secretary in April 1955, when Anthony Eden took over from Winston Churchill as Prime Minister, claimed that he had obtained 'a clear promise that if the Arab-Israeli tension could be reduced, America would join the Baghdad Pact' (Macmillan, 1969, p. 633). Moreover, Eden had convinced Eisenhower that both Great Britain and the United States should deliver tanks to Iraq, which was interpreted as further evidence of American support for the way British foreign policy regarded Iraq and the Baghdad Pact (Shuckburgh, 1986).

Clearly, British policy-makers considered the Baghdad Pact an American invention. They were aware that the United States was not ready to associate itself formally with the treaty, but noticed that the Americans were prepared to deliver arms to the adhering Middle Eastern countries, and that they were willing to participate in the Pact's structural organization. Not only had they appointed an observer, they were also present at the secret meetings of the Pact's security and economic committee (Heikal, 1986). By the summer of 1955, therefore, British objectives seemed to be within reach. A new treaty with Iraq had preserved British bases. Its adherence to the Baghdad Pact had affirmed its primary position in the Middle East. The Pact had been approved of, and even initiated, by the United States.[10] Within reasonable time, the United States would itself join the Pact. Why would British policy-makers consider their position in the Middle East to be seriously challenged by the United States?

**Images Shortly before the Crisis**

Escalation between Great Britain and Egypt took place in three steps. First, the Egyptian purchase of Czech arms in September 1955 after the West's continued refusal to sell arms to Egypt. Next, Jordan's King Hussein's dismissal of General Sir John Glubb, the British commander of the Arab Legion in March 1956, presumably at the instigation of Egypt in response to British attempts to have Jordan join the Baghdad Pact. Finally, Egypt's nationalization of the Suez Canal Company on 26 July 1956, after the cancellation of the Western loan for building the Aswan Dam. Interestingly, the response of British foreign policy-makers followed a familiar pattern. They engaged in attempts to obtain American support for their traditional Middle East policy, focusing on strengthening the position of Iraq and the Baghdad Pact. The American response seemed to confirm the common British perception that the United States continued to support Britain's Middle East policy.

The British response to the Czech arms deal was rather moderate. At the Cabinet meeting of 20 October 1955, Eden thought Nasser's 'decision to accept the Soviet offer understandable, if regrettable', considering his dependence on his army's support, and the West's unwillingness to supply him with any arms.[11] Great Britain stepped up its efforts to convince the United States of the danger of Soviet penetration in the Middle East. Eden and Macmillan accelerated their pressure on the Eisenhower Administration to sponsor the Aswan Dam project with a loan together with Britain and the World Bank (Aronson, 1986). In December 1955 Great Britain and the United States presented their offer to Egypt. The plan did not include a long-term guarantee of assistance, because the Western countries wanted to review the amount of aid each year, in an attempt to use the Aswan loan as a means to tie Egypt to the West. During Anglo-American talks in January 1956 Dulles said that Nasser's attitude towards the Aswan Dam proposal would give an important clue to Egypt's foreign policy in general, but warned that a solution to the Israeli-Egyptian dispute was a prerequisite for full American support of the Baghdad Pact (Aronson, 1986). Therefore, by 1 March 1956, when King Hussein dismissed General Glubb, Great Britain seemed to have been successful in making the Americans cautious about Egypt's relations with the Soviet Union and more appreciative of British efforts to strengthen the Baghdad Pact.

British policy-makers considered Glubb's dismissal a severe blow to British prestige in the Middle East. The event made a group of Senior Ministers decide on a full revision of Britain's Middle East policy on 5 March 1956. They decided that some examples of firm action should be set. It was thus agreed to deport Archbishop

Makarios from conflict-ridden Cyprus, and to consider an intervention in Bahrein, because stones had been thrown at Foreign Secretary Lloyd only two days earlier. In addition, they judged that once more an effort should be made to win over the Americans to the Baghdad Pact. Anthony Nutting's account of the Ministers' meeting in his telegram to Lloyd, who was on his way to a conference in Karachi, is quite revealing.

> Americans now seem ready to take additional responsibilities in ME and are looking to us for advice. Implicit in above policy is abandonment of appeasement of Nasser. This may be unwelcome to Americans but fact remains that appeasement has not paid and I suggest you should leave Dulles in no doubt about our suspicions of growing contacts between Egypt and Soviet Russia. Latest information on Aswan Dam negotiations suggests that Egyptians may well be playing double game.[12]

Two considerations are in order. First, the Cabinet's reaction was, rather predictably, to strengthen the Baghdad Pact and to try to cajole the Americans into more active support to that effect. Nutting's telegram reveals how much propaganda value British Government officials attached to potential contacts between the Soviet Union and Egypt as a means of influencing American opinion. Second, it shows that in March 1956 British policy-makers still expected the United States to look to Great Britain for advice on Middle Eastern affairs.[13]

Great Britain thus exploited the Glubb-crisis to intensify Anglo-American co-ordination of Middle East policy, expecting that in the near future a tougher line towards Nasser would be likely. The Aswan loan would be the first victim. When on 9 March the American Anderson-mission failed, which aimed at drawing Egypt and Israel closer by arranging a face to face meeting between Ben Gurion and Nasser, pressure to discontinue the offer quickly mounted (Aronson, 1986). Eisenhower and Dulles concluded that they could not build their Middle East policy on Nasser. Significantly, by that time British and American Chiefs of Staffs had started consultations about co-ordinating military emergencies in the area.

The Glubb-affair had provoked a reorientation of Britain Middle East policy. Yet, rather than developing an explicit strategy against Nasser, British policy-makers aimed at influencing the United States. The United States should become more appreciative of British interests in the area, less inclined to consider Egypt as the pivot of Middle Eastern stability, and more positive towards the role of British client states, notably Iraq. Clearly, on the eve of the crisis, British policy-makers still considered Great Britain the major power in the Middle East and expected the United States to respect that position.

## Conclusions

Throughout the post-war period until the outbreak of the Suez crisis, British policy-makers held an image of their country occupying a predominant position in the Middle East. Moreover, they were convinced that the United States accepted this position, and looked for a British lead to guide its own Middle East policy. The roots of these images can be traced to the late 1940s when British strategic assets, indispensable for containment policy, had made it possible to continue informal or formal rule in many parts of the world. This was possible in spite of American opposition to Britain's empire and despite Britain's economic weakness. In the early 1950s British foreign policy-makers remained unaware of a change in the American interests in the Middle East and its consequences for Great Britain's specific role. British policy-makers failed to learn from Anglo-American discord and co-operation over Iranian nationalism. They preferred to refer to Anglo-American co-operation during the concluding of an Anglo-Egyptian treaty regarding the Suez Canal Zone and the foundation of the Baghdad Pact. Such co-operation had been occasionally troublesome, but eventually serving British interests, not in the least because of perceived successful British diplomatic pressure.

It should therefore be expected that at the outbreak of the Suez crisis British policy-makers would be guided by similar images of Anglo-American relations, especially regarding the Middle East. British policy-makers are expected to start from the assumption that the Middle East is an exclusive zone of British interest. Moreover, they would expect the United States to recognize that exclusivity. As a matter of fact, British policy-makers would not expect an independent American position, as the United States is expected to wait for Great Britain to take the lead in Middle Eastern affairs. Finally, British policy-makers can be expected to believe that a constant explanation of British interests to the United States would eventually make the United States defend British interests in the area, especially if these could be presented as serving American anticommunist policies. During the crisis, therefore, British policy-makers had to go to great lengths to explain away American opposition to Britain's Suez policy.

## Notes

[1]    American paper, n.d. (November 1947); Memorandum in preparation of the Pentagon talks, n.d., *Foreign Relations of the United States* (FRUS), 1947, 5, pp. 575 ff.

[2]    Minute, Sir William Strang, 31 January 1951, PREM 8, pt. 4: 1405, PRO, quoted by Foot (1986, pp. 54-5).

[3]    Revisionist studies have challenged the traditional view that the United States imposed NATO on its allies. Great Britain played an influential role in cajoling the Americans into accepting the need to guarantee Western security. See for an overview of the literature Folly (1988, p. 60, footnotes 3-5).

[4]    NSC 155/1, 'US Objectives and Policies with respect to the Near East', 14 July 1953, *FRUS*, IX, pp. 400-401.

[5]    *Ibid.*

[6]    FO 800/839, US/53/67, Foreign Office to Washington, Telegram 1280, 19 March 1953.

[7]    FO 800/840, US/53/144, Eden to Dulles, 17 November 1953; FO 800/840, US/53/156, Churchill to Eisenhower, 19 December 1953; FO 800/840, US/53/158, Churchill to Eisenhower, 22 December 1953.

[8]    E.g., the Commander in Chief was intended to be British. Cf. Eden's summaries of his discussions with Acheson: FO 800/750, Af/51/3, Telegram 651, 7 November 1951; FO 800/750, Af/52/10, 26 May 1952.

9    FO 800/769, Eg/52/68, Eden to Churchill, 7 November 1952. FO 800/769, Eg/52/68, Eden
     to Churchill, 7 November 1952.
10   See, for a different interpretation, Reid (1988).
11   CAB 128(35)7, 20 October 1955.
12   FO 800/734, Telegram 531, Nutting to Lloyd, 5 March 1956.
13   The United States, however, had reached the conclusion that Nasser's nationalism was less
     useful to American interests in the Middle East. Yet, the Americans were not prepared to
     commit themselves to support the Baghdad Pact openly, as Dulles told Lloyd in Karachi on
     8 March 1956 (Lloyd, 1978).

# Chapter 4

# The Worldview of Sir Anthony Eden

## Introduction

This chapter will describe Anthony Eden's worldview by constructing his Operational Code on the basis of his public speeches as well as of utterances pronounced in environments of a more private nature. As explained in Chapter 2, the Operational Code differs from inductive methods to identify an individual's cognitive belief system, such as Cognitive Mapping, because it makes use of a previously designed classification of cognitive beliefs that are relevant to foreign policy-making. Categories are divided into philosophical beliefs, which deal with a policy-maker's assumptions and premises, and instrumental beliefs, which refer to matters of strategy and tactics (cf. Table 2.1 on page 29).

A previously designed scheme of classification can be very useful as a tool of comparative research in foreign policy-making. Thus far, comparative analysis of types of Operational Code has been limited to their link with differences in personality (Holsti, 1977) and to their variations in openness (Stuart and Starr, 1981/1982). Unfortunately, very few Operational Code studies have actually been used for the analysis of foreign policy decision-making (e.g., Walker, 1977; Starr, 1984). In this context, an additional aim of this study is to attempt to assess to what extent Anthony Eden's Operational Code adds to our understanding of British decision-making during the Suez crisis. However, before Eden's cognitive belief system can be reconstructed, it is necessary to solve several methodological problems. At the end of this chapter I will outline some expectations regarding Eden's handling of the Suez crisis, especially regarding his dealing with Egypt and the United States, on the basis of the knowledge of Eden's cognitive belief system.

## Methodological Considerations

Three methodological considerations are important in constructing a politician's Operational Code. First, the sources may include a politician's assessment of the very decision-making situation that one seeks to analyze. Second, an individual's belief system may reflect the role he or she is playing in the policy process (cf. Sjöblom, 1982). Third, an Operational Code may be constructed on the basis of a politician's public utterances, which may be tailored to his audience rather than reflect his or her true opinions (Holsti, 1976b; Stuart and Starr, 1981/1982).

*Avoidance of Rationalizations Afterwards*

In order to avoid using sources that might be influenced by Eden's experiences at Suez, the formulation of his Operational Code is based on those utterances that refer to the pre-crisis period. This implies that Eden's voluminous memoirs cannot be employed here. It is essential to try and reconstruct Eden's way of thinking at the beginning of the crisis. This study covers the period between 1924 and 1955, that is, from the moment that Eden became a Member of Parliament for Warwick and Leamington until he took over from Winston Churchill as Prime Minister on 6 April 1955. This still permits to deal with Eden's first attitudes towards Nasser as an opponent, as Nasser was part of the group of young officers that put aside King Farouk in 1952, and effectively became Egypt's leader in 1954.

*Accounting for Role Variables*

In a very orthodox way of reasoning one could object to the Operational Code approach that it assumes the individual's cognitive belief system to remain relatively stable and coherent throughout time. It would thus be impossible to take into account the possibility that a politician can learn from certain experiences, or, much more damaging from a methodological point of view, that his thoughts are not as much a reflection of his individual belief system but rather a reflection of the role he is playing in the political system at a particular moment of his career. It has been suggested that politicians who are involved in foreign policy-making will reflect opinions that are consistent with role expectations that surround the particular job they are occupying in the political system. A Minister of Defence is expected to display different attitudes towards a foreign policy problem from a Foreign Secretary or Prime Minister (cf. Walker, 1987; Roberts, 1988).

The possible influence of role variables can be accounted for by making a distinction between relevant political roles performed by Eden between 1924 and 1955 while analyzing the documents relevant to constructing Eden's Operational Code. A distinction is made between five relevant periods. (1) January 1924-December 1935. In this period Eden became a Member of Parliament for the first time, Permanent Parliamentary Secretary at the Home Office, Parliamentary Under Secretary at the Foreign Office, and Minister for League of Nations Affairs. (2) December 1935-March 1938. Eden served as Foreign Secretary under Neville Chamberlain. (3) March 1938-May 1945. In this period Eden, whether he liked it or not, became an important member of the internal opposition against Chamberlain's appeasement policy within the Conservative Party. Then he became Dominions Secretary (without a seat in the Cabinet) (1939/1940), Secretary of State for War (1940) and, finally, Foreign Secretary (1941-1945). (4) May 1945-November 1951. Member of the opposition against the Attlee Government. (5) November 1951-April 1955. Foreign Secretary under Churchill. Obviously, one would expect Eden to have different opinions on collective security as Minister for League of Nations Affairs than as Foreign Secretary. As a Foreign Secretary who had to compete with Churchill for dominance over foreign policy-making, especially from 1951 until 1955, one can expect different opinions than a stable

Operational Code would predict. By making a distinction between these five periods it becomes possible to control for role variables.

## The Problem of Intentions

Finally, a solution has to be found for the problem that an individual's utterances may not reflect his or her true intentions. It may rather be the case that they are pronounced because of their convenience at the time. Maybe a politician will try to please his audience, or will prefer not to show his real thoughts for political reasons. A distinction between Eden's public and private statements should resolve that problem. Public statements are more likely to be tailored to their audiences than private ones. Beliefs that can be derived from the latter type of sources will better reflect Eden's cognitive beliefs. The more they differ from public statements on the same subjects, the more likely it is that these public statements were pronounced for political reasons. A practical problem caused by this comparison of public and private utterances is the lack of private sources for those periods that Eden has not been in office.

## A Description of Anthony Eden's Operational Code

What follows is a description of Eden's cognitive beliefs, making use of the classification that has been developed by George and Holsti. The master belief of Eden's Operational Code consists of the idea that any international dispute can be settled if the parties involved recognize and respect their respective security interests. Several beliefs follow from this: those about international relations, the place of the United Kingdom in world politics, the nature of one's opponents, and the way to deal with them. Eden's worldview can explain to a certain extent his attitudes towards Germany and Italy in the 1930s and the Soviet Union in the 1940s, and as such may provide relevant clues to understanding his policies towards Egypt and the United States in the 1950s. In certain periods, however, significant differences in Eden's attitudes can be observed relating to the various roles he is performing in the British political system. Moreover, certain differences as to the use of military force are apparent in a comparison between public and private utterances.

## The Structure of Eden's Belief System

There can be no doubt that, for most of the period covered by the Operational Code (1924-1955), Eden's cognitive belief system was guided by the idea that conflict is a frequent feature of world politics, but that in the end any conflict can be accommodated as long as the parties involved are willing to recognize and respect their mutual security interests. A necessary precondition for conflict resolution, however, is respect for certain standards of international conduct which in turn form the basis of diplomatic negotiation. This view of international relations ran parallel to Eden's seldom expressed, general conception of politics (philosophical belief 1.1). Eden thinks of politics as:

> Essentially concerned with conflicting human claims: freedom and order, the individual and the state, tradition and change, personal security and adventure, ideals and reality, independence and interdependence. The art of statesmanship is to reconcile these claims and to build a way of life that gives them fair expression (Eden, 1949, p. vii).

Within that context the relation of the individual to the state is the most urgent problem of politics, and, according to Eden, it is exactly in this area that socialism is unable to provide a just balance between freedom and order (Eden, 1948, p. 5; 1949, p. 7).

The adherence to standards of international conduct, most notably the observance of treaties and the willingness to resort to free negotiations (Eden, 1939), furthers the growth of international confidence, which is a prerequisite for peace. This concept of the nature of world politics has important consequences for Eden's view of the opponent, his instrumental beliefs, both grounded in his modest historical optimism.

*View of the opponent*  Because of the predominance of the importance of standards of international conduct to Eden, his view of his opponents is derived from this principle rather than that the view of the opponent serves as a master belief itself around which other beliefs are centred. As long as states and their leaders adhere to certain conventions of correct behaviour, it will remain possible to come to an agreement with any country. That is, it is possible to accommodate international conflict irrespective of the type of political system or political ideology of the various international actors: 'International relations are guided not by forms of government, but by the manner in which governments observe their undertakings' (Eden, 1939, p. 175). This implies that, according to Eden, one can come to terms both with dictatorships, such as Italy and Germany, and with ideologically different nations, such as the Soviet Union. Indeed, class could not be a cause of international conflict as 'the interests of classes are not exclusive, but complementary' (Eden, 1939, p. 183). By consequence, Eden would change his cooperative attitude towards other nations, once these would have passed a certain threshold of international misbehaviour. Italy passed that threshold with its invasion of Abyssinia in 1935, Germany when it started pressing for a corridor to Danzig in 1939, and the Soviet Union after it mounted a blockade of the Western zones of Berlin in 1948. To Eden, this respect for a certain type of conduct was almost identical to interpersonal contact:

> We want, in our relations with all other countries, to try to maintain a standard of honesty, of fair dealing, and of international good faith. Foreign affairs are really not so very different in those respects from domestic affairs. Human intercourse is based on good faith, on the keeping of promises, on honouring the pledged word between man and man (Speech to the House of Commons, 25 May 1944, Eden, 1948, p. 258).

*Instrumental beliefs* This view of the nature of world politics and its consequences for the assessments of one's opponents similarly affects the way in which international diplomacy is practised. Eden preferred personal contacts with the relevant actors: 'I cannot help feeling that a direct approach to the men concerned is more likely to produce results than other methods' (Eden, 1948, p. 31). His approach as a diplomat can therefore best be described as pragmatic:

> He was interested in settling problems, in bringing people together, and working out agreements. His first reaction, when he heard the speeches which the Americans and Russians were making to one another in the United Nations in 1951, was that he must somehow reduce the shouting and persuade people to talk to and not at one another. His great speciality was to remember always the third parties and fourth parties in the international confrontations with which he was involved. His aim, he used to say, was 'to grasp definite and limited problems' and try to settle them bit by bit, one by one (Shuckburgh, 1986, pp. 15, 17).

Eden believed, indeed, that problems should be regarded as they arose, without politicians being guided by political doctrines and prejudices: 'all prejudices are equally fatal to good government' (Eden, 1949, pp. 5-6).

This pragmatism of Eden's is borne out in the way he dealt with international disputes as Foreign Secretary or Minister for League of Nations Affairs in the 1930s and the 1950s. Eden tried to confine the hostility between the disputants to a very specific issue thus ignoring all other differences between the countries. This allowed him to solve the 1934 Balkan crisis, when Yugoslavia's King Alexander was murdered by a Hungarian terrorist. It helped him find a solution for the Saar-problem, by pressing for an international police force under supervision of the League of Nations in order to hold a plebiscite on the future of the area in 1935 (cf. Peters, 1986). In similar fashion Eden helped solve the dispute between Italy and Yugoslavia over Trieste in 1954. He also succeeded in securing German rearmament after the French Parliament botched the European Defence Community in 1954 by incorporating Western Germany into the 1948 Treaty of Brussels, the common defence pact that constituted the Western European Union. In addition, he managed to formulate a compromise over Indo-China at the 1954 Geneva conference that satisfied all parties involved (cf. James, 1986).

*Modest historical optimism* Both Eden's conception of the nature of world politics and his subsequent views of opponents and the possibilities of diplomacy are matched by a sense of optimism as to the possibility of influencing the course of history: for Eden it was possible to understand the course of history: 'history is not a series of isolated and disjointed incidents, but a continuous process' (Eden, 1948, p. 169); the politician should not ignore historical development, nor try to master it completely: 'change is perhaps the only thing in the universe that is constant. By trying to thwart it, you only drive it underground. It becomes fitful and eruptive instead of ordered and continuous'. For Eden, politicians should attempt merely to 'guide development' (Eden, 1948, pp. 69-70).[1]

This conception of history, change, and the role of chance in human affairs and history (philosophical beliefs 2, 3, 4) thus fits Eden's view that interactions between international actors can, to a reasonably large extent, be manipulated and guided towards the accommodation of their disputes. Indeed, if countries adopted certain standards of international conduct, it would be possible to abandon the 'doctrine of force' which had dominated the interactions between states for so long. Then 'all outstanding questions would become possible to solve and international economic progress would bring happiness to every human being' (Eden, 1948, p. 37).[2]

Eden's optimism is confined by the limits that history has set on the role a country is bound to play in world affairs: 'nations, like human beings, are fashioned and moulded by their past. You cannot wholly escape from your past. You can improve on it' (Eden, 1948, pp. 169-70). For the United Kingdom this meant that its 'foreign policy is to a large extent dictated by our geographical position. Whether we like it or not, we are part of Europe. Whether we like it or not, we are also the centre of a great Imperial Commonwealth, and so we are, in that sense, a World Power too. Our duty is to act as a bridge, and there is nobody who can play that part but us – nobody else' (Eden, 1948, p. 178). In general terms, this role imposed by history points to another important component of Eden's belief system, already apparent is his master belief: nations can accommodate their disputes as long as they respect certain rules, and as long as they recognize their mutual legitimate interests.

*The role of the United Kingdom in world affairs*   Eden's view of the role of Great Britain in world affairs has been reasonably consistent throughout the period covered by the Operational Code. It contains two important elements. First, its geographical position which makes the Middle East and Mediterranean strategically important to preserving the British Commonwealth and Empire. Second, the recognition that the United Kingdom is not able to play the role of policeman of the world, and thus has been dependent on the United States ever since the early 1930s.

Its geography has made the United Kingdom part of Europe as well as leader of the Commonwealth. As most members of that Commonwealth are to be found on the shores of the Indian and Pacific Oceans, the Middle East and the Mediterranean form the crucial link between the Commonwealth and its centre. This is why Eden defined freedom of communication over the Mediterranean and Red Seas as a vital interest of the United Kingdom since he had become Foreign Secretary in 1935. During the Second World War Eden emphasized that Great Britain's interests lay more in the Mediterranean than elsewhere. After that war he still deemed the area essential, most notably because the Suez Canal was of vital interest to Great Britain for the transportation of its imports and exports.

Until the explosion of the Atomic bomb, Eden was convinced that the Middle East, and in particular the Suez Canal area, was the most important strategic area, and indispensable to win any large-scale war because of the control over the lines of communications. Eden had a clash with Churchill, who considered the area less vital, over the number of troops that Great Britain could afford to send to the area.

Eden was convinced that the Germans (until 1941 together with the Soviets, thereafter alone) would try to come down to the Canal and the Middle Eastern oil wells through the Caucasus. After the war, however, Eden was one of the first to realize, as early as 1945, that nuclear weapons upset traditional military strategy, because no natural barrier would be able to stop their delivery, and that therefore the Suez Canal would rapidly lose its extreme strategic importance. Eden had thus an early grasp of changing British interests in the area, which would eventually lead to his difficult, but successful, attempt to convince the Churchill Government of the need to withdraw British troops from the Suez Canal zone in the early 1950s. Despite its changed strategic importance, the Canal and, indeed, the whole of the Middle East remained an essential line of communication between the United Kingdom and its Commonwealth. Eden judged British economic weakness after the Second World War to be of a temporary nature and was convinced that preferential trading with the Commonwealth countries, even after Indian independence, would make it possible to rebuild the British economy. The transportation of these trading goods and of oil imports, however, required some guarantee that the Suez Canal remained open to free navigation. Ever since the mid-1930s Eden called the Canal and the Mediterranean Britain's arterial road.

According to Eden, British influence is first of all based on prestige. In its turn, prestige is based not simply on military and economic strength but as well on the respect the United Kingdom merits as one of the world's oldest democracies, as on its adherence to international law. However, it is clear that for Eden the Commonwealth and Empire form the main source of prestige in Britain's relations with major powers: speaking about Anglo-American and Anglo-Soviet relations, Eden told the House of Commons in May 1944:

> We cannot say to the world: 'you have got to do this; you have got to do that'. That is beyond the power of 45,000,000. But what we can do, in our own conduct, and by our own leadership, is to try to establish and maintain those standards of international conduct without which there cannot be peace. That I conceive to be the duty of British foreign policy. Though I have been in many negotiations with these two Powers alone, I have never felt any sense of inferiority, and I honestly do not believe that they felt any particular sense of superiority. The reason, of course, that, although we are only 45 millions, we have in this island a unique geographical position and a rather remarkable experience, and because we are the centre of a great Empire (Eden, 1948, pp. 258-9).

Throughout the 1930s, 1940s and 1950s Eden is aware of Britain's relative weakness. Early on in the 1930s he recognizes that it is unthinkable that Britain will be able to impose its will on other nations in the world whenever it feels like it. In 1932 already Eden eventually opposes strong measures against Japanese aggression in the Far East, because the British Pacific fleet would be too weak for a display of coercive diplomacy. Any effective countering of Japan's aspirations required intimate co-operation between the United States and the United Kingdom. In the late thirties Eden tried to persuade his colleagues that co-operation with the United States was indispensable to dealing with the European crisis that was unfolding.

It is exactly the recognition of relative British weakness, despite it still being a great power that determined Eden's policy dilemma as Foreign Secretary between 1935 and 1938. Given the consideration, shown in warnings from the Chiefs of Staff, that Great Britain would not have the resources to simultaneously fight three enemies, Japan, Germany and Italy, it was essential that the formation of blocs of countries be avoided, in order to prevent those countries from creating an alliance of their own. At the same time, the expansionist aspirations of each had to be dealt with. This resulted in a precarious policy of approaching Germany in a constructive mood which lasted well into 1939, while trying to oppose Italian aggression in Africa and the Mediterranean, but up to the point that she would be driven into Germany's arms. His Operational Code suggests that Eden's different approaches to Hitler and Mussolini can be explained by his master belief.

A permanent feature of Eden's belief system is therefore his recognition of relative British weakness, and the importance that Britain seeks co-operation with the United States. This concept is reinforced when it becomes apparent to him during the Second World War that the war would result in increased British weakness. Already in 1942 Eden thinks that the Americans should 'fulfil a leading role after the war and thus accept worldwide responsibility for maintaining peace' (Eden, 1948, p. 179). The prevention of aggression should then be trusted into the hands of those countries that have a monopoly of strength in the world: the United States, the Soviet Union, and the United Kingdom.

In sum, Eden's view of how international relations should be conducted is constrained by his belief that other nations should respect Britain's vital interests. Because of the economic importance of the Empire, the Middle East, the Suez Canal, and the Mediterranean are of vital interest to the United Kingdom. At the same time, however, Britain is not strong enough to impose its will on other nations, and should therefore seek co-operation notably with the United States.

*Impact of the Structure of Eden's Worldview on His View of His Opponents*

One of the advantages of the Operational Code's American intellectual origins is that in most Operational Code studies it has been clear where to look for an opponent in order to complete an individual's cognitive belief system. Usually, the Soviet Union appears as the main adversary. It is much more difficult to determine who should appear to be Eden's most important opponent. This study includes Eden's views of Italy, Germany and, to a lesser extent, Japan. These countries clearly were Britain's major challengers at the time Eden was in office in the 1930s. Second, of the Soviet Union, because it was to become the West's major adversary after the Second World War. Third, of the Middle East, especially the nationalist regimes in Egypt and Iran, because Nasser was to become Eden's 'obsession', as some authors claim. Finally, of the United States, because what actually was taking place was the decline of British power relative to American power and because of the rather peculiar pattern of Anglo-American relations during the Suez crisis. Eden's attitude towards Italy and Germany, and towards the Soviet Union until June 1948, fit his master belief well. His attitude towards the Middle East gives rise to some puzzling questions as to his handling of the Suez crisis. His view of the United States is blurred by the conviction that it would be possible to convince the Americans of the special nature of the British Commonwealth and Empire.

*Italy, Germany, and Japan* The most puzzling question of Anthony Eden's attitude towards Italy and Germany, is why he remained so positive about the possibility of a settlement with Hitler, while he was in favour of curbing Italian aggression almost from the beginning. One clue to an answer can be found in Eden's cognitive belief system. Towards the end of the war, in a speech to the House of Commons, in which Eden laid down the principles of his foreign policy, he made a remark that can easily be understood in the context of his worldview: 'why did the war become inevitable? It was because Hitler and Mussolini refused to observe the ordinary standards of international conduct in the day-to-day conduct of international affairs' (Eden, 1948, p. 258). Of course, these standards were: 'maintain a standard of honesty of fair dealing, and of international good faith, the keeping of promises, on honouring the pledged word between man and man' (*ibid.*). It should be noted that not even in 1944 did Eden speak of the evil of totalitarian dictators threatening democracies, or of inherently expansionist tendencies of Italy and Germany. He sticks to his belief that in principle the nature of the political system of other nations does not matter, as long as certain international rules are observed. Indeed, as Foreign Secretary, Eden was not extraordinarily alarmed by German's remilitarization of the Rhineland in March 1936. Although he thought it a violation of the sanctity of treaties (i.e., Versailles), Eden thought that international confidence could be restored by negotiation. Similarly, Eden was not too worried by German claims regarding the Sudeten-area in the autumn of 1937. Discussing the matter with his French colleague on 29 and 30 November, Eden said that 'there was a feeling here that the Sudeten Germans had certain grievances, which ought to be dealt with' and that 'the Czechs had certainly not yet done enough'.[3] Eden still believed that it would be possible to reach a settlement with Germany. As late as 10 February 1938, that is, shortly before his resignation, Eden wrote a memorandum suggesting that Germany could be induced to a 'contribution to general appeasement'. At the very least he expected 'that Germany would refrain from intervention against us should we be attacked in the Mediterranean or in the Far East'. He thought it reasonable to offer Germany colonial compensation for such a pledge.[4] Eden's attitude towards Germany did not even change after his resignation, as role theory would predict, being freed of the duty of daily compromising at the Foreign Office. Indeed, Eden was reluctant to condemn the 1938 Four Power-settlement of Munich, which he greeted in the House of Commons as the beginning of 'new hopes' and 'better things', or at least as 'breathing space' (Eden, 1939, pp. 287-8). Not until the summer of 1939, when Germany claimed Danzig, did Eden show a completely different stand:

> Nobody can foretell with precision what the tactics will be in the next few weeks. No doubt there will be many moves. We will be lulled and soothed, we shall be threatened and provoked, but in essence the Nazis' purpose remains the same-to impose on Poland this year the fate which they imposed upon Czechoslovakia (Eden, 1948, pp. 32-3).

The latter speech indicates, first of all, a change of terminology: Nazis instead of Germany. Second, it clearly points to the recognition that Germany no longer respected the standards of international conduct.

Eden had reached that verdict on Italy much sooner. As a Minister for League of Nations Affairs, he had recognized Italy's ambitions in Africa early in 1935. At the time he considered Italy a useful counterweight to German moves towards Austria and proposed League arbitration. But when Italy actually invaded Abyssinia in October 1935 Eden thought that the League should resort to collective security and impose effective sanctions. However, he was the only member of the Cabinet in favour of an arms boycott (James, 1986). As Foreign Secretary, from December 1935 onwards, Eden had to fight a constant battle within the Foreign Office and later against Sir Neville Chamberlain, who became Prime Minister in 1937, about policies towards Italy. Most people at Whitehall expected Germany and Japan to be the main adversaries, which implied that Italy somehow had to be appeased, for instance, by *de jure* recognition of her occupation of Abyssinia (Chamberlain's theme from 1937 on). Eden, however, thought Italy to be the real troublemaker, whose behaviour could trigger a large-scale war by inviting Germany to fish in troubled waters.

It is easy to see, knowing Eden's belief system, why he considered Italy much more dangerous than Germany: first, it was threatening the balance of power in the Mediterranean and the Middle East, thus threatening the arterial road between Empire and homeland. Second, Italy was not a trustworthy party in the game of international relations. In a minute, written in November 1936, Eden wondered:

> Does any in the Foreign Office really believe that Italy's foreign policy will at any time be other than opportunist? Any agreement with Italy will be kept as long as it suits Italy. Surely nobody can now place any faith in her promises. All this is not an argument against seeking to improve Anglo-Italian relations, but against placing an exaggerated valuation on any such improvement if and when we get it. We must be on guard against increasing the dictator's prestige by our own excessive submissiveness.[5]

Eden therefore does not want to know about *de jure* recognition: 'to grant him [Mussolini] *de jure* recognition as the result of a bargain seems to me rather sordid and might be dangerous to our reputation. To give him recognition without a bargain would I suppose be hailed as a considerable triumph for Mussolini'.[6] Over and over, Eden tried to convince Chamberlain to stop appeasing Mussolini. His different assessment of Germany and Italy is borne out by his letter to Chamberlain of 9 January 1938:

> There seems to be a certain difference between Italian and German positions in that *an agreement with the latter might have a chance of reasonable life, especially if Hitler's own position were engaged, while Mussolini is, I fear, the complete gangster and his pledged word means nothing.* But all this would not alone deter me. What worries me much more is the effect that recognition might have on our own moral position (emphasis added).[7]

The difference in attitude of Eden towards Italy on the one hand, and Germany on the other hand is thus rooted in two beliefs. First of all, his conception of international affairs as a world in which the accommodation of conflicts between states is possible, as long as certain standards are observed and mutual interests recognized. Second, the central position the Mediterranean and the Middle East occupy in his view of the relationship between the United Kingdom and her Commonwealth and Empire. A rival explanation would be that Eden had capitalized on his insistence on collective security through the League of Nations, when still a Minister for League of Nations Affairs, indeed had become Foreign Secretary on that quality, and thus would be interested in insisting on a hawkish position towards Italy in order not to lose popular support. Although this would provide an explanation for his general attitude towards Italy, it can not satisfactorily explain why Eden turned away from collective security as the correct approach to Italian aggression, nor can it explain the different attitude towards Germany. These can only be understood by Eden's master belief about international affairs.

*The Soviet Union* Anthony Eden's views of the Soviet Union until 1948 reflect his opinion that international relations should not be influenced by the nature of the political system of a particular country as long as that country respects certain standards of international conduct. Well into the Cold War Eden professes the idea that mutual respect for one's legitimate interests would make it possible to remain on speaking terms with the Soviet Union. The blockade of West Berlin would signify a watershed, the sign to Eden that no 'normal diplomatic deals' could be made with the Soviets. This would actually lead to a completely different definition of international relations: from 1948-1949 on, Eden considers world politics as a conflict between two opposing ways of lives instead of a world where ideology is of secondary importance.

After Churchill's famous Iron Curtain speech at Fulton, Missouri, in March 1946, which was followed by the announcement of the Truman Doctrine, Eden, now a Member of the Opposition, remained remarkably co-operative towards the Soviet Union: 'there is no reason why the two ideologies should not live together in peace if both will accept not to back their fancies in every other land. Restraint may be difficult to practice, but surely this is not too much to ask as the price for enduring peace' (Eden, 1948, p. 416).[8] This attitude was grounded in the conviction that the Soviets would obey the rules of international relations as long as all parties involved respect one another's legitimate security interest. W.P. Crozier reports of a conversation he had with Eden during the War:

> We have to make up our minds on Russia: either she was International Communist in her intentions or she was a Peter-the-Great Russia. Personally he [Eden] was convinced that Stalin's policy was that of a Peter-the-Great Russia and that we could, and therefore must, live with her in Europe. Stalin had convinced him that Russia was, and would be, reasonable in her aims (Crozier, 1973, p. 266).

The Moscow conference between the United States, the Soviet Union, and Great Britain in the Autumn of 1943 convinced Eden that the Soviet Union wished to adhere to 'normal' diplomacy:

> It is a common diplomatic experience to find that problems which seem to present insuperable difficulties when there is no confidence and no mutual trust can fall into a different perspective when once a real basis of goodwill has been established (Eden, 1948, p. 223).

Eden was prepared to sympathize with the perceived security dilemma of the Soviet Union. It had experienced several invasions from Europe and therefore looked for certain guarantees. To that purpose Eden was opposed to a paper on post-war arrangements in Europe that circulated in Whitehall which envisaged a Western European Union under British leadership in the framework of the British Empire. Eden argued that this would 'invite Russian animosity and a counter alliance in Eastern Europe. Frank co-operation and friendship with Russia is the proper course' (Colville, 1987, pp. 131-2). He more than once declared that Russian foreign policy was dominated by the German attack and by the wish not to see that happen again. He even stated that fears of Soviet domination over Europe were caused by wartime German propaganda. Well into 1948, even after events in Czechoslovakia, Eden repeated that

> While firmness and vigilance are indispensable, neither threats nor bluster are going to get us anywhere. To be unshakeable in essentials, to be patient in explanation of what is our point of view, even at the cost of endless repetition, to be cool and to leave the door open for agreement, these should be our present directives (Eden, 1949, p. 184).

This is not to say that Eden had an extremely naive attitude towards the Soviet Union. He recognized the shaking up of the European balance of power at an early stage of the Second World War. In January 1942 he wrote a memorandum to the Cabinet, in which he warned that

> On the assumption that Germany is defeated and German military strength is destroyed and that France remains, for a long time at least, a weak power, there will be no counterweight to Russia in Europe. Russia's position on the European continent will be unassailable. Russian forces would end the war much deeper into Europe than they began it in 1941. It therefore seemed prudent to tie the Soviet Government to agreements as soon as possible (Carlton, 1988, p. 193).

Eden was by consequence prepared to recognize the Soviet annexation of the Baltic States for the sake of an Anglo-Soviet treaty in April 1942. Interviewed at the time by W. Crozier, he defined the issue as:

> Did we or did we not desire to co-operate with Russia with regard to the future of Europe? He [Eden] believed that Russia was willing to co-operate and that we could work together and that he held that this would be of immense importance. If we now refused what Russia desired and maintained she was entitled to on the grounds of her bare security we should run the risk of alienating her and preventing what ought to be a most

fruitful co-operation in the future. Further, we could not, of course, prevent Russia from absorbing these (Baltic) States if she desired to (Crozier, 1973, p. 315).

Clearly, then, Eden was prepared to deal with other nations on the basis of the recognition of their mutual legitimate security interests. A fundamental change in his assessment of the Soviet Union did not occur until the Soviets started the Berlin blockade in June 1948. Eden believed it to be a complete break with the Soviet conduct: 'if there ever was a time to stand firm, it is now; if ever there was a course in which to stand firm, it is this' (Eden, 1949, p. 211). But, more importantly in terms of his worldview, Eden believed that the Soviet Union was undermining international stability, first by seeking to undermine the authority of a State from within (Germany), and second '*by a direct challenge to accepted international agreement*' (Eden, 1949, p. 212; italics added).

The Berlin blockade seems to mark a turning point in the structure of Eden's belief system: no longer does he consider the political system of the opponent as irrelevant to the conduct of international relations: The Berlin blockade showed that 'two opposing ways of life confront each other. Sometimes there is open conflict. Sometimes there is what is called cold war. But the challenge is always there' (Eden, 1949, pp. 131-2). The Soviet Union has made the United Nations, which Eden originally judged to be the institution through which the three Great Powers of the Second World were going to prevent or curb new forms of aggression, unworkable by what he called 'Soviet abuse of the veto' (ibid, p. 133). The fact that the Soviet Union no longer respected the rules of international conduct, and its attitude towards the United Nations 'has strengthened the need for regional arrangements' (Eden, 1949, p. 142).

In sum, Eden's view of the Soviet Union is marked by a rather constructive nature until the events of the Berlin blockade. Eden believes that the Soviet Union will respect the rules of international conduct, as long as the West recognizes her security interests, and as long as the Soviet Union respects the West's. The Berlin blockade, to Eden a violation of an international agreement, is a watershed. Eden's subsequent definition of international relations as divided into two opposite camps, is a rather puzzling development, which cannot be accounted for by looking at his belief system. He still refuses to see war as the inevitable outcome: negotiation from strength, 'the only basis which they understand', might still bring the Soviets to their senses (Colville, 1987, p.134).

*The Middle East*  The Middle East, especially the Suez Canal, was pivotal to Eden's view of the world's geopolitical configuration. In his view, the Middle East is the crucial connection between the United Kingdom and the largest part of the Commonwealth and Empire. Those few public references of Eden's to the Middle East, that do not stress the geopolitical importance of the area, show a remarkable assessment of the damaging role British interference with domestic politics in the Middle East could have on British influence in the area. At the same time, however, in private communications, Eden displays a much tougher attitude to the area whenever he feels that vital British interests are at stake.

When in the summer of 1945 the Iranian Government asked the British and Soviet Government to withdraw their troops from their respective zones of influence,[9] the British Government indicated its willingness to comply. Eden hailed Foreign Secretary Bevin's decision, recognizing that 'the last thing we want is a recurrence of the practice of zones of influence and matters of that kind which there were in Persia long ago, and which made us so intensely unpopular in that country for a generation' (Eden, 1948, pp. 365-6). A few months later, the Soviet Union refused to withdraw her troops until a satisfactory settlement regarding joint Soviet-Persian oil well exploitation and autonomy for Persian Azerbeidjan would have been reached. Indeed, the first Cold War confrontation was near hand and Eden judged it bad policy to work out a deal with the Soviet Government that would impose a government on Iran that would fit the interests of both the United Kingdom and the Soviet Union:

> Supposing we and the Russians did agree that one party was better than another, is it really our business to impose that party on Persia, and ought we to? In the time of Edward Grey, in 1906, we tried to do that sort of thing. It was a terrible failure and we ourselves were absolutely detested by every section of the Persian people (Eden, 1948, pp. 388-9).

It therefore seems that Eden was well aware of the negative consequences British interference with Middle Eastern regimes could have on British long-term interests. This was one of the reasons why in the 1952-1954 period he wanted to conclude a treaty with Egypt, providing for the withdrawal of British troops from the Canal Zone. Eden thought it unrealistic to assume that Great Britain could simply impose its will on Egypt, and tried to convince the Churchill Government of this point. From this perspective, it comes as no surprise that Eden's public reaction to regional crisis was firm, but conciliatory. This happened with Iranian Prime Minister Mussadiq's decision in April 1951 to nationalize British owned oil installations in his country, and when Egypt demanded the renegotiation of the 1936 Suez Canal Treaty with the United Kingdom. Eden thought the British should stay in Abadan and take the matter to the International Court of Justice at The Hague (James, 1986, p. 337; Carlton, 1988, pp. 289-90). Eden's private utterances at the time, however, suggest a very different, much tougher attitude. Gifford, the American Ambassador in London, reports of a conversation with Eden over lunch in May 1951.

> Eden told Morrison he felt oil sit(es) in other parts of (the) Near East w(ou)ld tend to degenerate if Iran won out which it might unless something constructive were done by (the) UK. Eden suggested that UK sh(ou)ld use force (regarding the) Suez Canal issue by sending destroyers with tankers thru Suez Canal and insisting on oil being transported freely thru Canal. He seemed to believe that UK w(ou)ld get away with Egypt and that it would convince (the) N(ear) E(ast) area that UK meant business and w(ou)ld have salutary effect on Iran. He was saying that the use of (a) big stick directly in Suez w(ou)ld be better than directly in Iran which might bring Soviets in from (the) North.[10]

American Secretary of State, Dean Acheson would not believe that Eden entertained such a hawkish opinion, but Ambassador Gifford replied to his chief that Eden had hinted at tougher policies in his Empire Day speech on 24 May 1951, communicating Eden's lines on Iran and Egypt:

> Giving away just international rights does not win peace. That is appeasement at its worst. We have been pushed around a little too much of late. That is bad for us and bad for other countries and it is bad for peace. For sometime past I have thought that we should call a halt to that process.[11]

*The United States*  Eden's attitude towards the United States is captured by three dimensions. First, a growing awareness since the mid-1930s that the preservation of British influence throughout the world was dependent on Anglo-American co-operation. Second, a growing awareness that the United Kingdom was economically strongly dependent on the United States after World War Two. Third, a growing awareness that the United States had a much different evaluation of the British Empire from Great Britain.

In 1937 Eden (and the Imperial Staff) had recognized that the United Kingdom alone could not handle Japanese aggression, and that American naval support would be needed. Towards the end of that year Eden wished to draw the United States into closer co-operation with the United Kingdom in order to deal with Mussolini and Hitler, and welcomed a secret initiative by Roosevelt on the matter.[12] Eden, however, warned against the idea that United States would be willing to co-operate because the countries were so much alike:

> I think it is a mistake to attempt to base those relations mainly upon sentiment. I think it is also a mistake to try to base them on common origin, or common percentage, or even common language, because there will be occasions when we differ one from the other. But I think it is desirable to base them on their true foundation, which is a common interest in the maintenance of world peace and in preventing a repetition of these catastrophic conflicts every twenty years (Eden, 1948, p. 187).

It was obvious that after the Second World War, the United States had become the leading nation (Eden, 1948, p. 353). Nevertheless, Eden was convinced that Britain was still a leading nation, thanks to its Empire. Unfortunately, exactly the Empire would be the cause of much misunderstanding.

Towards the end of the war Eden realized that the United Kingdom would be economically dependent on the United States for a while. He accepted the necessity of American economic assistance, but remarked that this could reduce British prestige, as the United States would now take most of the credit for winning the war (Ryan, 1987). The solution to escape from complete dependency was, again, the Empire. Discussing Marshall aid in the House of Commons, Eden remarked that 'we cannot become the permanent pensioners of the United States. We have a role of our own to play as the heart and centre of a great Empire' (Eden, 1949, p. 24). Preferential trading with Commonwealth nations and the Empire would furnish hard currency and guarantee the reconstruction of the British manufacturing industry. The Empire thus forms the pivot to Eden's thinking after the Second World War. First, it is a major source of prestige guaranteeing great nation status to Great Britain. Second, it is a crucial means of economic recovery. Unfortunately for Eden, the Empire was the source of much apprehension.

During the war Eden grew more and more aware that the United States held a different opinion on the British Empire. In general, Eden complained that the Americans did not understand, and did not take the trouble to understand, what, in British eyes, characterized the relationships between the nations of the Commonwealth. More in particular, Eden became weary that the Americans might develop an interest in one exclusively British sphere of influence, the Middle East.

Towards the end of 1942, Eden and Churchill did not understand why the Americans were complaining about the British (and Dutch) colonial Empires, while they had guaranteed the integrity of the French territories, 'which is more than we have done'. A report by Colonial Secretary Stanley, approved by Eden, suggested that much criticism was the result of 'complete ignorance regarding conditions in British colonial territories' (Sbrega, 1983, pp. 126-7). In a memorandum on the American attitude towards colonialism, Eden judged that the difference in opinion was fundamental, and could not be changed by, for example, Indian independence. While the United Kingdom considered the Commonwealth as an international organization within which complete self-government was taken for granted, the United States considered it a technique of oppression. In Eden's view, the Americans themselves disliked colonial rule for historical reasons, and had come to rely on different methods: 'as a great power (they) were in a position to press for such economic or political advantages as desired in a given area without assuming any responsibility for its administration'.[13] During and after the war, Eden therefore tried to persuade the American Government and the American public that the Empire was something else than harsh colonial rule, 'a family of free nations: free to stay, free to go', and that the world could learn from this example of peaceful coexistence (Eden, 1948, p. 416).

As to the British position in the Middle East during the Second World War, Eden felt that the Americans were trying to improve their position in the Middle East by capitalizing on their criticism of British imperialism. According to Eden, the Americans tried to increase their influence in Iran and Saudi Arabia at the expense of the United Kingdom. Moreover, he realized that after the war Great Britain would depend on the United States for the development of British oil resources in the Middle East (Sbrega, 1983; James, 1986). This fear would return in the early 1950s when the Americans tried to force the British to reach an agreement with the Egyptian government on the Canal issue. Evelyn Shuckburgh, Eden's private secretary between 1951 and 1954, noted that 'A.E.'s conviction is that all the Americans want to do is to replace the French and run Indo-China themselves. "They want to replace us in Egypt too. They want to run the world"' (Shuckburgh, 1986, p. 187).

## The Operational Code and Anthony Eden's Intentions

Two checks have been incorporated on the intentions that Eden might have had in making the utterances he made. First, a control for role variables was obtained by distinguishing different periods during which Eden played different roles in the British political system. Second, Eden's public and private utterances were separated, in order to account for the possibility that he would be tailoring his choice of words to his audience.

*Accounting for Role Variables*

Only on one issue, Eden's attitude towards collective security, can it be said that Eden displayed clearly different opinions in different roles. It seems that his enthusiasm for a system of collective security, in which all members of the international community react, whenever one country commits an act that could be called a severe breach of international law, is clearly linked to his role as a Minister for League of Nations Affairs. Eden made his name as Great Britain's representative at the League of Nations disarmament conference in the early 1930s, and became even more famous when appointed Minister of League of Nations Affairs. In this capacity he emphasizes in his speeches the obsolescence of the system of balance of power and the dangers of secret diplomacy, the classic themes of champions of collective security. The principle of balance of power could lead to both miscalculation and to misunderstanding and thus to war, as had happened in 1914. Eden considered the League's decision, at his personal initiative, to install an international police force that would keep an eye on the plebiscite in the Saar-area in 1935, as an example of successful collective security through the League. Similarly, he insisted on sanctions through the League against Italy after the latter had invaded Abyssinia, and was the only Cabinet member in favour of an arms embargo.

Despite his enthusiasm for collective security, he gave priority to the interests of the United Kingdom. Eden was opposed to sanctions against Japan, after its attack on Manchuria in 1934. Given the absence of the United States and Soviet Union from the League of Nations, Great Britain could not deal with Japanese aggression on her own: 'Britain and France were not capable of performing the role of an international police force' (Peters, 1986, p. 57). Eden thus was not willing to have British foreign policy determined by decisions made at the League in Geneva (*ibid.*, p. 26). It was argued above that Eden's willingness to impose collective security matters on Italy should be understood in terms of his worldview, which stresses the crucial role of the Middle East and the observance of standards of international conduct. After having become Foreign Secretary in December 1935, Eden no longer talks of collective security. Indeed, shortly before the outbreak of the Second World War he would claim that neither collective security nor balance of power politics are reasonable guidelines of foreign policy-making.

What must be concluded from this change of belief, which seems related to a change of political role? Given the fact that Britain's vital interests remain dominant, the change is not disturbing for an analysis that makes use of an individual's belief system. It points to the possibility, nevertheless, that Eden's assessment of international organizations is not as positive as his speeches seem to suggest. He probably conceives of international organizations as platforms where the world's major powers can work together on the basis of the recognition of their mutual security interests. He expected the United Nations to develop into machinery that would prolong the wartime alliance between the Soviet Union, the United States and the United Kingdom. Eden considered the United Nations a failure, possibly temporary, when the Soviet Union used its right to veto so often. International co-operation is therefore first of all a product of reasonable nation-states. International organizations are vehicles for their interactions but no independent source of co-operation.

No other differences in beliefs occur that can be accounted for by a variation of Eden's political roles. One might have expected a change of Eden's opinions on foreign policy, once he returned to opposition in 1945. But, consistent with his belief that it was a duty to keep foreign affairs out of political controversy, he stuck to his master belief.

*Public versus Private Utterances*

No real contradictions between public and private statements appear in the sources consulted. Two troublesome considerations can be made, however. First, a much more precise description of what Eden considers Great Britain's vital interests becomes evident in private rather than in public utterances, especially when documents from the Foreign Office are considered. It is obvious that he would not speak in public in favour of handing over the Baltic States to the Soviet Union simply because it was much more in the long term interest of the United Kingdom to try and reach an understanding with the Soviet Union about general post-war arrangements. Second, Eden appears much more hawkish towards Egypt and Iran in private than in public. Even though he adjusted his attitude towards Egypt on the consideration that the Suez Canal base was no longer of strategic importance and that Great Britain could not afford to reoccupy Egypt, his exact opinion as to the use of force in international affairs remains unclear.

*Implications for an Analysis of the Suez Crisis*

The identification of Anthony Eden's cognitive belief system makes it possible to formulate expectations about Eden's handling of the Suez crisis. The Operational Code construct does not pretend to be able to give exact predictions as to a politician's behaviour. Rather, it sets boundaries on the range of possible interpretations of the nature of a crisis and of incoming information, the number of options available, and their respective evaluation (George, 1979a; Walker and Murphy, 1981/1982). The central hypothesis of an Operational Code analysis suggests that in times of crisis a politician will rely on his most fundamental beliefs, his master belief.

This implies, first of all, that, in the case of Anthony Eden, the adherence to accepted standards of international conduct, taking account of nations' legitimate national interests will be the most important consideration. It implies that Eden will not be influenced by the nature of the political regime of his opponent, but rather by the latter's observance of certain agreements. It might thus provide a clue as to why the nationalization of the Suez Canal Company, rather than the Czech arms deal, or the sacking of Glubb Pasha by King Hussein, sparked off the crisis. Possibly Eden considered this the final proof that Nasser did not respect international agreements. Similarly, it might give a hint as to why the British Government decided to no longer consult the American Government on their policies on Suez.

Second, this respect for international norms is founded in a respect for mutual legitimate security interests. According to Eden, the Middle East was pivotal to the communication between the United Kingdom and the Empire. The Empire itself was crucial in determining British prestige in the world and in earning hard currencies that could help the British economy's recovery. At the same time, Eden recognized that the United States played first fiddle and that the United Kingdom needed the United States in retaining its influence in the world. This suggests that the act of nationalization of the Suez Canal Company will be linked to its function as a line of communication of Commonwealth and Empire. Moreover, Eden will recognize the need to co-operate with the United States until the moment that he feels that the United States are not properly assessing the nature of British interests involved, or that the United States is evaluating the situation in terms of English imperialism.

Third, Eden acknowledges that international organizations can play a modest role in world affairs, as long as the main powers of the international system co-operate on the basis of the recognition of their mutual legitimate security interests and are prepared to use international organizations on the basis of some consensus of international stability. By 1949 Eden has reached the conclusion that, for the time being, Soviet votes have made the United Nations useless. This suggests that in times of crisis Eden will be reluctant to take recourse to the United Nations.

It should now be ascertained to what extent Eden's worldview contributes to understanding British foreign policy-making during the Suez crisis.

## Notes

[1]   In this context of guided development should one understand Eden's claim that 'circumstances are, to a great extent, what we make them' (Eden, 1939, p. 281).

[2]   For Eden, peace was not equal to the absence of war: 'we do not believe in conflict. We believe in co-operation. The world has surely learnt enough, in its long history, to know that by patient collaboration man can steadily increase his standard of living (-). It can never be done by war' (Eden, 1939, p. 186).

[3]   *Documents on British Foreign Policy*, Volume 19, Record of a Conversation, 29 and 30 November 1937, C 8234/270/18, p. 600. Prime Minister Sir Neville Chamberlain made it clear during the same conversations that in the eyes of British public opinion 'we ought not to be entangled in a war on account of Czechoslovakia' (*ibid.*, p. 599), a remark that was not in any way modified by Eden.

4   *Documents on British Foreign Policy*, Volume 19, Memo by Eden on German contribution to general appeasement, C 1057/42/16, 10 February 1938, p. 873.

5   *Documents on British Foreign Policy*, Volume 17, Minute by Eden, No. 352, R 6646/226/22, 5 November 1936, pp. 513-14.

6   *Documents on British Foreign Policy*, Volume 19, Eden to Chamberlain, R 248/7/22, 1 January 1938, p. 711.

7   *Documents on British Foreign Policy*, Volume 19, Eden to Chamberlain, R 306/7/22, 9 January 1938, p. 723.

8   A speech Churchill thought far too friendly. He reproached Eden on it (see Carlton, 1981).

9   In the summer of 1941 Britain and the Soviet Union had forced the Shah to accept the temporary occupation of Persia in order to secure the oil fields, and the transportation of Allied arms to the Soviet Union.

10  *Foreign Relations of the United States 1951*, Gifford to Secretary of State, 11 May 1951.

11  *ibid.*, Gifford to Washington, 25 May 1951.

12  Eventually, Chamberlain rejected Roosevelt's proposal without consulting Eden. This triggered Eden's resignation in March 1938.

13  Memorandum by Eden, August 1943, FO 371/35927, F/4767/1943/61, quoted by Sbrega (1983, pp. 292-3).

# Chapter 5

# Six Decisional Conflicts

## Introduction

This chapter investigates in which way British policy-makers handled the six decisional conflicts distinguished in Chapter 2 (pp. 38-9). For each decisional conflict the data are presented in a similar fashion. First, each section starts with an overview of the structure of decision-making based on the chronology of meetings reported in Appendix 2. This is followed by a description of decision-making. Then, the available material is linked to the explanatory variables of this study: Groupthink, worldview of the leader, domestic political institutions, and organizational context.

## Decision 1: Diplomacy Instead of Immediate Attack

In the morning of 30 July 1956 the special committee installed to deal with the crisis, the Egypt Committee, decided to agree to an international diplomatic conference as a response to Egypt's nationalization of the Suez Canal Company four days earlier. On 1 August the Cabinet confirmed this decision. It was also agreed to invite those states that had signed the 1888 Constantinople Convention, which had established the Suez Canal as an international waterway. The Egypt Committee's choice in favour of diplomatic response raises the question why a conference was preferred to a military confrontation.

### The Structure of Decision-Making

A glance at Appendix 2 allows for three observations. First, the full Cabinet was only sparsely involved. It convened at the beginning (27 July) and at the end (1 August), but did not meet in between. Moreover, an informal meeting at 10 Downing Street preceded its very first meeting, which lasted more than five hours. Second, decision-making seemed dominated by meetings of the Egypt Committee. This ad hoc committee had been installed on 27 July. Its original members included Eden, Foreign Secretary Lloyd, Chancellor of the Exchequer Macmillan, Lord President of the Council Salisbury, Minister of Defence Monckton, and Commonwealth Secretary Lord Home. Third, Eden's phone call to Macmillan in the morning of 27 July shows Macmillan's weight within the Government. Eden and Macmillan discussed the phrasing of the short statement that Eden would pronounce at the House of Commons that morning at 11.[1] Despite Butler's illness at the time, it seems strange that Eden did not consult him, and that he did not include Butler among the original members of the Egypt Committee. Macmillan's presence (and Butler's absence) at informal meetings with French Foreign Secretary Christian Pineau, American Secretary of State John Foster Dulles, and his special envoy Robert Murphy, confirms Macmillan's influence. Moreover, Eden consulted Macmillan about the contents of the letter that would be sent to President Eisenhower, following the Cabinet meeting of 27 July.[2] It should also be noted that the formal tripartite conversations between the representatives of France, Great Britain, and the United States between 30 July and 1 August (not shown in the Appendix) are paralleled by meetings between American and British officials alone. This testifies to the uneasiness that both Americans and British felt about co-operation with the French (cf. Adamthwaite, 1989) and possibly of the traditional British view of privileged co-operation with the Americans.

*The Definition of the Problem*

It is of crucial importance to examine how British policy-makers defined the problem. This is likely to constrain discussions and decisions in subsequent meetings (cf. Sylvan and Voss, 1998). No full account exists of the first informal meeting after the news of the nationalization broke through. Eden is said to have declared Nasser's behaviour an act of aggression to which he wished to respond forcefully and immediately. The Chiefs of Staffs present (Mountbatten [Navy], Dickson [RAF], Templer [Imperial Staff]) reckoned that the United Kingdom's military forces were not prepared for this type of crisis.[3] Indeed, in the Commons next morning Eden made a very cautious statement, talking about rights and interests affected, and about consultations between Governments concerned, avoiding the question of force. At the first meeting of the Chiefs of Staff on 27 July at 9.15 a.m. Mountbatten reported that 'Ministers had already given consideration to the attitude the U.K. should adopt in the situation and had decided that until the views of other interested powers had been obtained no action should be taken which could be construed as threatening Egypt'.[4] British decision-makers thus did not want to strike immediately, even if such a *coup de main* had been possible given the doubts Mountbatten, Boyle, and Templer had presumably pronounced.

The Cabinet's meeting of 27 July was affected by the way Eden handled the discussion. Eden opened the meeting by giving an account of his meeting with the French and American representatives the night before.

> He had told them that Her Majesty's Government would take a most serious view of this situation and that any failure on the part of the Western Powers to take the necessary steps to regain control over the Canal would have disastrous consequences for the economic life of the Western Powers and for their standing and influence in the Middle East.[5]

He thus presented the Cabinet with some sort of *fait accompli*. By 'informing' France and the United States of 'Her Majesty's Government's' view of the situation, he attached importance to the crisis and imposed a sense of urgency on Cabinet members. Eden, however, did not impose the military option on the Cabinet. The minutes read: 'the Cabinet should now consider what courses of action were open to us to safeguard our interests'. What followed was a discussion of the Canal's economic importance and of legal aspects of the problem. Not until then did one discuss the factors related to the military option. Experts gave their view on various sides of the problem: Minister of Fuel and Power Jones (not a Cabinet member) had been invited to spell out some of the consequences of Egypt's move. The legal advisors of the Foreign Office had prepared a memo on considerations of international law. The Chiefs of Staff had been invited to discuss the military option.

Eden intervened only afterwards by saying that 'against this background the Cabinet must decide what our policy must be'. He led the Cabinet into formulating its objective: the Canal should be placed under international control. Next, he invited the Cabinet to face the fundamental question 'whether they were prepared in the last resort to pursue their objective by the threat or even the use of force, and whether they were ready, in default of assistance from the United States and France, to take military action alone'. The Cabinet agreed to this, taking into consideration that 'failure to hold the Suez Canal would lead inevitably to the loss one by one of all our interests and assets in the Middle East and, even if we had to act alone, we could not stop short of using force to protect our position if all other means of protecting it proved unavailing'.

These considerations reveal three important matters: first, British prestige in the area was perceived to be at stake rather than British lines of supply. Nationalization was thus considered a threat to long-term British interests in the Middle East. Second, Cabinet members sensed that the amount of time to respond was limited: failure to react to this slap in the face would have a disastrous effect on British standing elsewhere. Third, the agreement in principle to the use of force, even without assistance from the United States and France, reveals the prevailing assumption that, in that event, no opposition from the United States was expected, but at least tacit support.

*Explanatory Variables*

In the morning of 30 July the Chiefs of Staff told the members of the Egypt Committee that immediate military action would be risky because it could not be guaranteed that the initial troops occupying the Canal Zone would hold out until the arrival of reinforcements. At that same meeting the Egypt Committee agreed to organize a conference of those maritime nations that had an important interest in the canal. To what extent can one say that the first decision, not to take immediate military action, but to arrange a diplomatic conference first, was affected by the four explanatory variables?

*Eden's worldview and leadership* Eden's worldview provides an important clue to understanding why the Cabinet decided not to adopt a more conciliatory attitude first before responding vigorously to Egypt's act of nationalization. After all, the Cabinet had recognized that from a narrow international legal point of view nationalization 'amounted to no more than a decision to buy out the shareholders'. Why then did British policy-makers define the problem as an Egyptian threat to British interests throughout the Middle East? The minutes reflect considerations that can best be understood in terms of Eden's worldview. Egypt's recent behaviour gave no confidence that it would recognize its international obligations in respecting and running the Canal as an important international facility.[6] Within the frame of Eden's worldview, Nasser had passed an important threshold. He could no longer be considered someone who respected the rules of international conduct based on the mutual recognition of respective national interests. In his memoirs, Eden writes that in the many messages he despatched that day he wrote that 'a man *with Colonel Nasser's record* could not be allowed "to have his thumb on our windpipe"' (italics added) (Eden, 1960, pp. 425-6).

Eden's directive leadership at the beginning of the Cabinet meeting of 27 July, when the definition of the problem was narrowed down, reinforces this interpretation. Eden's leadership style clearly contributed to the Cabinet's sense of crisis. Yet, he did not impose his perspective on the Cabinet. After the initial presentation of the problem, he allowed for a relatively free discussion of the courses that were open to the Cabinet, after having asked for the opinions of three experts on economic, legal and military aspects of the problem. Three alternative courses of action were discussed: to refer the matter to the United Nations' Security Council, to take economic measures only against Egypt, and to put economic pressure on Egypt while at the same time threaten with the use of force. Two options were thus not even considered, that is, to do nothing, or to issue a strong diplomatic protest. As noted above, Eden had effectively excluded these options with his opening statement that failure to take the necessary steps to regain control of the Canal would ruin the Western powers' standing and prestige in the Middle East. During the first Cabinet meeting Eden flatly refused to refer the matter to the Security Council. He thought it would risk a Soviet veto. This view is fully consistent with his worldview. Eden had grown extremely distrustful of the United Nations since 1948 (a turning point in his attitude towards the Soviet Union) and thought it had become wholly ineffective because of Soviet vetoing.

During the Egypt Committee meeting in the afternoon of 30 July, Lord Home again suggested taking the matter to the Security Council in an attempt to have Egypt charged with aggression. This would give more time to prepare other measures and prevent Great Britain from being labelled as an aggressor itself. This option was rejected because a vote at the United Nations would put the Arab countries in a most difficult position, as they would have to side with Egypt while they might secretly support the strong action being taken against Egypt. The records do not show who formulated these considerations (they are recorded as 'Cabinet discussion'). However, Eden's worldview is not the only factor accounting for the attitude adopted towards the United Nations. Narrow calculations of national interest and strategy seem to have been equally important.

It is thus difficult to indicate Eden's impact on decision-making with precision. Nevertheless, it has been significant for the definition of the problem and for the subsequent formulation of British objectives in this crisis. Mountbatten suggests that Eden was much more straightforward about the stakes than the official records reveal. Apart from the restoration of international control of the Canal, Eden's 'object was to get rid of Colonel Nasser personally and his regime which he regarded as the principal enemies'.[7] Clearly, however, the decision to link Great Britain's response to the downfall of the Egyptian Government, which the Egypt Committee explicitly formulated as immediate objective,[8] was the origin of the principal dilemma that the British Government would face during the entire crisis. It would prove very difficult to get rid of Nasser if one preferred to use the veil of international control of the Canal as a pretext for intervention. Control of the Canal could be only obtained with support from the United States and public opinion. Neither would support military action explicitly aimed at toppling Nasser. Therefore, the principal cognitive failure made by the British Government was the assumption that taking strong action regarding the Canal would automatically cause Nasser's downfall.[9] This assumption was indispensable, however, in order to prevent a formal acknowledgement that the toppling of Nasser was the real objective.

Curiously, however, the objective of Nasser's downfall was not mentioned during the Cabinet discussions on the day after the nationalization. It reoccurred at the Egypt Committee of 30 July, when it was concluded that 'while our ultimate purpose was to place the Canal under international control, our immediate objective was to bring about the downfall of the present Egyptian Government'.[10] It seems likely that Mountbatten's account of Eden's objectives refers to the informal meeting in the evening of 26 July at which he had been present. If correct, this puts a heavy burden on Eden who led the Cabinet into accepting the use of force in principle without full discussion of the question whether its objective should include the downfall of Nasser. Of course, the genesis of the Egypt Committee might point to Eden's preference to withhold certain objectives from the Cabinet. The installation of such an ad hoc body was rather unusual (cf. Seymour-Ure, 1984). Butler afterwards declared that it was Eden's personal wish to have a small committee of trusted collaborators around him in order to avoid opposition from the full Cabinet (Butler, 1975).

If Mountbatten's account reflects the informal meeting of 26 July, then Eden can be said to have directed the Cabinet towards the use of force without clear objective for such action, leaving the formulation of military and political objectives to the Egypt Committee, originally intended as a very small group indeed. However, if Mountbatten's account refers to the Cabinet's first meeting during the crisis, as he claims himself, then it must be concluded that the Cabinet unanimously accepted the toppling of Nasser as the immediate objective of the whole enterprise.[11] Even if criticism against such an objective emerged, it must have been rather clear, given Eden's personal statements of goals (as recorded by Mountbatten), that in deciding in favour of an extremely small decision-making body to deal with the situation, all Cabinet members knew perfectly well into which direction such planning would go.

*Groupthink* One is struck by the extent of unanimity that arises from the records of the meetings. Neither the Cabinet nor the Egypt Committee shows much dissension on the formulated aims or the methods to be employed, including the possible use of force. Even later critics, such as Monckton and Butler,[12] raised no objection. Moreover, every policy-maker appeared to agree to the essential consideration that failure to hold the Canal would inevitably lead to the loss of all British interests in the Middle East. Both Cabinet and Egypt Committee were also unanimous in their assumptions about the Egyptian attitude. Egypt was considered incapable of running the Canal by itself. Moreover, it was 'evident that Egypt would not yield to economic pressure alone'. It was thus essential to concert diplomatic pressure on Egypt with France and the United States.[13] Neither decision-making body felt like verifying whether Egypt might yield to economic pressure alone, and whether the Egyptians would be capable of running the Canal without help from the Company's pilots. Failure to examine the latter question especially would prove a fundamental mistake later in September when the British and French Governments thought they could bring matters to a head by having the Company recall its pilots. When eventually the Egypt Committee accepted the idea of a users' conference in the morning of 30 July 1956, after it had become clear that no immediate military action would be possible, its members engaged in some dangerous wishful thinking. The users' conference was to re-establish international control of the Suez Canal. 'If Colonel Nasser failed to accept it, military operations could then proceed'.[14] No one thought of the possibility that the outcome of the Conference might be ambiguous, instead of Egypt's unequivocal acceptance or rejection of Western demands.

Dissension focused on possible recourse to the United Nations. On 30 July Home argued that Egypt should be condemned as an aggressor before the Security Council in order to anticipate a similar move by Egypt or the Soviet Union against the United Kingdom. The other Egypt Committee members feared it would bring Arab countries into a difficult position because a resolution would force them to take a public stand. At the full Cabinet on 1 August the issue of the United Nations was brought up again. Lloyd stressed that the United States in particular had been against recourse to the United Nations. The United States feared implications for the status of the Panama Canal, which it regarded as American property rather than an international entity, such as the Suez Canal Company. Rather than a U.N.O.-sponsored conference, it preferred a conference of signatories to the original 1888 Convention of Constantinople, which had established the Suez Canal as an international waterway. The American position raises the question of the importance of a small group of individual Ministers. Only a restricted number of British policy-makers met with the American envoy Robert Murphy and Dulles who had arrived on 1 August: Eden, Lloyd, Salisbury, and Macmillan. British perceptions of the American attitude towards the dispute were based on the interpretation of a small number of individuals. Moreover, both the Egypt Committee and the Cabinet were dependent on these four individuals in making an assessment of the American position.

In a meeting at the Foreign Office on 27 July the American *Chargé d'Affaires* Foster[15] had made it clear to Lloyd and the French Ambassador Chauvel that American understanding of the British and French position did not mean giving them *carte blanche* to engage in military adventures.[16] Even more alarming was next day's message from British Ambassador in Washington Roger Makins that the Americans did not want to be entangled in the conflict. He suggested therefore impressing upon Murphy that France and Great Britain took the matter very seriously.[17] It must therefore have been deliberate policy of Eden, Lloyd and Macmillan to emphasize the immediate use of military action to Murphy (Carlton, 1988).

In an attempt to co-ordinate French and British policies, Lloyd told Pineau on 29 July, 15 minutes before they were to meet with Murphy for the first time, that the

United States was very reluctant to talk about military force. It would therefore be better to discuss restoring international control of the Canal 'to fill the gap until we were prepared militarily'.[18] During their meeting with Murphy, Lloyd talked of the threat to Great Britain's vital interests, and Pineau stressed Nasser's influence on North African politics, comparing him with Hitler. Murphy answered that attention would have to be paid to world opinion, adding that American public opinion was 'not yet prepared'.[19] The French were clearly afraid that Murphy had come to London only to delay drastic measures. The French Ambassador told Lloyd on 29 July that his Government was afraid that the Americans would take the same position as they had over the Iranian crisis of 1951 (see pp. 52-3).

On 30 July Eden, Salisbury, Lloyd, and Macmillan had lunch with Murphy. That evening Murphy dined with Macmillan, Foster, and Lord Alexander at 11 Downing Street. On both occasions British ministers tried to convince Murphy that Great Britain meant business. Macmillan made his famous remark that Britain could not become a second Netherlands (Macmillan, 1971). Murphy's account of these conversations to Eisenhower prompted the American President to send Secretary of State Dulles to London (Murphy, 1964). In a private discussion, however, Lloyd and Eden had already drawn conclusions from the talks with Murphy. In case the United States would not join in with military action, they argued, 'we should rely upon them to "watch the bear"' and ensure that the United States 'should use all their influence to keep the Israelis out of it'. Lloyd and Eden took account of another message from Makins who had reported that Dulles had sent for him, and had told him that he saw no basis for American military force, partly because it would need the approval of Congress, which was by no means a certainty.[20] British policy-makers thus still assumed that an American refusal to actively participate in military action implied tacit approval of, and support for, such a policy.

When Dulles arrived on 1 August, he carried a letter from Eisenhower, in which the President stressed the exploration of diplomatic solutions. Dulles had recognized that Eisenhower's phrasing was rather ambiguous and handed over another letter of his own. It explained that Eisenhower's text 'refers not to the going through the motions of having an intermediate conference, but to the use of intermediate steps as a genuine and sincere effort to settle the problem and avoid the use of force'.[21] On 1 August Harold Caccia reported to Eden of a meeting between him and Dulles at the Foreign Office that morning. Caccia told of Dulles's words that the aims of the United States and the United Kingdom were the same, but that 'if the attempt were to be made by force alone, he saw great difficulties'.[22] This one word 'alone' may have left Eden enough room not to take Dulles's correction of Eisenhower's letter too seriously and to conclude: 'The President did not rule out the use of force' (Eden, 1960, p. 436). Lloyd's conversation with Dulles and Murphy at noon that day left the Foreign Secretary with the same impression even though he truthfully reported that Dulles suspected the British Government was not taking diplomatic steps seriously.[23] In general, Lloyd displayed a rather bellicose attitude in these early days. He privately told Pineau on 31 July that it would be wise for France and Great Britain to go forward together: 'the Americans often followed where others took action. It was important not to get held up in discussions longer than suited us militarily'.[24]

Two main conclusions can be drawn regarding the possible influence of small group factors. First, both Cabinet and Egypt Committee acted rather unanimously in their assessment of the problem, the objectives to be pursued and the means to be employed. By consequence, many assumptions on which their decision-making was based were not discussed. Second, contacts with the United States and France were maintained by a small group of four policy-makers, two of which, Macmillan and Salisbury did not formally belong to the foreign policy-making system. This is a first indicator of the presence of an even smaller inner circle. Dealing with the Americans, Eden, Macmillan, Lloyd, and Salisbury acted on the assumption that it would be possible to cajole the United States into a policy that would best benefit the United Kingdom. In doing so, they applied a technique that had been practised during the concluding of the Suez Canal treaty, the Iranian crisis, and, most recently, after the Czech arms deal and the Glubb affair. This approach had two important consequences. First, British policy-makers did not conceive of the possibility that American reluctance to support military action might actually signal their opposition to it. Lloyd and Eden thought the Americans would rather not join in military action, but would no doubt cover British and French manoeuvres. Second, by consequence, British policy-makers went to great lengths to ensure that their interpretation of messages from Dulles and Eisenhower fitted their own assumptions regarding the American attitude.

Did the inner circle affect decision-making at the level of the Cabinet or Egypt Committee? In the Egypt Committee Eden was fair about the conversations with Murphy. He said that Murphy had come only to hear what the trouble was all about. Eden mentioned that he had said to Murphy that he hoped that the Americans would keep a watchful eye on the Soviet Union and would restrain Israel.[25] Selwyn Lloyd's account to the Cabinet on 1 August, when the Government was to accept the proposal for the London Conference, was less qualified. Lloyd said that the United States and the United Kingdom were thinking along the same lines. Both wanted to make Nasser 'disgorge' what he had swallowed.[26] He added, however, that Dulles had made it clear that the Americans would 'strongly deprecate "any premature use of force"'.[27] Unsurprisingly, no Cabinet member wondered whether the United States' attitude implied fundamental opposition to the use of force.

Can the Cabinet, or Egypt Committee, or the small group that met with Murphy and Dulles be said to have displayed symptoms of Groupthink? The Cabinet's decision of 27 July to be prepared to go it alone eventually testifies to an illusion of invulnerability. The decision not to go to the United Nations may be symptomatic of the same. Neff reports that on that same day Cabinet members felt as if they had taken a weighty decision, one of great righteousness (Neff, 1981). If correct, this would indicate a belief in the inherent morality of the group. To a certain extent, the original exclusion of Butler from the Egypt Committee, and from the group of four that spoke to the Americans, might qualify as a self-appointed mindguard. The evidence is rather poor, however. Moreover, efforts to rationalize collectively (e.g., about the American attitude) are not linked to this particular decision, but reflect the general strategy the British had adopted towards the United States. They thus testify to the influence of the images of the United States that British foreign policy-makers had developed previously.

*The organizational context* The British Government was unable to send a military force forthwith because the British Armed Forces were unprepared for a limited war. This condition constrained British decision-making considerably. Mountbatten told the Chiefs of Staff that in the night of 26 July Ministers had already decided not to take any action 'which could be construed as threatening Egypt' until the views of other interested powers had been obtained. It remains unclear whether the lack of readiness induced the Ministers to embark on consultations first, or whether they had deemed consultations the proper move anyway. Anyhow, on 27 July the Cabinet must have been under no illusion regarding the immediate use of force. The Chiefs of Staff pointed out that military supplies would take weeks to arrive by sea. Preparations would thus take several weeks.[28]

The military plans, presented to the Cabinet by the Chiefs of Staff on 1 August entitled *Action against Egypt*, stressed the unready state of notably the paratroopers who lacked adequate parachute training, because they had been fighting against Cypriot guerrillas since the Summer of 1955 (Lamb, 1987). Any swift airborne occupation of (part of) the Canal therefore seemed unlikely.[29] Much more important, however, was the military's belief that airborne troops should be reinforced within reasonable time. Even though it might be possible, with French support, to move an armoured division to the Canal area, it would take too long to have them relieved by the main task force, which would have to sail from Malta, the closest harbour for landing craft.

Decision-making was thus strongly affected by the conditions of military preparations. Possibly, British military forces were caught by surprise by the nature of the task assigned to them, being prepared only for large scale or guerrilla wars. This made them engage in traditional, meticulous, planning, as for the 1944 Normandy invasion. In that effort they relied on standard operation procedures. This was Eden's view, when he recalled 'constantly urging' on the military that planning against Egyptians was not as difficult as planning against Germans (Eden, 1960, p. 430). Although a plausible interpretation, it should be qualified. For one thing, contingency planning had included operations against Egypt. Since 23 April 1956 British and American Joint Chiefs of Staff had been engaged in preparing contingencies to act against aggression in a war between Israel and Arab countries. On 13 April 1956, in preparing themselves for these talks, the British Chiefs of Staff had come up with four situations that might arise. One possibility was an attack by Israel on Egypt, another was an Egyptian attack on Israel; a third, a situation in which the aggressor would not be evident, and fourth, a limited military action to safeguard nationals and vital interests, notably the Canal base. Apart from plans to install a maritime blockade, combined with air and land operations, a worst case scenario was developed. This aimed at keeping open the Suez Canal by dropping paratroopers, followed by a swift build-up of air transported forces in order to secure the airfield, to occupy Suez, and to seize bridges and ferries across the Canal. Port Said was a deep-water port that could be used for the arrival of reinforcements.[30] Interestingly, Mountbatten asked for guidance on political objectives, because British involvement in an Arab-Israeli conflict could have consequences for British relations with the Arab world. He thought it wise, however, to hold these joint planning sessions on the assumption that the protection of oil interests would be the ultimate purpose of the planning.[31] The Chiefs' report of the joint planning talks with the Americans in Washington between 25 April and 3 May clearly shows that the seizure of the Canal Zone by employing paratroopers and launching a naval assault was judged to be possible. British and Americans did not differ in their assessment of plans and requirements, only regarding the command structure of such an operation.[32]

This suggests that contingency planning for other wars than those on a worldwide or local scale actually took place. Even the employment of paratroopers for an action against the Suez Canal had been contemplated. The Chiefs of Staff expressed their preference for a maritime blockade, possibly combined with air operations in order to minimize the alienation of Arab allies, who might think that seizure of the Canal would amount to British support of Israel.[33] No reference is made to unready paratroopers, or to problems regarding the amount of time that would be needed to relieve the airborne troops. It certainly raises the question of the nature of decision-making among the Chiefs of Staff. For the purpose of this study it is important to note that the range of options presented by the Chiefs of Staff constrained British policy-makers considerably.

*Conclusions*

How to explain the British decision to agree to an international diplomatic conference instead of immediate military action? Two elements stand out. First, the consideration that at least tacit American consent was needed before starting any military action. This meant that the principal American foreign policy-makers (Eisenhower, Dulles, and Murphy) had to be convinced of the seriousness of the situation. Second, the presumed lack of readiness of British military forces. Eventually, this meant that a conference became indispensable in order to keep up the pressure while military plans were being worked out. The military's position actually caused a domestic problem for the Government, because public opinion in Great Britain might accuse the Government of inactivity. This explains the explicit haste with which troops were sent to Tobruk in Cyrenaica on 31 July and why 20,000 reservists had been urgently recalled forthwith on 28 July.[34]

In sum, the organizational context has set the time frame within which British decision-makers had to operate. The group factor emerged during the crucial meeting of 26 July, which was attended by only a small group of ministers. Also, contact with the representatives of the United States and France was entrusted to almost the same small group. Moreover, apart from the issue of reference to the United Nations, both the Cabinet and the Egypt Committee were unanimous in their analysis of the stakes involved, the preferred objectives, and available options. Their unanimity prevented them from questioning several important assumptions employed in their deliberations. Nevertheless, only few symptoms of Groupthink could be found. Part of the decision-making process, at least during the important first full Cabinet meeting on 27 July should be explained by the way the group's leader, that is, the Prime Minister, conducted the meeting. In that sense, directive leadership has been of some relevance. More importantly, Eden's worldview partly explains the sense of crisis that occurred after Nasser's move (contrary to earlier Egyptian acts against

British interests) as well as the attitude that was adopted towards the possibility of referring the dispute to the Security Council.

## Decision 2: The Menzies Mission

The Cabinet expected that the outcome of the London Conference, which was to open on 16 August, would amount to either Nasser 'disgorging' the Canal or obtaining permission to restore the international character of the Canal by force. Evidently, a more ambiguous outcome was not anticipated. Eighteen of the 22 countries present supported a proposal reflecting Dulles's strong opening speech in which he asked for international control of the Canal. Great Britain and France preferred Dulles to head a delegation. This would reinforce the commitment of the United States to their cause and confront Nasser with something that looked like an ultimatum. Dulles, however, declined travelling to Egypt to present the so-called Eighteen-Powers Proposals to Nasser. Towards the end of the Conference, therefore, British policy-makers suddenly became aware of the possibility that, unless a strong delegation was sent, Nasser might procrastinate for a little while, making it impossible for Great Britain and France to take stronger action. The solution to this dilemma was found in the early morning of 22 August, when the Australian Prime Minister, Sir Robert Menzies, agreed to head the delegation to Cairo.

British policy-makers' growing apprehension that the London Conference would have an unfortunate ending is shown in Salisbury's letter to Eden on 9 August. Salisbury suggested that the Conference might have many different endings than acceptance or refusal by Nasser of its proposals.

> There are an infinite number of gradations in between. For instance, the conference may break up without agreement. Or Colonel Nasser may not entirely turn down some proposal that is put to him, but may make suggestions that go some way to meet us, but not nearly enough for it would be claimed by Colonel Nasser as a success, and we cannot afford that he should have a success. [Contingency planning was thus] the more necessary as we shall we have, if we are to proceed to force, to try to carry the bulk of our own public opinion with us, and at present I doubt whether we have more than half the country behind us; and the official Labour Party are steadily sliding away. This may well entail further intensive propaganda during the next few days as to the issues involved and the danger of weakness. Finally, there is the position with regard to Parliament. If we are likely to have unhappily to proceed to extremes [i.e., use of force], a debate in Parliament is going to put us in an almost impossible position. This is, as I see it, an entirely new position, at any rate so far as recent times are concerned [in which] we should certainly not want to disclose our intentions or our plans.[35]

Salisbury's letter illustrates two increasingly pressing developments confronting British policy-makers, the decrease in public support for a tough policy towards Egypt and the possibility of an equivocal outcome of the Conference. This dilemma would eventually lead a small group of Ministers to conclude that some provocative action by Nasser would be needed, if force were to be justified. This conclusion was furthered by a third factor, which after 10 August constrained the decision-making process. That day the Chiefs of Staff suggested that the invasion should not take place at Port Said, but rather at Alexandria, thus making it less seem a response to the nationalization of the Canal company, and taking the risk of a larger number of civilian casualties. This plan of attack was therefore less easily justifiable under international law, and added to the sense of facing a dilemma.

Appendix 2 allows for three conclusions regarding the structure of decision-making. First, the Egypt Committee dominates decision-making. Second, two informal meetings between Senior Ministers take place. One such meeting takes place at an important moment, shortly before the important Cabinet meeting of 21 August, at which the official British attitude towards the development of the London conference had to be determined. Third, further evidence exists of a restricted number of ministers, Eden, Macmillan, Salisbury, and Lloyd, who meet informally with representatives of the United States (Aldrich, Dulles) during the conference. Furthermore, some of these ministers (Eden, Lloyd, Salisbury) keep in touch with the opposition. It thus seems that only a few Ministers provided both Cabinet and Egypt Committee with information on the attitude of both the United States Government and the Labour Party.

*Constraints on Decision-Making before the Start of the Conference*

As the day of the Conference's start approached, three factors made British decision-makers realize that military action might not yet be possible in the event of Egypt's rejection of the conference's outcome. Domestic opposition to the use of force was growing. Nasser might not equivocally accept or reject the conference's outcome. Moreover, the military came with a change of plan.

*Domestic public opinion*  In the Commons debate of 2 August, the Labour Party had vigorously denounced Nasser's act of nationalization (James, 1986). Labour leader Hugh Gaitskell met Eden that same day, in order to find out about the Government's intentions regarding the use of force. Next day he wrote Eden a letter emphasizing that the majority of his Party would not agree to force unless it was in line with the United Nations Charter. Eden's reply did not entail specific assurances about the use of force, upon which Gaitskell instantly sent another letter to Eden, repeating his party's reservations (James, 1986). Further erosion of Labour support for a tough line occurred when Eden, Salisbury, and Lloyd met with a Labour delegation on 14 August. Gaitskell again stressed Labour's opposition to the use of force. Eden reported this to the Cabinet meeting which opened immediately afterwards, but Eden significantly added that the Labour party delegates 'recognized that if any new incidents occurred, such as the interference with ships using the Canal, a new situation would arise in which force might be justified'.[36]

British policy-makers also had to take account of international public opinion. On 7 August the Egypt Committee, discussing Lloyd's draft instructions to the British Ambassador to France, Sir Gladwyn Jebb, discussed the possibility of both Nasser's downfall and the occupation of entire Egypt as a possible outcome of strong action. Nevertheless, it was considered most important 'from the point of public opinion, especially in the United States and in Asia, that the purpose of our action should appear to be confined to establishing the security of the international waterway across the isthmus of Suez, and not as being complicated by political designs against the Egyptian regime. It follows that the leakage of a document appearing to define our objective in wider terms could be disastrous'. Therefore, and in order not to alienate pro-Western Arab states, Israel should be restrained and France should moderate her attitude towards the Algerian situation, which had made her unpopular with Arab states.[37] The Egypt Committee was very anxious not to appear too bellicose, while a diplomatic conference was at hand. Any significant military measures were therefore to be played down, much to the annoyance of the French who, because of domestic concerns opposite to those of the British Government, wanted to give as much publicity as possible to any sign of vigour.

It does not come as a surprise therefore that the first two weeks of August witnessed an increased effort to impress domestic and international public opinion with the brutality of Nasser's act and of the strength of the Anglo-French case under international law. On 8 August Eden went on television to make a speech in which he compared Nasser with dictators from the Thirties. On 13 August the Australian Prime Minister Sir Robert Menzies, arriving for the London Conference, also broadcast, at Eden's request, a condemnation of Nasser's action under international law (Menzies, 1967). Lloyd followed next day (Lloyd, 1978).

*Apprehension of the conference's results* Salisbury's doubts about the outcome of the conference were a response to discussions in the Egypt Committee meeting in the evening of 9 August, at which only Eden, Salisbury, Macmillan, Lloyd, Home, Thorneycroft, and Secretary to the Cabinet Sir Norman Brook had been present. The group had been discussing the dilemma that, while wanting to appear willing to accept a diplomatic solution, the government would have to set the military machine in motion while the conference was still going on. Furthermore, it was recognized that a division of the House might reveal only a small majority for the Government. The Senior Ministers realized that a provocative act by Egypt would be a solution.[38]

This solution was the central thought of Eden's later reply to Salisbury's letter of 9 August. Eden stated that the Conference should produce some form of international control of the Canal. In case Nasser rejected this arrangement, the other nations should refuse to pay their shipping dues. If Nasser would then refuse passage through the Canal, 'an incident would have been provoked by him which would justify our using force'.[39] The full Cabinet adopted this line of reasoning at the Cabinet meeting of 14 August, specifying that the United States should co-operate by withholding shipping dues. The causal chain at the end of which Nasser would be willing to provoke an incident was never questioned.[40] Later that afternoon Brook submitted a provisional timetable to the Egypt Committee, which met after the full Cabinet. It suggested that Nasser should respond to a note, asking him to accept the majority recommendation of the Conference, within four days. Egypt's counter-proposals could then be rejected one week later, and after two days (on 7 September) ships could sail (James, 1986).

*Military planning* British Task Force Commanders had objections to the original plan of the Chiefs of Staff. They reckoned Port Said unsuitable for a rapid build-up of forces and preferred Alexandria instead. The new plan, presented on 10 August, proposed a landing of 80,000 troops at Alexandria who would advance on Cairo. This threat alone, it was assumed, would provoke the fall of the Egyptian Government and, with a new Government installed, British and French troops could march to the Canal Zone (Kyle 1989). The Egypt Committee endorsed the new plan despite Eden's initial objections because of its military risks (Beaufre, 1969). With its clear objective to topple Nasser, this operation would become much harder to defend in front of national and international public opinion. This consideration made American support at the conference more important. Therefore Eden suggested on 14 August, when he told the full Cabinet that military planning had been completed, that 'there would be a difficult question of timing'. Indeed, he recognized that American support of economic sanctions against Egypt, including the withholding of shipping dues, would be necessary.[41] After the Cabinet, later that afternoon, when a timetable was presented to the Egypt Committee, he suggested that a final decision to launch any attack should be delayed. Clearly, the new military plans demanded an unequivocal outcome of the Conference, including firm American support.

British decision-makers, both informally (correspondence Eden-Salisbury) and in the Egypt Committee, thus initially entertained rather simple visions of what the Conference would be like. Once they became aware that things might not work that smoothly, and that the new military plan had serious consequences, they reasoned that Egyptian provocation was needed. This induced them to think that simply withholding shipping dues would provoke Nasser into further action. These considerations set the tone for the British approach to the London Conference that opened on 16 August. Some preliminary conclusions can be made about the decision-making process. First, the Cabinet was not informed of the details of military planning. However, when before the Cabinet meeting of 14 August it had become clear that decisions about the use of force might have to be taken at some nearby stage, few Cabinet members seemed worried about the small circle to whom decision-making had been entrusted. Only Duncan Sandys would write to Eden complaining about the lack of information (James, 1986). Second, the role of an even smaller group of Ministers within the Egypt Committee becomes increasingly important. Important considerations were made at a meeting at which a small group of Ministers, most of whom had met informally during the period of Decision 1, were present. Moreover, a kind of circuit of letters emerges between Salisbury and Eden. Similarly, Macmillan writes memos to Eden before putting things, such as Israeli involvement, to the full Egypt Committee. Also, Salisbury and Lloyd are present at Eden's meeting with Gaitskell and other Labour MP's on 14 August. The Cabinet therefore appears as a body that authorizes Committee decisions rather than a place of genuine discussion.[42] These patterns were to be reinforced during the days of the Conference.

*The London Conference*

Between the opening of the Conference on 16 August and the moment that Menzies accepted the chairmanship of the delegation to Cairo, the situation became increasingly difficult for those who had thought that the Conference would produce either Egypt's retreat or military action. First, Lloyd's paper on the legitimate use of force under international law, which was discussed at the Egypt Committee on 20 August, demonstrated that armed intervention was justifiable only in four situations:[43] interference with a British warship, an action which endangered the lives of British subjects, the refusal to let a ship pass because of a refusal to pay her dues, or seizure of the Suez Base.[44] Second, policy-makers realized that at some stage it would become very difficult to employ military force, because of the international support that Nasser would have mounted during and after the Conference. Brook suggested to Eden that after 15 September support for Egypt would outweigh support for military action. Third, at home voices urging that reference of the dispute to the United Nations should precede military action gained strength. However, the United States did not show much enthusiasm for such a move. Moreover, military preparations would be ready soon (30 August), so that a final decision could be taken by 27 August.[45] By consequence, decision-makers were desperately looking for a way out.

Four key players (Eden, Salisbury, Macmillan, and Lloyd) seem to have virtually prepared the meetings of the Egypt Committee and the Cabinet. Their actions were influenced by their contacts with Dulles who had come to the London Conference. One day before the start of the conference Eden had already defined the stakes. 'PM said at one point this morning people still talk about the danger of our alienating India, or worrying Africa, but the fact is that if we lose out in the Middle East we shall be immediately destroyed.'[46] Three days later, Macmillan, in a similar analysis, contemplating 'the end of British influence and strength for ever', wondered 'on what principle can we base a "casus belli"? How do we get from the Conference leg to the use of force?' That evening he dined with Dulles, and once more tried to convince Dulles that 'in the last resort, we must use force and defy opinion, here and overseas. [Dulles] really agreed with our position. But he hopes (and he may be right) that Nasser will have to yield in due course. This again lights up the frightful problem of how to keep a military expedition "all dressed up and nowhere to go"'.[47]

Next day Macmillan and Salisbury met U.S. Ambassador Aldrich. They wanted to know the American attitude towards referring the dispute to the United Nations. Aldrich said that Dulles was strongly opposed to this course. Macmillan reasoned that the American position was explained by the American fear that the Panama Canal would be drawn into a U.N.O.-discussion of international control of waterways (Macmillan, 1971). Macmillan noted in his diary that both he and Salisbury found Dulles 'rather "sticky"', and that he could not 'help feeling that he really wants us "to go it alone", and has been trying to help us by creating the right atmosphere'.[48]

At the same time, pressure was put on participants at the conference in lunches on 16, 17, 21, and 22 August with Eden and apparently handpicked Cabinet members.[49] The pressure on the Americans, however, was to no avail. Dulles was not prepared to lead the delegation to Nasser. Moreover, Eden told the Egypt Committee on 20 August that Dulles had said to him that the United States could neither increase her economic pressure on Egypt nor block the payment of transit dues by American ships 'since this would lead to difficulties with the U.S. Treasury over the control of Egyptian Government holdings in the United States'.[50] The withholding of transit dues had been seen as a way of provoking Nasser into retaliation. Yet, American support of this measure was obviously indispensable.

Under these bleak conditions a small group of Senior Ministers met just before the mid-day Cabinet on 21 August. The crisis-like proportions of the situation are evident from Macmillan's diary notes of that day. Macmillan clearly opposed the possibility that a committee, which would be sent to Nasser, would engage in negotiations. It should only give 'explanations and elucidations'. Negotiating would be 'very alarming. It's too much like Canossa' (Macmillan, 1971, p. 108). The informal meeting therefore clearly faced an equivocal outcome of the situation; once again, provocative action against Egypt was seriously considered.[51] The dilemma was resolved with the decision to ask Menzies to head the delegation to Nasser, but without giving him the authority to negotiate with the Egyptian Government. This was co-ordinated with Dulles. Menzies reluctantly agreed. Next day was used to put pressure on other countries' delegations to accept the proposal that had been worked out by Eden, Dulles, and Lloyd. Eventually, 18 out of 22 nations would adopt their proposals.

*Explanatory Factors*

*Groupthink*  Given the structure of the decision-making process Groupthink is likely to have played a role in the period regarding decision 2 (2 August to 22 August, 2 a.m.). Notably the Egypt Committee meeting of 9 August with only a small group of Ministers and the informal meeting 45 minutes before the Cabinet meeting on 21 August suggest that decision-making was increasingly concentrated in the hands of a group even smaller than the regular Egypt Committee.

Three Groupthink symptoms can be observed. First, self-censorship of personal doubts. On 9 August Salisbury wrote a letter to Eden about the possibility of an equivocal outcome of the Conference. In his reply Eden suggested the withholding of shipping dues as a solution to Egypt's refusal of international control of the Canal. The problem that Salisbury brought up was therefore ignored until it resurfaced when during the Conference it became clear that Dulles did not want to head a delegation. Rather than discussing the matter in the Egypt Committee, Salisbury preferred discussing this matter privately with Eden, and seemed temporarily relieved after Eden's reply. Had the matter been discussed right away, a new, surprising situation around 20 August might have been avoided.

Two instances of the illusion of unanimity can be found. When the Chiefs of Staff presented their first military plan to the Egypt Committee on 2 August, the members of the Committee disagreed on the importance of going to the United Nations. That night Salisbury wrote Eden a reassuring letter, comforting him that unity was not lost. 'My dear Anthony, I felt today that we were very unhelpful with our ifs and ands over the United Nations etc. But, tiresome though all these things are – & short though the time is in which decisions have to be made – I really think we made some progress.'[52]  A second example occurred when during the London Conference delegates of important nations were lunching with Eden, only hard-line British Ministers (or people not yet known to be dissenting, such as Monckton) were asked to join in. Most important absentee was Butler, who happened to be on holiday.

Third, the illusion of invulnerability may have played a part. Some members of the inner circle around Eden were clearly irritated by criticism. When Eden, Salisbury, and Lloyd met with a Labour delegation on 14 August, Salisbury had an outburst, according to Eden's diary: 'Gaitskell gave us a donnish lecture about the situation of inordinate length but of unremarkable quality. We listened with all the attention we cd command but suddenly Bobbety [Salisbury] cd take no more & burst out with indignation that he and the Prime Minister, having spent all their lives in foreign policy, cd not see the purpose of this lecture'.[53]

*Leadership* The small group of Salisbury, Macmillan, Lloyd, and Eden was also responsible for communicating the American attitude to the Cabinet in this period. While it was therefore an inner circle that actually formed opinion on the United States' position, it was primarily Eden who informed the Egypt Committee and Cabinet. Interestingly, from the point of decision-making, at the Cabinet meeting on 21 August Eden discussed the American attitude only because he was asked to do so. In his discussion Eden referred to the American attitude towards economic measures (withholding shipping dues, etc.) but not to the question of military action.[54] He had been much more straightforward in the Egypt Committee the day before.

> It had been pointed out to him [Dulles] that the Government of the United Kingdom could not accept a long delay in any settlement, since once the military preparations had been completed, the forces involved could not be maintained in a state of readiness for an indefinite time. Mr. Dulles had recognised the value of these military preparations in evincing the determination of the United Kingdom to reach a satisfactory settlement, but he was not in favour of provoking Colonel Nasser into taking further action which would justify the use of military force. He had indicated that if the United Kingdom and France became involved in war, United States forces would not be able to join in military operations, since the United States Government could not justify going to war over oil in the Middle East.[55]

Nevertheless, Dulles had told Eden that he had warned the Soviet Union's Foreign Secretary Shepilov that the United States would provide material support to Britain and France in case of hostilities. This suggests that Eden had come close to Macmillan's (and possibly Salisbury's) opinion that Dulles had implicitly conveyed the message that they wanted the United Kingdom and France to go it alone, but that indirect support would be forthcoming.

*The organizational context* Part of the decision-making process had been affected by the military's change of plans. The Forces' Commanders who would have to do the actual fighting had rejected the original idea of landing at Port Said, because they found it too risky. The alternative that the Chiefs of Staff formally presented on 10 August brought further complications, because landing at Alexandria and marching in the direction of Cairo was much harder to defend to domestic and international public opinion. This clearly was an additional factor that caused the inner circle of Ministers to think that somehow provocative action by Egypt would be needed in order to justify the use of force against Egypt. For the time being, however, the Menzies mission gave them some breathing space.

## Decision 3: The Users' Association and the Withdrawal of the Pilots

The London Conference thus sent Menzies with the Eighteen Powers' Proposal to Cairo. The British Government assumed that Nasser would either accept internationalization of the Canal, or flatly reject the proposals. Dulles, meanwhile, who had hoped that his diplomatic efforts would cause such a long delay that the feeling of crisis would have faded and force could thus be avoided, thought that France and the United Kingdom were not inclined to accept further delay. Dulles knew that a crisis might be precipitated if Menzies had to leave Cairo empty-handed. He came up with the idea of an Association of Users of the Suez Canal (later to be baptized S.C.U.A.) to which shipping dues should be paid, a fair share of which would be handed over to Egypt.

France and Great Britain were uncertain of Dulles's intentions. Was this a proposal to *de facto* internationalize the administration of the Canal, and thus a slap in the face of Nasser, or just another stalling technique? Eventually the British Cabinet would adopt the S.C.U.A. proposal on 11 September and agreed that another Conference should be held in London in order found this association. But, directly related to this decision, the Egypt Committee had taken another important decision on September 7, that is, to ask the Suez Canal Company to withdraw its pilots from the Canal, expecting traffic in the Canal to come to a standstill. Both decisions should be analyzed in the context of uncertainty about the outcome of Menzies mission as well as about the American position. The decision to withdraw the pilots was a deliberate attempt to bring matters to a head and provoke military action, despite the adherence to another diplomatic effort.

Regarding the structure of decision-making Appendix 2 allows for three preliminary conclusions. First, the decision to ask the Suez Canal Company to recall its pilots from Egypt was taken by the Egypt Committee without consulting the Cabinet. Second, the decision to accept Dulles's proposal of a users' association was made after bilateral diplomatic exchanges between the United States and Great Britain (thus excluding France) in which neither the Egypt Committee nor the Cabinet were involved. Third, the number of informal meetings increased, especially during the last week of August. All this suggests that by then the inner circle of Senior Ministers rather than the Egypt Committee constituted the central unit of decision-making.

*How to Respond to the Outcome of the Menzies Mission*

*Groupthink* The prospect of using force was beginning to cause uneasiness among members of both the Egypt Committee and the Cabinet. On 22 August Butler returned from holiday and must have understood that military intervention had come much closer during his absence. He did not raise any objections at that time, but aired his doubts to Home.[56] Other Cabinet members had the same impression as Butler:

Duncan Sandys complained to Eden about the lack of information to the Cabinet about the use of force. At the same time, the Minister of Defence, Sir Walter Monckton, doubted the wisdom of the use of force at this moment, and spoke up during the Egypt Committee's meeting of 24 August. The full Cabinet meeting of 28 August therefore was meant to obtain a new mandate. The decision-making process in this period shows the occurrence of three symptoms of Groupthink. First, the illusion of unanimity. Aware of Butler's anxiety, Home wrote to Eden on 22 August.[57] His letter clearly shows that until that moment Butler must have been outside the inner circle of decision-makers, and must have had little contact with Eden. Second, the letter testifies of the conviction among members of the inner circle that dissenters were just having difficulties with the timing of force, but still fully supported the original analysis and decisions. Next day (23 August) Butler was invited to an informal meeting after the full Cabinet. Those present, besides Butler, included Eden, Salisbury, Macmillan, Edward Heath (Chief Whip), and Anthony Head. The small group discussed the possibility of provoking Egypt by taking away equipment from the Suez Base, the role of the United Nations and the right moment to recall the House of Commons after any decision to send in the troops.[58]

An even clearer example of the same phenomenon occurred after Monckton's sudden outburst of opposition against the use of force at the Egypt Committee on 24 August. Immediately after the meeting at least three participants wrote reassuring letters to Eden. One of them, Secretary to the Cabinet Sir Norman Brook, told him not to worry too much about Monckton's behaviour.

> I don't think that W[alter] M[onckton]'s statement, at the Friday meeting, need be taken too seriously. I think he [unreadable], that it was ill judged and ill timed. He was provoked into it by H[arold] M[acmillan]'s speaking as though we were deciding there and then on the date of the operation. As I see it, the position is this. All the members of the Cabinet, without exception, are solidly in agreement with you that we cannot afford to let Nasser get away with this. The Cabinet are therefore agreed that we must stop this at all cost and that, in the last resort, if all other methods fail, we must be ready to use force.[59]

Salisbury and Home were clearly worried that support for a tough line was weakening. Home saw 'a definite wavering in the attitude of some of our colleagues towards the use of force'. Home, Salisbury, and Brook pointed out to Eden that some Cabinet members, notably Butler, Monckton, MacLeod, Selkirk, and Amory, were anxious not to use force before all diplomatic means had been exhausted. 'The anxieties of some, Rab [Butler] for instance, might be removed if we didn't have to go on thinking in terms of button pushing and dates and had plenty of time for diplomatic manoeuvre'. All three warned Eden not to rush things and to avoid creating too large a distance between the full Cabinet and the Egypt Committee.[60]

Second, self-censorship of personal doubts. Although Butler discussed his doubts with Monckton and Home, he never raised them openly or explicitly until the full Cabinet meeting on 28 August when he said that more time was needed before military action could take place. That means that Butler had accepted the idea of provoking Egypt into an incident that might justify the start of hostilities, as discussed at the informal meeting of 23 August. Home later recalled that 'Rab was constantly asking us all what we thought. In the end he always supported the Prime Minister's decisions with the rest of the Cabinet' (Lamb, 1987, p. 206).

Third, direct pressure on dissenting group members. After Monckton's outburst at the Egypt Committee meeting of 24 August, Macmillan made an attempt to get him back in line. Eden's press secretary, William Clark, talked with Monckton on Monday 27 August: 'He [Monckton] told me [Clark] that he had spent the day with Macmillan on Sunday being toughened up. What PM [Eden] and HM [Macmillan] seem to want is agreement to go in if Nasser refuses to accept internationalization. WM [Monckton] refused'.[61] Macmillan's pressure was of no avail. Monckton would repeat his objections at the Cabinet on 28 August. Yet he too would finally agree to the Cabinet's decision that day that '[a]s soon we were satisfied that a just settlement could not be secured through the machinery of the United Nations, we should ourselves take other steps to secure it'.[62] Not even Monckton therefore would go as far as rejecting force outright, and, presumably, resigning from the government.

*Leadership* Butler's and Monckton's protests seemed related to the way Eden, and to a certain extent, Macmillan dominated the decision-making process. William Clark, who had lunch with several key participants on a regular basis throughout the crisis, noticed a hurried decision-making style. After lunch with Home on 23 August he records: 'he [Home] regrets the hurry with which the PM pushed that vital decision [to use force] through [the] Cabinet without time for a proper decision'.[63] A few days later he had a conversation with Walter Monckton, who made it clear to him 'that PM is pressing Cabinet to decide for force. WM said that at last Friday's Cabinet he had to speak up when PM and Chancellor were trying to rush things through'.[64] Indeed, Brook and Home warned Eden not to push the full Cabinet too hard. Brook wrote that '[a]ll this leads me to the view that it would be a mistake to put the Cabinet at the final fence too soon'. Home suggested Eden to use the planned Cabinet on 28 August to 'get their [the doubters'] feelings off their chest so that you should know where you are. You will know how to handle all this, but I am sure you should encourage those who have not been on the Egypt Committee to be frank and outspoken'.[65] All this suggests that Eden (and Macmillan) were in a hurry to have permission to move into Egypt without much delay. Moreover, it testifies to the relative isolation of Eden (and his inner circle) from the rest of the Cabinet. What considerations had caused all the haste?

*Perceptions of dilemmas* The most pressing dilemma between 22 and 28 August was the need to respond to Nasser's expected refusal of the 18 Powers Proposals. In a note, given to Eden just before the Egypt Committee meeting of 24 August, Salisbury sketches the dilemma. On the one hand diplomatic moves would be advisable, given international and national public opinion. On the other hand further diplomacy 'would weaken our power to resort to force' and entailed the danger that Nasser could 'get away with it'.[66] One way to soothe public opinion would be to refer the matter to the United Nations. Indeed on 23 August, the Egypt Committee had recognized that recourse to the Security Council seemed unavoidable, but that it would compromise military planning. The Committee 'invited the Foreign Secretary to consider how the machinery of the United Nations could best be used to present the case of the United Kingdom for any military action against Egypt'.[67] Yet neither these considerations nor this invitation were mentioned to the Cabinet meeting that started 45 minutes after this Egypt Committee meeting. The informal meeting immediately after the Cabinet at 3 p.m. discussed the best date to recall Parliament so as to avoid too much opposition.[68]

Obviously then, Lloyd's assignment to see how the use of force could best be reconciled with reference to the U.N.O. was an illusory attempt to satisfy both public opinion and the need to quickly proceed after the Menzies mission. Lloyd immediately asked Sir Pierson Dixon, British Ambassador to the United Nations, who happened to be in London, what to do. Dixon suggested simply informing the Security Council of the dispute. If not, other nations would try 'to prolong the period of negotiation and possibly also to extract some commitment from us in regard to not using methods of force'. The best thing would be to let the meeting of the Security Council end without it voting on any resolution, an unusual, but not illegal move.[69] On 26 August, after having read Dixon's suggestion, Eden wrote to Lloyd and Salisbury that he thought the Security Council far too dangerous a place, and wondered whether referring the matter to NATO or the Western European Union would not be a solution. In their responses Lloyd and Salisbury wrote that sooner or later they would have to go to the United Nations anyway.

The acute problem of having to anticipate Nasser's rejection of the 18 Powers Proposals underlined Britain's fundamental dilemma. Macmillan recorded in his diary:

The truth is that we are caught in a terrible dilemma. If we take strong action against Egypt, and as a result the Canal is closed, the pipelines to the Levant are cut, the Persian Gulf revolts and oil production is stopped - then U.K. and Western Europe have 'had it'; if we suffer a diplomatic defeat, if Nasser 'gets away with it', Nuri [Prime Minister of British client state Iraq] falls, and the Middle East countries, in a ferment, 'nationalise oil', we have equally 'had it'. What then are we to do? It seems clear that we should take the only chance we have – to take strong action, and hope that thereby our friends in Middle East will stand, our enemies fall, and the oil will be saved, but it is a tremendous decision.[70]

The Cabinet meeting of 28 August therefore had to deal with internal opposition, with international and national public opinion against the background of having to take a decision that dealt with the expected failure of the Menzies mission. Hard-liners, such as Macmillan, Home, Salisbury, and Kilmuir, clashed with Monckton and, to a lesser extent, Butler. Nevertheless, Monckton's objections were not as strong as those he had raised at the Egypt Committee four days earlier. Now, he agreed that if all other methods proved unavailing, force would have to be used. On the other hand the Cabinet should weigh the disadvantages of using force.

This Cabinet meeting was well prepared, if not stage-managed, by a small group of Ministers in order to sway the Cabinet so as to reduce the possible harm of an intervention by Monckton. Eden opened with a concession by accepting referring the matter to the United Nations, thus relieving those Cabinet members, such as Duncan Sandys, who were afraid that the button would have to be pushed any minute. Only then an important memorandum was distributed, instead of handing it out before the meeting, followed by a speech by Macmillan illustrating the high stakes, backed up by Lennox Boyd, another hard-liner, After Monckton had raised his objections, Salisbury drew a parallel with Hitler and Mussolini. The minutes of the Cabinet and Egypt Committee seldom show this analogy. Here it was an instrument in an attempt to persuade the full Cabinet to continue supporting the original line of policy. Kilmuir's subsequent exposition on the lawfulness of military action falls into the same category. The inner circle had thus preserved unity and expected to carry public opinion by referring the matter to the United Nations.

*Dulles Launches the Users' Association*

Two assumptions had guided British decision-making: Egypt's quick and clear rejection or acceptance of the Menzies mission and American support for going to the United Nations. No sooner had the Cabinet agreed to go to the United Nations, than both assumptions were proven false, thus creating another problematic situation. First of all, Nasser had taken his time in receiving Menzies and discussing and answering the proposals he carried. This delay much angered Eden. He called Macmillan on 29 August, after the news had broken that Nasser had finally agreed to see Menzies on 3 September, and judged the delays intolerable (Horne, 1988). Intolerable they were: for the British military timetable, that is. Nasser's eventual rejection of the proposals would not come until 9 September. By that date, events had been overtaken by a surprising American reaction to Lloyd's invitation to Dulles on 28 August to co-ordinate an approach to the United Nations (significantly without France). On 4 September Dulles communicated through the British Ambassador in Washington, Roger Makins, his idea of a users' association. British policy-makers were puzzled by this new American move.[71] How to explain their reaction?

*Leadership*  The decision to refer the matter to the United Nations was meant to remain a secret until the Menzies Mission had completed its task. Moreover, the negotiations between the American Government and the United Kingdom on a users' association were conducted through diplomatic exchanges. Therefore, decision-making during the first week of September shifted to the highest level, as Eden wished to be closely involved with Lloyd's foreign policy. By consequence, the dynamics of Anglo-American relations in this period, and therefore the acceptance of the principle of a users' association carries Eden's personal mark.

Eden was worried about a letter from Eisenhower written on 3 September. Clark judged its contents 'most devastating': 'it is this which has brought the PM racing back almost in despair'.[72] Eisenhower's telegram argued against the use of force, because 'American public opinion flatly rejects the thought of using force, particularly when it does not seem that every possible peaceful means of protecting our vital interests has been exhausted without result'. Worse, Eisenhower rejected recourse to the U.N.O. at this very moment and preferred proceeding with the Menzies mission, even if it 'may fail to give the setback to Nasser that he so much deserves'. Eden was clearly disappointed by Eisenhower's opposition to the use of force. That same day, the American President dealt another blow to British optimism when he declared to the American press that 'we are committed to a peaceful settlement of this dispute, nothing else'. This clearly undermined Menzies's position in Cairo. Eden must therefore have welcomed Dulles's idea of a users' association as a possible way of extracting a commitment of the United States to a hard-line policy, which Eisenhower's letter seemed to exclude. Eden judged that by endorsing a users' association the United States would be obliged to pay its shipping dues no longer to Nasser but to the new association.[73] In addition, he still expected the Americans to go to the United Nations with the United Kingdom and France.

At the Cabinet meeting on 6 September Eden gave a reasonably correct summary of Eisenhower's position. He explained that the United States Government was worried that Britain and France would use force before all other means had been tried. However, he did not tell his Ministers that Eisenhower doubted whether force should be used at all. Significantly, Eden preferred to rely on Dulles's message on the users' association and told the Cabinet that Dulles's letter showed 'that our continued firmness was having the effect of encouraging the United States' Government to consider further means of bringing pressure to bear on Egypt'.[74]

Meanwhile, France had reluctantly agreed to go to the United Nations, and a draft resolution was already circulating between Washington, London, and Paris. On 7 September, however, Dulles had changed his mind and judged it unwise to go to the United Nations. He preferred to exhaust the possibilities of the 1888 Constantinople Convention first, implying that one should first try the users' association. This left the British completely in the dark as to his real intentions. Dulles had said that a resolution in the Security Council would make the parties engage in new negotiations. Egypt would 'prolong it and finally break it off and then we would be precisely where we are today'. Eden must have been uncertain as to Dulles's intentions: did he want a tough policy on Nasser, or was this just another stalling technique?[75] That day Dixon warned Eden not to go to the United Nations without the Americans, as they might then 'even feel obliged to support another country's resolution not to use force without further recourse to the Council'.[76] Lloyd responded, with Eden's approval, that 'Mr. Dulles's response is most disappointing. We seem to be further apart than at any time since July 26. Any further dawdling along will be fatal'.[77] Clearly, Eden and Lloyd must have been in despair about the American attitude. Against this background the Egypt Committee decided that the Company's pilots should be pulled out of the Canal in order to create chaos, and possibly, a pretext for military intervention.

Later that day, 8 September, Roger Makins sent Eisenhower's reply to Eden's letter of 6 September. Eisenhower told Eden that he was 'making Nasser a much more important figure than he is'. Force was to be avoided because it would make Nasser an Arab hero. But, ambiguously, Eisenhower wrote that there was no public support *as yet* (italics added) for military intervention. In short, Eisenhower recommended a slow approach through the users' association (Carlton, 1986). Eisenhower's letter of restraint was delivered together with Makins's account of his conversation with Dulles that day. Dulles's words clearly differed from Eisenhower's.

You must not think that the United States Administration were not as deeply concerned as Her Majesty's Government, but they saw no end to the consequences of military intervention. It would be possible to occupy several key points, but in the President's view there were not enough troops and resources to put out all the fires that would be started. [Nevertheless,] 'the President did not exclude the use of force in the last resort [margin marked by Eden]. Between us we could get Nasser down and the United States Administration were quite determined that this should happen. If Nasser obstructed the Canal and used force, they would use it too. But they did not believe that the methods and the tempo which we were advocating were the right ones. Mr. Dulles said he regards his proposal [users' association] as a temporary one which might perhaps last for a year' [double line in the margin by Eden]. He [Dulles] believes that there were acceptable courses between occupation of the Canal and yielding to Nasser, and he was trying to work one out. On parting he said he realised our need to collaborate with the French. Nevertheless, this was a complication for the administration. It was much easier for them to work these problems out with us. They distrusted French security in general, not only from the technical standpoint.[78]

Now this must have been a puzzling situation: Eisenhower rejecting force, Dulles accepting it under specific circumstances. Moreover, Dulles seemed to exclude the occupation of certain key points on practical military grounds, but not on political. More importantly, Dulles suggested that the Americans agreed to the immediate British objective, that is, Nasser's downfall. Last, but not least, Dulles referred to Anglo-American co-operation. Undoubtedly, the latter was an attempt by Dulles to separate the British from the much more aggressive French. However, given the prevailing British perception of the nature of Anglo-American relations (see chapter 3), British policy-makers would be more likely to interpret this as the United States asking the United Kingdom to lead the dance.

In this context the solution to recall the Company's pilots, while simultaneously abandoning the idea to go to the United Nations forthwith, and adopting the idea of a users' association, must have seemed ideal. Compliance with the United States' preference for diplomatic means would make the Americans become more closely involved through the paying of shipping dues to the association. American consent to stronger measures might still be won if the shipping in the Canal would break down due to the absence of competent pilots. Moreover, it would satisfy the French who were becoming impatient. Thus, the withdrawal of the pilots was finally announced on 11 September. A fortnight later it would appear that Egypt could perfectly manage the traffic in the Canal.

Eden, and, to a lesser extent, Lloyd were thus at the centre of British communications with the United States regarding the United Nations and the users' association. Eden, and Lloyd, for that matter, perceived the American attitude according to the images widely shared by British key decision-makers. They assumed that Great Britain and the United States had the same objectives in the Middle East. Traditionally, the United States always had to be cajoled into supporting British policies in the area. The users' association and the withdrawal of the pilots seemed two perfect methods to bring the Americans over to the British side.

*The organizational context* When Eden and Monckton met with the Chiefs of Staff in the morning of 7 September 1956, they discussed another change of military plans. The Chiefs of Staff had abandoned the idea of landing at Alexandria, and had returned to their first choice of Port Said. The Chiefs of Staff feared a high number of civilian casualties would harm British international prestige. Moreover, they expected fierce Egyptian resistance, which would prevent the capturing of Cairo before international public opinion would have been mobilized. At the same time, the Chiefs of Staff's report indicated that bad weather conditions in the Eastern Mediterranean in autumn left only ten days to decide to send in the troops. On the one hand Eden was much frustrated by the comments of his military staff. He interpreted their report as an urge to move ahead at a time when international and national support was not yet sufficient.[79] On the other hand Mountbatten's papers suggest that on 7 September he managed to persuade Eden of the political and military disadvantages of landing at Alexandria and advancing on Cairo (Grove and Rohan, 2000). The Chiefs of Staff clearly tried to impress the Egypt Committee with the problem of civilian casualties and the need for strengthening moral support for action, while at the same conveying the message that military operations might soon be thwarted by bad weather. It is possible that they made an attempt to persuade the politicians that force might not be a real option after all. Certainly, the *volte face* in the planning of the Chiefs of Staff seems peculiar. The point of civil casualties clearly was relevant, but hardly new. The timing of the presentation of the new plan (called Musketeer Revise) certainly limited the number of options available to British policy-makers, because the plan's implementation required a delay of fourteen days.

*The Decision to Agree to a Users' Association*

On 9 September the news came through that Egypt had rejected the 18 Powers' proposals presented by the Menzies Mission. A strong response was impossible because military action was not an immediate option, due to *Musketeer Revise*, and because the Americans seemed opposed to it for the moment. Dulles's idea of a users' association, combined with the withdrawal of the pilots, seemed an attractive way out. The consequence, however, was a new set of dilemmas. First, no full commitment had yet been obtained from the Americans that they considered a users' association an instrument of keeping pressure on Egypt. Yet, the failure of the Menzies mission required the Government to show quickly that the United States, France, and Great Britain were able to make a powerful diplomatic move. Second, the end of the Menzies mission obliged the Government to answer questions in Parliament. The opposition was expected to try to extract a promise from the Government not to use force unless recourse to the United Nations had been taken, an option to which the United States was strongly opposed.

The aspect that worried British policy-makers most was the prospect of 'Nasser getting away with it'. Between the Egypt Committee's meeting of 7 September and the Cabinet's agreement to a users' association on 11 September perceptions of what was at stake were narrowed down to the loss of British prestige, should Nasser seem to have successfully resisted Western diplomatic pressure. Macmillan pointed the gloomiest picture and, once again, sketched a choice between two negative outcomes: 'We shall be ruined either way; but we shall be more inevitably and finally ruined if we are humiliated'.[80] Sir Ivone Kirkpatrick, who had drafted Eden's response to Eisenhower's letter of 3 September, wrote of his disappointment at

Eisenhower's reaction to that response. Kirkpatrick predicted that Great Britain would be wrecked within a year, or two. He thought Dulles's users' association scheme impractical, which 'would leave us with no other choice, but the use of force or to surrender to Nasser'.[81]

It was therefore important to try to obtain a commitment from the Americans to pay shipping dues to the new organization and to use that money as a leverage over Egypt. Moreover, at this instance it was necessary to act united with the Americans. Hence Lloyd's flow of telegrams to Washington to attain both objectives, in which Lloyd pointed out that if the Government were not able to offer a users' association to the House of Commons, it would not be able to refuse Parliament's expected request to go to the Security Council. This was meant to put pressure on the Americans, as the Cabinet had already accepted to go to the United Nations before Dulles came up with his new idea. No decisive American commitment to the payment of shipping dues was obtained, however. The decision of the Egypt Committee to adopt the plan for a users' association may therefore be explained by British confidence that Americans could be cajoled into accepting such strong measures. Macmillan wrote on 8 September: 'it is vital to keep the pressure up on our American friends'. The next day he noted: 'the more we can persuade them [the Americans] of our determination to risk everything in order to beat Nasser, the more help we shall get from them'.[82] Macmillan's analysis illustrates the common orientation of British foreign policy-makers, which centred on the belief that the United States could be persuaded to defend British interests in the Middle East.

When the Cabinet adopted Dulles's proposal on 11 September, it became immediately clear, that a users' association was only a temporary compromise. Macmillan thought that if the users' association plan failed, Britain could and should resort to force. Kilmuir and Salisbury who thought force permissible under the U.N.-Charter under such circumstances supported him. Monckton argued that the users' plan could be no more than a prelude to negotiation or an appeal to the United Nations, and warned against resorting to force without full American support.[83] Much depended on full American co-operation regarding the implementation of the users' association scheme. Unfortunately, no sooner had the Cabinet adopted the proposal, and the House of Commons started assembling in the morning of 12 September, than the news from Washington seemed to convey only a qualified American commitment. This was to be the first element eventually adding up to the British Government's growing annoyance with the American attitude and eventually its decision to go it alone.

### Decision 4: Reference to the Security Council

September 1956 was characterized by an increased British effort to persuade the United States to consider the Suez Canal Users' Association (S.C.U.A.) as a tool of leverage over Egypt's Middle Eastern policy. The Americans, however, were very reluctant to agree with this view and remained hesitant to pay their shipping dues to this newly established authority. At the same time it became clear that the withdrawal of the pilots had been of no avail and that Egypt was perfectly capable of managing the Canal. In this context Great Britain decided to refer the matter to the Security Council despite Dulles's resistance. It thus added to the growing apprehension and misunderstandings between Washington and London.

Appendix 2 reveals three important characteristics of the structure of decision-making. First, the decision to refer the dispute to the Security Council is taken without a formal meeting of either the Cabinet or even the Egypt Committee. Only Macmillan seems to have been consulted, by telegraph, as he had left for Washington on 21 September in order to attend the yearly meeting of the International Monetary Fund. It is therefore probable that Eden and Lloyd and Macmillan took this decision.[84] Second, the central place of Macmillan is evident. He speaks to Eden on the phone, he meets with Dulles, and is present at informal meetings. Third, it appears that British decision-makers meet the representatives of the American Government independently from the French, probably in an attempt to reach a bilateral agreement first.

*Explanatory Factors*

The decision to refer the matter to the Security Council without American consent can be explained by considerations of domestic politics and by growing British impatience with the attitude of the United States Government. The latter factor appears to have been more relevant to the matter. Both factors, however, are intertwined with processes at the individual and group level.

*Domestic politics* In September Parliament was about to return from recess. A small group of British policy-makers (Eden, Macmillan, Salisbury, and Home) was afraid that Parliament would force the Government to promise that no force would be used unless recourse to the United Nations had been taken. They hoped to be able to avoid this by offering the users' association backed by a strong American commitment. The full Cabinet meeting of 11 September, however, had revealed a severe split as to whether the users' association should be seen as a prelude to force or to the Security Council. A small group, consisting of Butler, Kilmuir, Salisbury, and Macmillan, convened after the Cabinet in order to work out the wording of the pledges the Government could make without committing the Government to the Security Council, while keeping together hawks and doves within the Conservative Party (Macmillan, 1971).

The debate in the House of Commons opened on 12 September with the Government's official announcement of the concept of a users' association. Next day the Labour Party and the Liberal Party asked the Government to refer the matter to the United Nations. The Conservative Party was internally divided between MPs who considered a users' association too soft an approach and MPs who held reservations about the use of force. A small group of Ministers met on the following day. Butler suggested to give the pledge not to use force without recourse to the United Nations, but the other Ministers present followed Macmillan in his fear that the appearance of climbing down under Socialist pressure would be fatal to the Prime Minister's, and Government's, reputation (Macmillan, 1971).

During the debate Eden only just managed not to give such a pledge. It did not qualm unrest among the Tories. On 19 September Chief Whip Edward Heath reported to Eden 'a good deal of trouble in the Party'. The Tory group that was opposed to force even as a last resort, might be large enough to put the Government in a minority position in the House.[85] Possibly, therefore, the inner group of Ministers felt pressed to give up its hesitancy regarding the United Nations. It does not explain, however, why this important step was taken without American consent, or even, against American opposition. British policy-makers had become a little nervous about the American attitude towards the dispute. The day of the S.C.U.A. Conference was approaching and Dulles still seemed unwilling to commit the United States to making use of the users' association as a stick to beat Egypt. At the start of the Conference on 19 September the mood around 10 Downing Street was glum. 'Everyone seemed to feel that somehow the Americans were letting us down.' Dulles's speech at the conference cheered the party up: 'Selwyn [Lloyd] came in [with news of Dulles's speech]. This seemed to restore morale a bit though the odour of defeat is still pretty pervasive'. Next day, Clark saw 'great dangers in the strong anti-Dulles movement which is building up'.[86] The last day of the conference, which heralded the foundation of the Suez Canal Users' Association (S.C.U.A.), 'was a ghastly day with all the worst expectation turning up. Dulles pulled rug after rug from under us and watered down the Canal Association till it was meaningless'.[87]

*Groupthink*  The inner circle of Salisbury, Kilmuir, Butler, Eden, and Macmillan dealt with the threat posed by Parliament. The one thing that had to be avoided was the impression to have given in to the opposition over the U.N.O. issue. At the informal meeting on 13 September, just before Eden's wind-up of the debate, Butler had been in favour of meeting the opposition. The group's majority, however, judged the anticipated loss of prestige of heavier consequence than the break-up of the bipartisan consensus on the Government's policy, which had existed until then. Some evidence of Groupthink can be observed in the days after the debate. Two days later Eden phoned Macmillan about Hugh Gaitskell's letter to The Times in which the Opposition Leader complained about the Government's obscure position on the use of force. Eden 'seemed rather concerned', but Macmillan said that he 'felt very relieved that Mr. G[aitskell] should take this line, as it entirely destroyed the argument that P.M. had "climbed down"' (Macmillan, 1971, p. 127). This is a clear example of a common effort to rationalize, which was repeated next day when Eden rang Macmillan once more. 'He seemed a little depressed, so I did my best to cheer him up. We *are* in a difficult position. But we must have the courage to play the hand through.'[88] Another example is the effort by Macmillan and Salisbury to put pressure on Dulles before the start of the users' conference. Macmillan and Salisbury thought it 'vital that the Americans should not think that we are weakening, in spite of the Socialist Opposition and the other defeatist elements here' (Macmillan, 1971, p. 128). Both thus stuck to the common assumption that the Americans could be persuaded to follow if given a firm lead.

*Leadership*  Evidence of growing impatience with the United States mainly comes from a witness at 10 Downing Street, William Clark. This points to Eden's leadership, even though he must have stayed in close touch with on the one hand Macmillan and Salisbury, who had been talking with Dulles, and on the other hand Lloyd, who represented the United Kingdom at the conference. In the course of the conference, Eden developed doubts regarding the idea of a users' association. 'He [Eden] seems to feel that the Users' Association has been a bit of a mistake though if we can make the clause on payment of dues effective, he said, it will be just worthwhile.'[89]

The decision to refer the matter to the Security Council despite American opposition had been made without having taken into consideration two possible consequences. First, it might arouse American anger. Indeed, Dulles was enraged when he heard of it, Dulles claimed that Eden had promised him not take such a step without co-ordination with the United States (Spaak, 1969). Second, it might stir up dissenters within the Egypt Committee and the Cabinet, who had considered the users' association as a prelude to negotiations, and who might consider this sudden rush to the United Nations without consulting the full Cabinet amounting to manipulation by a small inner group. Significantly, Monckton, who had already expressed his worry to Clark that 'PM would use [a] loophole [in the idea of a users' association] to start trouble',[90] sent his letter to Eden, in which he announced his coming resignation as Minister of Defence, on 24 September, the day after the announcement to refer the matter to the United Nations.[91]

The decision to act independently from the United States was thus furthered by a sense of frustration with American unwillingness to consider the users' association as a tool of curbing Nasser. The urge to refer the matter to the Security Council was prompted by considerations of domestic politics. Eden was increasingly interested in uniting the Conservative Party behind him rather than in preserving some kind of national unity. Indeed, he was worried to appear weak and permissive in face of Labour's opposition. Eden's reaction to the news of the strength of the Tory group opposed to force, was one of cognitive closure: 'P.M. seemed quite determined. It was 1938 over again, and he could not be a party to it'.[92] Eden would not agree to Clark's suggestion of what public opinion would regard as an 'unfair' resort to force, but agreed with the analysis that part of the trouble was the impression that Great Britain was meekly responding to Dulles's delaying tactics.[93]

In conclusion, the decision to refer the dispute to the United Nations was taken by a small group of ministers (Eden, Lloyd, and Macmillan) provoked by growing disappointment with the American attitude towards the users' association. Of the various independent variables only a limited amount of evidence of the existence of Groupthink can be traced. Considerations of domestic politics favoured the decision to refer the dispute to the United Nations.

## Decision 5: Accepting the Challe-Plan

At the beginning of October British policy-makers were facing a complicated situation. A diplomatic solution seemed possible, but would not reduce Egyptian influence in the Middle East. The users' association might be a means to put pressure on Egypt in the future, but the United States were very reluctant to consider it as a tool of leverage. Some policy-makers wanted to get rid of Nasser, but Britain's formal objective of international control over the Canal made military action unlikely, if a settlement could be negotiated at the United Nations. In the first week of October, Nasser seemed to 'get away with it' unless the users' association could be presented as a victory over Egypt. On 25 October the British Cabinet decided to agree to an occupation of the Suez Canal Zone if a conflict between Israel and Egypt were to occur. How to explain the decision to accept the far from remote possibility of war against Egypt when at the same time promising negotiations between Egypt, France, and Great Britain were being conducted at the United Nations?

Appendix 2 reveals that the level of decision-making shifted away from the Egypt Committee towards the informal level of meetings of Senior Ministers. Note that after General Maurice Challe had disclosed his plan to intervene as policemen in case of an Israeli-Egyptian war, the Egypt Committee met only once (on 17 October). Moreover, informal meetings precede, or follow on, Cabinet meetings. It is likely that these informal meetings were held in order to reach consensus among the most important ministers, before putting the matter before the full Cabinet. In order to understand the circumstances that led to the decision to intervene in case of an Israeli-Egyptian war, it is useful to make a distinction between the period before Challe's arrival on 14 October and the period afterwards.

*Conditions Favourable to the Adoption of the 'Challe-Plan'*

The conditions that favoured the adoption of the 'Challe-plan' had been created by a fundamental change of British perceptions of the American attitude towards the dispute in general, notably because of Dulles's talk of neo-colonialism on 2 October.

*Leadership*  Two important developments set the stage for the adoption of the 'Challe-plan'. First, Eden was growing impatient with American reluctance to use the users' association as a means of pressure against Egypt. Second, at a press conference on 2 October Dulles would accuse France and Great Britain of colonialist practices in their handling of the dispute. Although Eden's formal reaction was rather restraint, the way he presented the matter to his fellow Ministers testifies to the serious impact Dulles's speech must have had.

Although Eden had been able to report to the Cabinet on 26 September that the United States seemed willing to pay their shipping dues to the new Canal Authority[94] American reluctance became evident two days later. Anglo-American bickering over implementation would continue until Israeli forces invaded the Sinai on 29 October. Anglo-American differences on the users' association regarded four issues. First, American reluctance to put pressure on Liberia and Panama to make their ships pay to the users' association. British officials regarded these ships as 'American-controlled'.[95] Second, American hesitancy in considering the payment of shipping dues to S.C.U.A. as a tool of bearing pressure on Egypt. It had been agreed that part of the shipping dues would be transferred from S.C.U.A. to Egypt for the financing of development projects, but the British Government was very eager to make such money transfers dependent on Egyptian good behaviour. The United States never committed themselves to any percentage of shipping dues that might be used for such purposes. Third, the Americans had indicated that they preferred waiting with payments to S.C.U.A. until agreement would have been reached with the Egyptian Government about the 18 Powers' Proposals. These were being negotiated at the United Nations as a result of the Anglo-French decision to refer the matter to the Security Council. Finally, the United States were wary of being identified too closely with S.C.U.A. They thus wavered over participating in the association's administrative body.

By the time Eden met Challe and Gazier, therefore, a feeling of strong disappointment with the American attitude towards the users' association had been built up. The optimism of late September had been replaced with the strong conviction that the United States would not use S.C.U.A. as a tool of pressure against Egypt. Anthony Nutting, Minister of State at the Foreign Office, wrote to Lloyd on 12 October that the Americans were 'deliberately exaggerating the danger of Egypt closing the Canal to ships paying their dues to S.C.U.A. It is difficult to avoid the impression that the Americans are doing their best to put off this issue [shipping dues] as long as possible'.[96] Final proof of this came three days later when Dulles wrote to Lloyd that S.C.U.A. was not meant to be a means of pressure, but 'of practical working co-operation with the Egyptian authorities which would seek to establish de facto international participation in the operation of the Canal'.[97]

The Egypt Committee's opinion of the American attitude over the users' association thus shifted from moderately positive via 'highly unsatisfactory' (29 September) to 'defeating the whole purpose of the S.C.U.A. exercise' (8 October).[98] The Egypt Committee depended for its information on Eden and, to a lesser extent, Nutting. Both were in close contact with Lloyd who conducted the negotiations at the United Nations. Eden and Nutting co-ordinated British negotiations with on the one hand the Americans on S.C.U.A. and on the other hand France, the United States and Egypt on a peaceful settlement.

On 2 October Dulles held a press conference in Washington that would have an enormous impact on the decision-making process in Great Britain. He told journalists that 'there is talk about teeth being pulled out of the plan [S.C.U.A.], but I know of no teeth in it, so far as I am aware'.[99] Moreover, Dulles compared the Anglo-French attitude with colonialism by stating that the United States could not always be expected to identify automatically with either so-called colonial powers or independence-seeking nations. The effect of these words was that Eden felt completely let down. Apparently he told Nutting: 'Now what have you got to say for your American friends!'[100] Clark, meeting Macmillan at 11 Downing Street, was summoned to see Eden. 'He was bitter about Dulles's press conference in which JFD seems to have accused us of "colonialism" over Suez - however, we agreed to say nothing publicly.'[101] Indeed, Eden sent messages to the British Embassy in Washington and to Lloyd at the United Nations reassuring that 'Mr. Dulles knows that not one of us would ever want to make difficulties over Anglo-American relations'.[102]

Eden, however, decided to have Dulles's speech passed from hand to hand round the table at the full Cabinet meeting next day,[103] a clear example of structuring the decision-making process and influencing his colleagues' opinion on the American attitude. Eden denied Roger Makins's claim that the colonialist theme 'is common to so many Americans, [and] welling up inside Foster [Dulles] like lava in a dormant volcano'. He was outraged by a newspaper article, enclosed by Makins, which suggested that Dulles's policy amounted to no more than simply trying not to wreck American relations with Great Britain, France, the Netherlands, Belgium, and Portugal. Eden thought the article 'describes the most dishonest policy I ever read'.[104]

Clearly, then, Eden was enraged by Dulles's remarks, despite his restrained official reaction. This is clear from the change of tone in his messages to Lloyd, who was present at the negotiations at the United Nations in New York. On 6 October Eden wrote to Lloyd: 'I think we must never forget that Dulles's purpose is different from ours. The Canal is in no sense vital to the United States and his game is to string us until Polling Day'.[105] Two days later Eden feared that 'our position is being eroded. We have been misled so often by Dulles's ideas that we cannot afford to risk another misunderstanding. That is why a negotiating committee [Dulles's latest diplomatic move] would be so dangerous. We should lose control of the situation and justifiably be accused by the French of betraying them. Time is not on our side in this matter'.[106]

In terms of his worldview, Eden's changing attitude towards American policies, at least those formulated by Dulles, could be explained by Dulles surpassing a certain threshold. At the beginning of October Eden must have felt that Dulles could be relied upon no longer. Having suggested so regularly that American aims coincided with British objectives, and never having excluded force as a last resort, while having obstructed British policies so often, Dulles may have driven Eden to the conclusion that he should no longer have confidence in Dulles's diplomacy.

*Groupthink*  During the first weeks after the agreement to a users' association several symptoms of Groupthink can be observed. The initial optimism over the American attitude (until Dulles's devastating press conference) is illustrative of the inner circle's over-optimism. Re-assurance about the American position came from Macmillan who was attending the yearly conference of the International Monetary Fund in Washington. Macmillan and Ambassador Makins saw President Eisenhower in private. Makins recalls that he was 'amazed' by their conversation. 'I was expecting Harold to make a statement, say something important on Suez – but in fact he said nothing. I was very much surprised. Nor did Ike say anything' (Horne, 1988, p. 421). Macmillan, however, felt confident enough to report to Eden that 'I feel sure the President understands our problems about N[asser], but he is, of course, in the same position now as we were in May 1955 [elections]'.[107]

In terms of symptoms of Groupthink, Macmillan may have fallen prey to self-censorship of personal doubts. He did not have the courage to risk a negative reply from Eisenhower, and thus did not bring up the issue. The fact that Eisenhower did not either, added to the fact that Macmillan and Makins were ushered in and out through a side door in order to avoid the press, and that the talk lasted some 35 minutes, must have reinforced Macmillan's perception that a difference existed between American public and private utterances. Similarly, Macmillan reported on two different meetings with Dulles, one official and the other private. About the latter he wrote to Eden that 'some of the things he said were very helpful, but might be dangerous to him if they got about in the electioneering atmosphere'.[108] Moreover, Macmillan once more reassured Eden that American objectives coincided with

British aims: 'the American Government was prepared to do everything it could to bring Nasser down'.[109] On his return to London, Macmillan had a long talk with Eden. Afterwards, Eden picked up his correspondence with Eisenhower, and sent him a letter in which he argued that Nasser was 'now effectively in Russian hands, just as Mussolini was in Hitler's. It would be as ineffective to show weakness to Nasser now in order to placate him as it was to show weakness to Mussolini'.[110] Dulles's press conference next day was to change the mood considerably.

Its impact was felt at the Cabinet's meeting of 3 October. It was concluded that the British position was weakened because of Dulles's statement.[111] Similarly, at the Egypt Committee's meeting of 8 October, Nutting expressed the fear that United States might not want to be involved in a S.C.U.A. scheme that was designed to put pressure on Egypt.[112] Between late September and half October, therefore, a definite change had occurred at the level of the inner circle, and probably at the level of both the Cabinet and the Egypt Committee also, in the estimation of the American attitude towards the users' association. Dulles's press conference had the impact of reducing British optimism that they could count on forthcoming American support in 'cutting Nasser down to size'.

*The Organizational Context*   The political decision-making process at the end of September and the beginning of October was conditioned by the military's view of the desirable conditions under which an operation against Egypt could be mounted. At the beginning of October the Chiefs of Staff issued the order to draw up a so-called Winter-plan. Its aim was to reduce the state of readiness of the forces that had been ready to initiate an invasion from early September. The new plan envisaged the troops to be ready to fight at ten days' notice. The change of plan had occurred because the military judged it difficult to keep the troops in a state of readiness for a long period of time. Moreover, it was thought that meteorological conditions in the Eastern Mediterranean were likely to worsen towards the end of October, so that a different type of operation might be required. On 12 October Headquarters issued the new Winter-plan. Four days later, Monckton wrote a memorandum for use in the Egypt Committee in which he observed that 'it now seems probable that military operations against Egypt will not be required in the immediate future, but that there will be further negotiations which may well be protracted'. Monckton, therefore suggested that, following a more relaxed state of readiness of the forces as suggested in the Winter-plan, it would be advisable to release some ships that had been used to carry troops and return them to the merchant fleet.[113]

Clearly then, by the time that Gazier and Challe arrived in Great Britain on 14 October, British decision-makers faced a difficult situation. The United States was reluctant to 'put teeth' into the users' association. Uncertainty prevailed about the question whether the negotiations at the United Nations could be presented as a clear defeat of Nasser. On top of that, the military foresaw increasing difficulties in implementing their operational plans, as time elapsed.

*The Challe-Plan*

The Israeli attitude towards the crisis had been part of British discussions from early August on. In military planning it had always been taken into consideration that Israel might take advantage of an Anglo-French operation and make a move to secure the Straits of Tiran. Macmillan had even presented a memorandum to the Egypt Committee in which he urged to take advantage of 'noise' that could be made by Israel so that a considerable amount of Egyptian forces would be tied up in the Sinai, unable to defend Alexandria or the Canal Zone. Eden, however, had always wanted to keep Israel out of the picture, because he did not want Great Britain to be seen lined up with Israel against an Arab country; this would do irreparable harm to the basically pro-Arab foreign policy of Great Britain. The question is why British decision-makers, Eden in the first place, were prepared to accept the Challe-plan, which involved Israeli operations, and thus accepted the risk of long-term damage to British relations with the Arab world.

Contacts between France and Israel had been established as early as 22 June 1956, when top officials of the Army and Ministry of Defence of both countries met to discuss the co-ordination of an anti-Nasser policy. In the second half of September an Israeli 'high level' delegation flew to Paris and met with French policy-makers in order to co-ordinate a joint French-Israeli operation against Egypt. French Interior Minister Bourgès-Manoury had obtained Cabinet approval of such a move on 19 September (Bar-On, 1989). On 8 October Bourgès-Manoury asked General Paul Ely to study the possibility of a French-Israeli intervention. General Maurice Challe who flew to New York to discuss it with Pineau eventually produced this plan. The French Foreign Secretary showed remarkable enthusiasm and, so as to avoid the *Quai d'Orsai*, sent Challe to London, accompanied by Acting Foreign Secretary Albert Gazier, to consult Eden (Ely, 1969). Eden and Nutting received Challe and Gazier at Chequers on 14 October. Challe pointed out his plan for Anglo-French military intervention in case of an Israeli attack on Egypt and subsequent threat to the Suez Canal (Challe, 1968). Eden said he would have to discuss the matter with the Cabinet. The sequence of events has become well known since (Adamthwaite, 1988; Warner, 1989; Bar-On, 1989).

On 16 October Lloyd returned from New York in order to participate at a meeting of Senior Ministers. It was decided that Eden and Lloyd should fly to Paris that afternoon to have talks with Mollet and Pineau. Next day the Egypt Committee approved of the Challe-plan in principle, followed by the full Cabinet the following morning. On 21 October Israel had indicated that it had wanted to discuss the exact terms of agreement with Great Britain and France. Lloyd went to Sèvres, near Paris, to meet with representatives of France and Israel. On 23 October it looked as if the deal was off. Indeed, that day the Cabinet was told that it now seemed unlikely that an Israeli attack on Egypt was imminent.[114] On 24 October, however, agreement between the three Governments' representatives was reached, and next morning the die was cast when the British Cabinet

> agreed in principle, that, in the event of an Israeli attack on Egypt, the Government should join with the French Government in calling on the two belligerents to stop hostilities and

withdraw their forces to a distance of ten miles from the Canal; and should warn both belligerents that, if either or both of them failed to undertake within twelve hours to comply with these requirements, British and French forces would intervene in order to enforce compliance.[115]

*Explanatory Factors*

*Groupthink* The Egypt Committee met only once (on 17 October) during the crucial period between the French officials' visit and the Cabinet decision of 25 October. During those twelve days the Cabinet convened four times. In addition, at least four informal meetings of Senior Ministers were held. This suggests that the Cabinet's approval of a weighty decision was needed; that policy-makers felt a sense of urgency; and, most importantly, that Cabinet meetings were structured by informally reached consensus among Senior Ministers. What is known of these informal gatherings?

The first informal meeting took place on 16 October shortly after noon. According to Nutting, those present, besides himself, were Thorneycroft, Head, Monckton, Kilmuir, Eden, and Lloyd, who had returned from New York at 11.15 that morning (Nutting, 1967). Butler, Salisbury, and Macmillan were absent. The Challe-plan must have been presented frankly to all participants. Before the meeting Lloyd thought 'the idea of *our inviting* Israel to attack Egypt a poor one' (Lloyd, 1978, p. 166, italics added). Nevertheless, despite his reservations he chose not to express his doubts at the meeting, a clear example of self-censorship. Those who did protest against the plan were Nutting and, less vigorously, Monckton.[116] According to Lloyd, however, the meeting was no more than a 'general discussion of a rather indeterminate nature' (Lloyd, 1978, p. 167). It was decided that Lloyd and Eden should go to Paris to discuss the matter further with Mollet and Pineau. Possibly, the absence of three Senior Ministers made it impossible to commit the British Government to the Challe-plan.

A second informal meeting took place at Chequers on 21 October, at which Butler, Macmillan, Head, Kilmuir, Lloyd, and Eden were present, as well as General Keightley, Brook, and Permanent Secretary to the Ministry of Defence, Richard Powell. The French Government had indicated that Israeli leaders would be coming to Paris, who thought that a British representative would be needed (Lloyd, 1978). At the meeting it was decided that Lloyd should go to Paris the next day, travelling incognito. Clearly then, by 21 October another regular critic, Butler, had accepted the use of force and collusion with Israel.

A third informal meeting was held on 23 October at 10 in the morning, one hour before the full Cabinet would meet. Lloyd describes the meeting as 'in effect the Egypt Committee' (Lloyd, 1978, p. 185). Therefore, Eden, Butler, Macmillan, Salisbury, and Home, must have been present. The Foreign Secretary reported of troubles he had encountered in reaching agreement with the French and Israeli. The Cabinet was told no more than that an Israeli attack on Egypt now seemed unlikely, but that the French were unwilling to reach a settlement by compromise. No decision was taken.

A fourth informal meeting was held in the evening of 24 October. Patrick Dean, instructed that morning by Eden to go to Sèvres accompanied by Donald Logan, reported of his negotiations with the French and Israelis to a meeting of Senior Ministers at 10 Downing Street. They included Eden, Butler, Lloyd, Macmillan, Head, and the First Sea Lord, Mountbatten. Lloyd remarks that it was decided to 'recommend the contingency plan to the full Cabinet' (Lloyd, 1978, p. 188). The Cabinet minutes of next morning's meeting indeed suggest that Eden proposed the plan as a contingency plan. However, as Dean must have reported that Israel now agreed to pose a threat to the Canal in exchange for Anglo-French protection against the Egyptian air force, the informal meeting must have agreed to present it to the Cabinet in that way. This implies that another critic, Mountbatten, must have decided not to speak up against it.

Very little is known about the considerations that were put forward at these informal meetings. It seems probable, however, that the meetings of 21, 23, and 24 October must have dealt with the exact terms of the agreement with France and Israel. If not, Eden would not have been able to present to the Cabinet of 25 October the plan of confronting Israel and Egypt with an ultimatum to withdraw their troops to a distance of ten miles from the Suez Canal. One can only guess the nature of the discussions, but some clues can be found in the records of the four Cabinet meetings between 18 and 25 October. The full Cabinet met on 18, 23, 24, and 25 October. In order to reconstruct the decision-making process regarding decision 5, attention will be paid first to the decision-structure of each meeting and next to the factors that played a role.

The Cabinet meeting on 18 October followed a curious order.[117] First, Lloyd reported that negotiations at the United Nations might eventually lead to a satisfactory settlement. Then, Eden told the Cabinet that Israel might make a military move soon against either Jordan or Egypt. Eden said that 'it would be far better from our point of view that they should attack Egypt; and he had reason to believe that, if they made a military move, it would be made in that direction'. He had even 'therefore thought it right to make it known to the Israelis, through the French' that the United Kingdom would not defend Egypt under the 1950 Tripartite Declaration. According to Lloyd's personal notes, Eden asked the Cabinet whether they agreed that no obligation existed to defend Egypt against an Israeli attack: 'there was no adverse comment'.[118] Raising the question of what should be done in such a situation, Eden suggested that fighting over the Canal should be avoided.[119] Significantly, 'he said he had discussed this with some of his senior colleagues and they had agreed to this view. No one in the Cabinet disagreed'. Clearly then, Eden made a successful attempt at carrying the full Cabinet and at avoiding a detailed discussion of the plan's advantages and disadvantages by confronting his ministers with consensus among his Senior Ministers.

On 23 October Eden structured Cabinet discussions with his opening. Considering that an Israeli attack on Egypt now seemed less probable, he sketched a choice between an early attack and prolonged negotiations before the Cabinet. The latter possibility ran the risk of slowly weakening the British bargaining position because, following the Winter-plan, military preparations would have to be relaxed. In the discussion that followed, it was conceded that the Egyptians were willing to continue negotiations. Then, Lloyd spoke up and said that France was unwilling to fully co-operate to reach a diplomatic settlement. He added that no settlement was likely that would diminish Nasser's influence throughout the Middle East. Eden and Lloyd thus seemed to prepare the Cabinet to accept the use of force even without an Israeli attack on Egypt.

This suggestion came up the very next day when Eden and Lloyd reported on Pineau's visit to London. Eden told the Cabinet that the French Government preferred early military action, but saw no sufficient grounds to embark on such an operation at the present time. Eden informed the Cabinet that the troops 'could not be held in readiness for many days longer', and that adoption of the Winter-plan weakened the British bargaining position. What followed was an open discussion of the objectives of such an operation and the reaction of the Arab world. Eden explicitly intervened in this debate, by stating 'we should never have a better pretext for intervention against him [Nasser] than we had now as a result of his seizure of the Suez Canal'. The effects on the Arab world and the international community would be limited if the operation were 'swift and successful'. The Cabinet then considered the possibility to bring the issue to a head by issuing an ultimatum to Egypt to comply with the Eighteen Powers Proposals. No final decision would be taken, however, until the French Government's attitude would be fully known.

Next day (25 October) Eden and Lloyd dominated decision-making. Eden told the Cabinet that an Israeli attack on Egypt had now become very likely, and presented Challe's proposal to intervene if either party refused to withdraw to ten miles from the Canal. He even anticipated the risk of being accused of collusion, but thought this inevitable because Israel was likely to take advantage of any future Anglo-French intervention. Next Lloyd spoke up, supporting Eden's analysis, adding that Egypt had stepped up its attempts at undermining British influence in the Middle East. Only then did the Cabinet discuss the situation, and even in that discussion Eden seems to have played a dominating role in claiming that 'our action would be defensible in international law' and that military action now would be more effective than at some later moment. In the discussion several drawbacks were mentioned. Anglo-American relations might suffer lasting damage. Also, it would seem odd to ask Israel to remain at ten miles from the Canal and thus allow her to occupy Egyptian territory. Moreover, France and the United Kingdom did not have any 'specific authority of the United Nations' separating the fighting parties. Nevertheless, the Challe-plan was adopted.

Clearly then, Eden and Lloyd dominated Cabinet discussions. Two meetings probably did not even involve a full discussion, but were gatherings at which information about recent developments was given. At the meeting of 18 October this must have led to the acceptance of the Challe-plan in principle, without a formal decision being recorded. It would be wrong, however, to suggest that these dynamics pertain to the conclusion that Eden imposed 'his war' on the Cabinet. For one thing, the decision of 18 October was the result of consensus previously reached among Senior Ministers. Eden used that argument to carry the whole Cabinet. Moreover, all three remaining Cabinet meetings were co-ordinated by parallel informal meetings of Senior Ministers at which the details of the negotiations with France and Israel were agreed upon. It can thus be safely concluded that collusion with Israel was based on broad consensus among those Cabinet members that really mattered. On the other hand, it is evident that the Cabinet decision-making process was structured in such a way that the two individuals with most information, and presumably authority, regarding international developments led the discussions at the Cabinet meetings. During at least two meetings the role of the chairman has been decisive: Eden structured the debate by not leaving room for an exhaustive analysis of the issue and deferring final decisions to later sessions.

*Groupthink*  The remarkable amount of consensus in the Cabinet as well as during informal meetings points to the illusion of unanimity. This has been especially relevant on 18 October when Eden swayed the Cabinet by arguing that 'several senior colleagues' had agreed to his suggested line of action. Silence from traditional opponents of force, such as Monckton and Butler, must have given the impression to Junior Ministers that no line of division existed any longer within the inner cabinet. Their silence also testifies to self-censorship. Lloyd also had decided not to express his doubts, either at the informal or at the Cabinet meetings. Indeed, he must have acted as a catalyst of raising support for the Challe-plan, when he expressed doubts as to the effectiveness of any diplomatic settlement with Egypt. Another Minister who certainly fell prey to self-censorship was Walter Monckton. He had sent his letter of resignation on 3 October, but had already written to Eden that he was reluctant to leave the Government as 'I think it would do harm if I went altogether now'.[120] Significantly, Eden accepted his resignation on 18 October only, when he knew the Challe-plan had been accepted in rough lines, and offered Monckton the post of Paymaster-General.[121] Monckton knew that his resignation deprived him of his usual influence as Senior Minister. On 25 October he wrote to Lady Violet Bonham Carter that 'I cannot expect to carry the same weight or to have the same intimate knowledge of what is going on as I had before'.[122] Monckton too had accepted the Challe-plan. On 18 October Monckton and Lloyd had lunched at Brook's home, the Secretary to the Cabinet. Probably then Lloyd told Monckton that he was 'unhappy about the whole thing, but he had decided that he could not stand against it'.[123] Therefore, even though Lloyd and Monckton had their doubts, they preferred not to ventilate them and thus furthered the impression to Junior Ministers that the inner Cabinet was unanimous.

Another observable symptom of Groupthink is the self-appointed mindguard. Salisbury advised Monckton to leave the Government. 'It would be very embarrassing for you if, after having changed offices but stayed in the Government, you were then compelled to resign on a question of principle, which was already above the political horizon when you made your first decision.'[124] The same symptom can be observed in the refusal of Eden, Lloyd, and Macmillan to meet with Roger Makins, after the latter had returned on 11 October from his post as Ambassador in Washington to take up his new job as Permanent Secretary at the Treasury (Kelly, 2000). Makins had warned against misinterpreting the American attitude throughout the crisis. Meeting him would spoil the optimism about bringing the crisis to a head.

The last Groupthink-symptom that pervaded the decision-making process since the visit of Challe and Gazier was a collective effort to rationalize. What must have appealed to most ministers, and which may have persuaded doubters like Butler, was the suggestion that Great Britain and France would intervene in order to separate the belligerent parties, and thus might appear as policemen, defending international law. Indeed, on 25 October Eden explicitly argued that the proposed plan would be acceptable under international law, 'for we should be intervening to prevent interference with the free flow of traffic through the Canal, which was an international necessity'.[125]

*Leadership*   Eden's handling of Cabinet meetings affected the decision-making process significantly. At least on two instances Eden's leadership seriously affected the course of events. The first occasion was the reception of the Challe-plan. Eden, (together with Nutting) had been the first British policy-maker to learn of the Challe-plan. He had been urged by a message from Mollet to meet with Gazier and Challe. According to Nutting, Eden refused to be assisted by anyone from the legal department of the Foreign Office, because this would have been Fitzmaurice, a known opponent of the use of force (Nutting, 1967). Eden's reaction after Challe's exposition of the plan is very interesting. Challe recalls him to be have been 'delighted' (Challe, 1968, pp. 28-9). Taking account of the situation on 15 October, the Challe-visit must have been welcome to Eden. The Chiefs of Staff were about to issue the Winter-Plan, which would weaken the Anglo-French bargaining position at the negotiations at the United Nations. At the same time, it was becoming clearer every day that the American Government was not willing to use S.C.U.A. as a tool of pressure on Egypt. Each day uncertainty increased whether a solution would be found, either diplomatic or military, which would amount to a credible loss of prestige for Egypt. Challe's plan offered a way out of the dilemma.

Eden exercised directive leadership also in forging consensus among his Senior Ministers. On 18 October Eden told the Cabinet that he had reached consensus with several of his Senior Ministers. We know that at 16 October's informal meeting, Monckton, Lloyd, and Kilmuir had been the only Senior Ministers present. It is unlikely that Eden would have decided in favour of a drastic course of action without the consent of at least Macmillan and Salisbury, and probably Home. Indeed, Eden did not give a full pledge to Mollet and Pineau in Paris on 16 October, but said that he would give a definite answer the next day. This implies that Eden must have consulted his Senior Ministers on 16 or 17 October, because Lloyd's personal notes tell that a confirmation was sent from London to Paris on 17 October.[126] Geoffrey McDermott, one of three Foreign Office officials who were informed of political and operational plans,[127] reports that after Eden's and Lloyd's flight to Paris on 16 October, Eden 'saw a number of Cabinet colleagues taking the precaution to interview them individually' (McDermott, 1969, p. 148). Eden's insistence on receiving his colleagues *individually* testifies to his personal preference to go through with the Challe-plan. Meeting his Ministers separately served to persuade them to go along with the French plan.

Both leadership and Groupthink have played an important role. Cabinet meetings were structured by Eden's leadership style and by previously reached consensus among Senior Ministers. The Challe-plan made possible the avoidance of a probable loss of prestige due to prolonged negotiations without strong American support and the likelihood that military preparations would have to be relaxed soon. The presentation of the Winter Plan by the Chiefs of Staff suggests that the organizational context conditioned the decision-making process.


**Decision 6: Military Action Despite International and National Pressure**

After Israel's attack on Egypt on 29 October, which included a drop of parachutists near the Mitla-pass as a token threat to the Canal, Mollet and Pineau flew to London on 30 October. The projected ultimatum was put to both belligerents by the English and French Governments, and the armada started sailing from Malta and Cyprus. For a moment, everything seemed to be going as planned. In the evening of 30 October, however, the United States would not support the Anglo-French case before the Security Council. The next surprise was the adoption of the Uniting for Peace Resolution, sponsored by Yugoslavia, which undid the effect of the French and British vetoes at the Security Council and transferred the debate to an emergency session of the United Nations' General Assembly. British decision-makers now faced an unanticipated contingency: how to resist international pressure until the Armada would have arrived? Only now was it fully grasped that it would take the fleet seven very long days to sail to Port Said. On 2 November 1956 the Cabinet decided to continue the operations as planned, but announced that it would welcome a United Nations intervention force in the area. The next day it was decided that the Minister of Defence should go to Cyprus to urge for an earlier drop of French and British airborne troops. Military commanders at Cyprus, however, were against it, because these troops would face strong Egyptian resistance while the main assault would not start for another 48 hours. On 4 November the situation worsened, when Israel seemed willing to comply with the United Nations resolution that called for a cease-fire. This would deprive France and Great Britain of their pretext to intervene in order to protect the Canal. Operations could proceed, only when Israel announced that it would not agree to a cease-fire after all, after strong pressure from Mollet on Israeli Prime Minister Ben Gurion. On 4 November the British Cabinet decided that parachutists would be dropped the next day, 24 hours earlier than planned, and one day before the main assault.

The British Cabinet was trapped by her decision of 25 October. At the time the Challe-plan seemed an ideal way out of obtaining its objectives without seriously offending the United States and international public opinion. When these fundamental assumptions proved incorrect, a painful dilemma arose: on 4 November it seemed inevitable that remaining loyal to one's pretext implied that no occupation of the Canal Zone could take place at all. The objective of provoking Nasser's downfall seemed further away than ever.

Appendix 2 allows for three observations regarding the structure of decision-making. First, foreign policy was conducted from 10 Downing Street rather than from the Foreign Office. Lloyd's diary of engagements demonstrates that much of the Foreign Secretary's time was spent at the Prime Minister's office. This is by itself an indication of Eden's strong influence on the formulating and sending of diplomatic exchanges. Eden's role should not be exaggerated, however. It is very likely, and sometimes demonstrable, that Macmillan cleared major messages, such as those to Eisenhower. Second, a relatively large number of meetings of both the Cabinet and Egypt Committee were held. On the whole, the political decisions to go ahead with military operations and to accept a United Nations emergency force (including Anglo-French forces) were taken by the Cabinet on 2 and 4 November. Both meetings were preceded, however, by meetings of the Egypt Committee, which each lasted for about three hours. It seems that the Egypt Committee was dealing primarily with the implementation of military strategy, such as the decision of 1 November not to bomb Egyptian oil installations. As soon as politically relevant questions emerged, discussions were transferred to the full Cabinet. Third, it is difficult to give a plausible assessment of the amount of informal meetings taking place. The only unequivocal example is the meeting in Lloyd's room at the House of Commons on 1 November. More puzzling are the meetings at 10 Downing Street on 30 October, 3 and 4 November.[128] The sources show that Macmillan and Lloyd were present on 30 October too.[129] This suggests that throughout this period a small group of ministers were present at 10 Downing Street, or were at least contacted.

*Entrapment*

In the morning of 30 October the Cabinet agreed unanimously to issue an ultimatum to Egypt and Israel and to consult the French Prime Minister and Foreign Secretary. The remaining time was spent discussing the probable attitude of the United States Government. It was generally considered unlikely that the United States would respond to an appeal to support the action that would be taken. However, the Cabinet thought it possible 'to reduce the offence to American public opinion' and not to alienate the U.S. Government 'more than was absolutely necessary'. This was considered indispensable because of the expected reliance on American economic assistance, as British 'reserves of gold and dollars were falling at a dangerously rapid rate'.[130] Although active American support was thus not anticipated, the Cabinet did expect economic assistance. It thus seems probable that the Cabinet expected silent American approval combined with some public noise.

Until late afternoon all seemed to be going according to plan. Eden and Lloyd were 'curiously euphoric'.[131] Then, however, news of the American public reaction and the debate at the Security Council came off the tape. Most disturbing was the American attitude at the United Nations, once the news of the Anglo-French ultimatum broke through. The Americans introduced a resolution calling for an Israeli withdrawal and stated that compliance would remove the basis for the Anglo-French ultimatum. At 10 p.m. Dixon, British Ambassador to the United Nations, called Lloyd at 10 Downing Street, and made it clear that the Americans were 'gunning for us hard', and was afraid he would have to veto.[132] That same evening news came in that Dulles had said that the United States had 'noticed a rapid build-up of our forces in Cyprus which had started before the Israeli move'. He considered the ultimatum a 'pretty brutal affair' and added that 'we were facing the destruction of our trust in each other'.[133] At 9.15 p.m. Aldrich delivered a very cool message from Eisenhower. Eden and Macmillan, however, stuck to their curious rationalization of

American behaviour (see the next chapter). Later that night Yugoslavia introduced a Uniting for Peace Resolution which called for an emergency session of the General Assembly. Lloyd was very disappointed that the Americans supported this resolution, because their abstention would have been enough to reject the proposal, which would have given France and Great Britain some breathing space (Lloyd, 1978). Now, however, the General Assembly would convene at 10 p.m. on 1 November, and it was evident which side the United States was likely to take in that debate. Furthermore, the British veto and the start of the bombing of Egyptian targets by the Royal Air Force on 31 October had caused great turmoil in the House of Commons. Even the Conservative Party was increasingly divided, as the Whips reported (James, 1986).

In this context a meeting took place between Lloyd, Home, Lennox-Boyd, Monckton, Kirkpatrick, Assistant Secretary to the Cabinet Trend, as well as the three service ministers in Lloyd's room at the Commons at 10 a.m. on 1 November. They discussed developments at the United Nations. Kirkpatrick said that he expected the United Kingdom to leave the United Nations, or to be expelled. The party discussed the possibility of asking the United Nations to continue Anglo-French operations as a peacekeeping operation under U.N.O.-flag and with a U.N.O.-commander.[134] The idea was presented to the Egypt Committee that evening.

At this point it became clear how much the British Government was trapped in its own pretext. Originally, the Challe-plan had seemed an ideal solution, because France and the United Kingdom would appear to be acting under international law, or at least international morality, and would thus easily solicit the support of public opinion, especially at home, at the United Nations, and in the United States. Moreover, the plan offered the possibility of reducing the offence to pro-English Arab countries. Because Israel was bound to profit from an Anglo-French military attack on Egypt in any case, the Cabinet preferred to be seen as holding the balance between Egypt and Israel rather than as acting together with Israel.[135] When the Egypt Committee faced unexpected domestic and international opposition on the evening of 1 November, the solution of transferring the responsibility for the Anglo-French 'police action' to the United Nations seemed the only way out within the rationalization that British policy-makers had created themselves. By consequence, they lost sight of their main objective, which was reportedly noticed by the Minister of Defence, Anthony Head. He 'kept on reminding us [committee] that the first objective of this whole operation was to get rid of Nasser; that would never be done by [the] UN'.[136] Because it had been decided to use policing as a pretext to achieve its real objective, the British Government was constrained to present its case in the form of its chosen justification. The issue of handing over the matter to the United Nations was transferred to the Cabinet meeting next day. Actually, the Cabinet met twice, the interval allowing for a meeting between Pineau and Lloyd (and probably Eden). The Cabinet minutes reveal the worries about a split within the Conservative Party. Hard-liners would consider the transfer of responsibility to the U.N.O. as an excuse for abandoning an invasion altogether. Soft-liners would not understand why an attack on Egypt would be launched with the U.N.O. invited to take over. To make things worse, Pineau had made it clear that the French would not accept halting the operation, even though U.N.O.-policing could be discussed. The Cabinet thus decided that it would agree to stop operations if a U.N.O.-force could be constituted provided Anglo-French forces would be part of it.[137]

Meanwhile, the ships' slow speed had made the dilemma even more pressing. How to 'get the invasion started before the UN can make it too hot for us'. Eden reportedly kept on repeating that the United Nations was 'our only real danger now'.[138] The French were in a similar hurry. Pineau urged the landing of the troops before the vote in the General Assembly would take place. Pineau and General Ely flew to London to convince the British of swift action. Ely recalls strong hesitation among the British Chiefs of Staff, notably Mountbatten (Ely, 1969). At the political level,[139] it was decided to advance the drop of airborne troops to 4 November. This met with heavy resistance from the military who thought it militarily unsound.

The decision to intervene as policemen who would protect the Suez Canal from an Egyptian-Israeli war constrained the freedom of Anglo-French action in another way. Although at an early stage it had already been decided to try to minimize civilian casualties as much as possible in view of the effect on public opinion, the success of such efforts became all the more pressing, once policing had become the preferred pretext. The Cabinet thus decided to issue a public warning advising to keep clear of all Egyptian airfields. When news came through that the United States was evacuating its citizens by a road which ran through the Cairo West airfield, an R.A.F. target, it was decided that every effort should be made to postpone the particular attack until evacuation would have been completed. Similarly, Minister of Defence Anthony Head and General Templer were sent to Cyprus on 3 November to tell the Commanders that damage to civilian objects and civilian casualties had be minimized, and, logical consequence of the policeman pretext, to confine military operations to the Canal zone. This meant that an advance on Cairo was out of the question (Beaufre, 1969). Would that be enough to produce Nasser's downfall?

The consequences of entrapment were again clear on 4 November when news came through that Israel and Egypt had accepted the United Nations resolution calling for a cease-fire. This would deprive an Anglo-French invasion of its pretext, as both belligerents posed no longer a threat to the Canal. Faced with this situation, and worried by talk of U.N.O. oil sanctions against France and Great Britain, the Cabinet met in the early evening of 4 November.[140] Three courses of action seemed open. One was to go on as planned, accepting a U.N.O. force as long as French and British troops would be part of it. Another was to suspend operations for 24 hours and wait for the U.N.O. to accept Anglo-French troops as 'an advance guard of the Ultimate United Nations force'. The third option was to stop operations indefinitely. When a formal vote was taken, three ministers favoured the last course, four ministers the second, while twelve were in favour of going on. Eden did not consider this enough, although only Monckton had indicated that he would not accept a majority decision and 'must reserve his position'.[141] A governmental crisis, however, was averted by the news that Israel had decided not to accept the terms of the United Nations Resolution after all. The pretext was restored, and operations could continue.

*Explanatory Factors*

*Groupthink*   At least four symptoms of Groupthink can be observed during this period of entrapment. First, in the safety of the pretext of a policing operation, several indications of the presence of the illusion of invulnerability among Senior Ministers and even the full Cabinet can be found. First, on 30 October, when the Cabinet decided to issue the ultimatum to Egypt and Israel as planned, Eden and Lloyd acted in a 'curiously euphoric' manner.[142] Second, at the Cabinet meeting of 4 November, when the news broke of Israel's refusal to accept a cease-fire, and thus the pretext was restored, a split in the Cabinet avoided, and operations could proceed, 'tension round the table was immediately relieved' (Butler, 1971, p. 193). 'Everybody laughed & banged the table with relief – except Birch and Monckton, who looked glum'.[143] A third element of a feeling of invulnerability can be observed in the fact that in the evening of 5 November, the day of the first landings of French and British parachutists, a sherry party was held at 10 Downing Street.[144]

A belief in the inherent morality of the group transpires through Home's letter to Eden, written after the crucial 4 November meetings of the Egypt Committee and the Cabinet.

> My dear Anthony, The stakes you were playing for yesterday [4 November] were the highest – to lose all or to win all. We are not out of the wood, but we have won a decisive round. If our country rediscovers its soul and inspiration your calm courage will have achieved this miracle. With my unstinted admiration, Yours ever, Alec.[145]

Third, pressure was exerted on dissenters. On 1 November already, Monckton told Clark that he had wanted to resign from the Government. Nevertheless, 'WM said he only stayed with the ship at the strong request of the PM'.[146] Indeed, Monckton's eventual decision to stay on counts as an example of self-censorship. All Cabinet decisions on 30 and 31 October, 2 and 4 November were taken unanimously. When Israel appeared to accept a cease-fire on 4 November, Monckton had said he must reserve his position if military operations were not deferred indefinitely. Nevertheless, once it became known that Israel did not accept the U.N.O. resolution, Monckton remained silent. His self-censorship surfaces in the letter he sent to the Cabinet after Anglo-French operations had been halted.

> I have remained in the Cabinet without resignation because I have not thought it right to take a step which I was assured would bring the Government down. I have always felt that in as much as my opinion was not shared by any of my colleagues, a certain measure of humility demanded restraint in action on my part. Moreover, I did understand the danger of doing nothing because Nasser was succeeding in undermining our position throughout the Middle East and North Africa. I have lived on from day to day in the hope that I could within the Cabinet contribute towards a settlement as soon as possible.[147]

The fact that those ministers who favoured stopping altogether (Salisbury, Buchan-Hepburn) or postponement (Butler, Kilmuir, and Heathcoat-Amory) (Jones, 1986), happily joined in the general relief about Israel's refusal to accept a cease-fire testifies to the power of the idea of operating as a policeman. Indeed, it should thus count as a collective rationalization of one's behaviour.

*Leadership* From the records it is difficult to conclude that Eden, as the chairman, manipulated the discussions of the Cabinet. Especially, the minutes of the 4 November meeting suggest that Eden solicited a thorough discussion of the consequences of the situation that had occurred now Israel seemed willing to abide with a U.N.O. resolution. At first, a search for alternative courses of action was held. Next, the respective advantages and disadvantages were looked into. Only then did Eden invite each of his colleagues to indicate his view on the three alternative courses set out.[148] He reportedly did not vote himself (Lamb, 1987). The Cabinet appeared strongly divided, with two Senior Ministers (Kilmuir and Butler) voting in favour of postponement, and one (Salisbury) in favour of stopping. Eden is said to have taken Butler, Macmillan, and Salisbury aside and to have told them that 'if they wouldn't go on then he would have to resign'.[149] Eden thus attempted to direct the decision-making process, as these three 'most Senior' Ministers agreed that in that case no-one would be able to form a government.[150] However, it proved unnecessary to discuss the consequences of the vote with the full Cabinet, as the news broke that Israel would not accept the cease-fire after all.

*The organizational context* Decision-making was severely constrained by the logistics of the military plan, once the fleet had left Malta, Cyprus, and Algiers. It would take the ships seven days to arrive at Port Said. British military planners objected to a rapid occupation of Port Said by airborne troops, because the lightly armed parachutists would not be able to hold out against the Egyptian army, while reinforcements would still be far away at sea. Moreover, the Israeli advance in the Sinai had caused Egypt to withdraw parts of her troops from the Sinai and re-deploy them near the Canal. Indeed, at the Egypt Committee meeting of 3 November the Chiefs of Staff argued that therefore Port Said had to be heavily bombed before the Anglo-French assault, which conflicted with the political objective of limiting damage and civilian casualties. However, the next day the original plans could be implemented, when air reconnaissance had revealed that Egyptian forces were withdrawing towards Cairo.

*Domestic politics* Little evidence exist of the effect of growing domestic opposition on the decision-making process. It seems, however, that British policy-makers were worried by a potential division within the Tory Party rather than by public opinion at large. The risk of a divided Conservative Party affected the Cabinet's decision of 2 November to request the participation of Anglo-French troops in a U.N.O. emergency force.

The decision to continue operations despite growing international and domestic opposition should thus be understood in terms of the constraining influence of, especially, the organizational context, and, to a lesser extent, domestic politics. The decision itself has been influenced by Groupthink. British decision-makers preferred to stick to the rationalization that the Challe-plan had offered them. The presence of a large number of symptoms of Groupthink testifies to their entrapment in their legal pretext. On 5 November airborne troops landed at Port Said, the next day followed by the rest of the troops in order to safeguard the Suez Canal as international policemen. Within 48 hours American financial and diplomatic pressure would force Great Britain and France to stop the operation. Since Egypt's nationalization of the Suez Canal Company on 26 July British policy-makers had founded their policy on the assumption of at least silent American support. With their responses to six sequential decisional conflicts between July and November they found themselves entrapped in their legalistic pretext.

## Notes

1    Macmillan (1971, p. 101).

2    *Ibid.*

3    Kyle (1991, pp. 136-7). Kyle suggests that Eden dominated this meeting, quoting Clark; Clark's original diary, however, does not allow for that conclusion: 'Then I went down to No. 10 about 10.30 p.m. and met the King of Iraq just leaving. From then till 4 a.m. it was frantic. It was badly organized, said Guy, with French and Americans listening while we discussed how and whether to take military action. All that emerged was a dullest statement for use in the House at 11 this morning', Clark 'Whitehall Diary', p. 101, entry 26/27 July 1956. It seems thus more likely that Clark was not present at all and received his information from Guy Millard, Eden's Private Secretary.

4    DEFE 4/89, COS(56)73, 27 July 1956.

5    All quotes from the Cabinet meeting on 27 July are from CAB 128/30, CM(56)54.

6    *Ibid.*

7    ADM 205/117, 27 July 1956. These are Mountbatten's phrasings, which do not occur as such in the records of the EC's meeting of 27 July.

8    CAB 128/1216; EC(56)3, 30 July 1956.

9    The records of the third EC meeting on 30 July 1956 reveals the perception of this dilemma very clearly: 'This [Nasser's downfall] might perhaps be achieved by less elaborate operations than those required to secure physical possession of the Canal itself [e.g., air raids on Alexandria and Cairo]. On the other hand, it was argued that our case before world opinion was based on the need to secure international control over the Canal'. EC(56)3, 30 July 1956.

10    *Ibid.*

11    Two arguments speak in favour of the first interpretation. First, as a rule the Chiefs of Staff would be seen into the Cabinet Room when military planning was the subject of discussion. Second, on 27 July the Cabinet discussed military requirements for the occupation and running of the Canal in the light of Egyptian military strength, not in the context of an attempt to topple Nasser. It seems therefore unlikely that Mountbatten had been present at the beginning of the Cabinet meeting, when the definition of problem and the objectives were discussed.

12    Butler was absent due to illness until 30 July. Although he later claimed otherwise (Butler, 1975), the official records show that Butler was present at both crucial meetings of the Egypt Committee that day, when the aim of toppling Nasser was approved, EC(56)3, 30 July 1956.

13    CAB 128/30, CM(56)54, 27 July 1956.

14    CAB 128/1216, EC(56)3, 30 July 1956.

15　Ambassador Winthrop Aldrich had coincidentally left for Washington on 26 July 1956 (Aldrich, 1967, pp. 541-2).

16　PREM 11/1098.

17　*Ibid.*

18　PREM 11/1098.

19　*Ibid.*

20　PREM 11/1098, Makins to Foreign Office, 30 July 1956.

21　PREM 11/1098, 31 July 1956.

22　PREM 11/1098, 1 August 1956.

23　*Ibid.*

24　PREM 11/1098, 31 July 1956.

25　CAB 128/1216, EC(56)4, 30 July 1956.

26　CAB 128/30, CM(56)56, 1 August 1956.

27　*Ibid.*

28　CAB 128/130, CM(56)54, 27 July 1956.

29　AIR 8/1948, JS(56)135 (final), 1 August 1956.

30　DEFE 6/35, JP(56)70 (final), 13 April 1956.

31　DEFE 4/86, COS(56)44, 25 April 1956.

32　DEFE 4/86, COS(56)187, 9 May 1956.

33　DEFE 6/35, JP(56)70 (final), 13 April 1956.

34　ADM 116/6097; CAB 128/1216, EC(56)2, 28 July 1956, EC(56)6, 31 July 1956.

35　PREM 11/1099, Salisbury to Eden, 9 August 1956.

36　PREM 11/1099, CM(56)59, 14 August 1956.

37　PREM 11/1099, EC(56)10, 7 August 1956.

38　PREM 11/1099, EC(56)13, 9 August 1956.

39　PREM 11/1099, Eden to Salisbury.

40　PREM 11/1099, CM(56)59, 14 August 1956.

41　*Ibid.*

42　Although it would be incorrect to say that Eden, or other Egypt Committee members, misled the Cabinet. He, certainly, did not hesitate to use emotive persuasion. For instance, at the Cabinet meeting of 14 August Menzies held, *at Eden's request*, a vigorous speech in which he portrayed Nasser as a familiar military dictator. PREM 11/1099, CM(56)5, 14 August 1956.

43　PREM, 11/1099, Memorandum by the Foreign Secretary, 18 August 1956.

44　When Great Britain left the Suez Canal Zone in June 1956, it remained entitled to leave supplies that could be used whenever a situation would occur in which troops could legally re-enter the area, as provided by the 1954 Canal Treaty.

45　PREM 11/1104, EC(56)16, 16 August 1956.

46　Clark, 'Whitehall Diary', entry 15 August 1956, p. 113.

47　Diary entry 18 August 1956, quoted in Horne (1988, p. 408).

48　Diary entry 19 August 1956, quoted in Horne (1988, p. 409).

49　De Zalueta to Monckton, 15 August 1956, Monckton Papers, 6 (139-41).

50　PREM 11/1099, EC(56)18, Confidential Annex, 20 August 1956.

51　The only record which gives a bit of insight into what happened can be found in the files of Anthony Head. C.E. Key reported to Head that 'Sir Norman Brook spoke to Sir Richard Powell this morning and said that a small group of Ministers thought that it might be a good thing to take some provocative action against Egypt and suggested that we might start moving munitions out of the [Suez Canal] Base in a rather big way'. WO 32/16709, C.E. Key to Head, DUS(A)/BM/425, 21 August 1956.

52　Quoted in James (1986, pp. 483-4).

53　Eden's diary, entry 14 August 1956, quoted by James (1986, pp. 492-3).

54  PREM 11/1099, CM(56)60, 21 August 1956.
55  PREM 11/1099, EC(56)18, Confidential Annex, 20 August 1956.
56  Letter Home to Eden, 22 August 1956, quoted in Lamb (1987, p. 206).
57  It is worth quoting his letter in full length: 'My dear Anthony, I sense that Rab is very unhappy. I know your time is full but if you could see him alone it would be well worth while. He is not against the use of force, but he fears that we have got ourselves into a position where we shall press the button before we have a moral basis for action which will carry conviction in this country, the free world and the Conservative party. He feels that there should be more flexibility so as to allow time for the fullest diplomatic action the extent of which cannot be foreseen. I have told him that the pressing of the button is entirely within our control and that an intensive study is being made of the "casus belli" and the justification for armed intervention. I think his anxiety derives very largely from the fact that he was away for a fortnight and feels that possibly irrevocable decisions have been taken before the full implications of the use of force have been weighed. I may be wrong about this diagnosis but I am certainly right about his state of mind and I think if you can see him you can put everything into perspective and he will feel he has had a chance to tell you what he feels. I am sorry to add this to your preoccupation but I thought you should know. Yours, Alec. Rab, of course, does not know I am telling you of this.'; Lord Home to Eden, 22 August 1956, PREM 11/1100.
58  PREM 11/1100, 23 August 1956.
59  PREM 11/1152, Brook to Eden, 25 August 1956.
60  PREM 11/1152, Home to Eden, 24 August 1956.
61  Clark, 'Whitehall diary', entry 27 August 1956, p. 121.
62  CM(56)62, 28 August 1956.
63  Clark, 'Whitehall diary', entry 23 August 1956, p. 118.
64  *Ibid.*, entry 27 August 1956, p. 121.
65  PREM 11/1152, Brook to Eden, 25 August 1956. Home to Eden, 24 August 1956.
66  PREM 11/1100, Salisbury to Eden, 24 August 1956.
67  PREM 11/1100, EC(56)20, Confidential Annex, 23 August 1956.
68  PREM 11/1100, Record of a meeting of Ministers, 23 August 1956.
69  PREM 11/1100, Dixon to Lloyd, 23 August 1956.
70  Diary entry 25 August 1956, quoted in Horne (1988, pp. 410-1).
71  Before Dulles's move, some members of the inner group had already started doubting the American attitude. Macmillan, who had been confident of American support for going to the U.N.O., wrote to Eden on 27 August that the United States Government did not block private Egyptian accounts or 'fresh accruals to the Egyptian Government. This does not seem to be a very logical course' (Macmillan 1971, p. 108).
72  Clark, 'Whitehall diary', entry 5 September 1956, p. 125. Eisenhower's letter is printed in Carlton (1988, pp. 118-20).
73  PREM 11/1100, Eden to Washington Embassy, Telegram 4032, 5 September 1956.
74  PREM 11/1100, CM(56)63, 6 September 1956.
75  PREM 11/1100, Washington Embassy to Foreign Office, Telegram 1823, 7 September 1956, Telegram 1829, 8 September 1956.
76  PREM 11/1100, Dixon to Foreign Office, Telegram 650, 8 September 1956.
77  PREM 11/1100, Foreign Office to Washington Embassy, Telegram 4102, 8 September 1956.
78  PREM 11/1100, Washington Embassy to Foreign Office, Telegrams 1839 and 1840, 8 September 1956.
79  Eden's comments in the margins of his copy of the Chiefs' report testify to this interpretation. PREM 11/1100, EC memo EC(56)43, 6 September 1956.
80  Diary entry 9 September 1956, quoted in Horne (1988, p. 415).

81    FO/800/740, Kirkpatrick to Makins, Telegram 4144, 10 September 1956.

82    Diary entries 8 and 9 September 1956, quoted in Horne (1988, pp. 413, 415).

83    CAB 128/30, 11 September 1956.

84    Cf. Lloyd's account: 'it became clear to the Prime Minister and myself that we must act. The Prime Minister sent a message to Macmillan explaining our reasoning' (Lloyd, 1978, pp. 148-9).

85    Macmillan diary entry 20 September 1956, quoted in Horne (1988, p. 128).

86    Clark, 'Whitehall diary', entries 19 and 20 September 1956, pp. 132-3.

87    *Ibid.*, entry 21 September 1956, p. 134. Clark added that later 'Pineau came in and seemed almost at the edge of dissolving the Alliance'.

88    Diary entry 16 September 1956, quoted in Horne (1988, p. 402; emphasis in the original).

89    Clark, 'Whitehall diary', entry 20 September 1956, p. 133.

90    *Ibid.*, entry 14 September 1956, p. 130.

91    Draft of a letter from Monckton to Eden, final letter sent on 24 September 1956, Monckton papers, 6 (210-1).

92    Macmillan diary entry 20 September 1956, quoted in Horne (1988, p. 418).

93    Clark, 'Whitehall diary', entry 20 September 1956, p. 133.

94    CM(56)67, 26 September 1956.

95    PREM 11/1121, EC document EC(56)55, 29 September 1956.

96    PREM 11/1121, Nutting to Lloyd (at the United Nations, New York), Telegram 1160, 12 October 1956.

97    PREM 11/1121, Dulles to Lloyd, 15 October 1956.

98    EC(56)55 memorandum, 29 September 1956. EC(56)33 Minutes, 8 October 1956.

99    *The Times*, 3 October 1956, quoted by Thomas (1986, p. 101)

100   Horne (1988, p. 425). Horne quotes from the original manuscript of Nutting's *No End of a Lesson*, which apparently had been purged at the request of the Cabinet Office.

101   Clark, 'Whitehall diary', entry 2 October 1956, p. 137.

102   PREM 11/1174, Eden to Washington Embassy, Eden to New York, 3 October 1956.

103   Nutting, allegedly purged paragraph from *No End of a Lesson*, quoted by Horne (1988, p. 426).

104   PREM 11/1174.

105   FO 800/741, Eden to Lloyd (at United Nations), Telegram 1063, 6 October 1956.

106   FO 800/741, Eden to Lloyd (at United Nations), Telegram 1078, 8 October 1956.

107   FO 800/740, Macmillan to Eden, Telegram 2004, 25 September 1956.

108   FO 800/740, Macmillan to Eden, Telegram 2003, 25 September 1956.

109   PREM 11/1121, Macmillan to Eden, Telegram 2001, 25 September 1956.

110   FO 800/726, Eden to Eisenhower, 1 October 1956.

111   CM(56)68, 3 October 1956.

112   EC(56)33, 8 October 1956.

113   PREM 11/1103, EC memorandum EC(56)60, 16 October 1956.

114   CM(56)72, 23 October 1956.

115   CM(56)74, 25 October 1956.

116   Nutting in a conversation with Lamb (Lamb, 1987, p. 233).

117   Quotes refer to CM(56)71, 18 October 1956.

118   FO 800/828, 18 October 1956.

119   This is known from Lloyd's personal record of the discussion. The official Cabinet minutes do not even record this issue being brought up and simply record that the Cabinet took note of Lloyd's and Eden's report of their conversations with Pineau and Mollet in Paris on 16 October; FO 800/728, 18 October 1956; CM(56)71, 18 October 1956.

[120] Monckton's letter of resignation can be found in the Monckton papers, 7(249-50), 3 October 1956. Quote from a letter sent to Eden on 1 October 1956 (in effect another draft of his resignation letter), Monckton papers, 7(238), 1 October 1956.

[121] Eden to Monckton, 18 October 1956, Monckton papers, 7(310-311). At the same time, Anthony Head was appointed Minister of Defence.

[122] Monckton to Lady Violet Bonham Carter, Monckton papers, 7(384), 25 October 1956.

[123] Clark's record of a conversation over lunch with Monckton on 2 November 1956. Clark, 'Whitehall diary', entry 2 November 1956, p. 149.

[124] Salisbury to Monckton, Monckton papers, 7(226), 28 September 1956.

[125] CM(56)74, 25 October 1956.

[126] FO 800/728.

[127] The other two were Patrick Dean and Sir Ivone Kirkpatrick. Actually, McDermott was no longer informed after August.

[128] The principal source is Kilmuir (1964, p. 275).

[129] Clark records that at 9.15 P.M. U.S. Ambassador Aldrich handed over Eisenhower's cool reaction to the Anglo-French ultimatum. The draft reply to Eisenhower, which was sent that evening, shows suggestions by Macmillan. At 10 P.M. Lloyd talked on the phone to Dixon, British Ambassador to the United Nations. Clearly then, both Lloyd and Macmillan were present at 10 Downing Street. Clark, 'Whitehall diary', entry 30 October 1956, pp. 143-4.

[130] CM(56)75, 30 October 1956.

[131] Clark, 'Whitehall diary', entry 30 October 1956, p. 144.

[132] Lloyd answered 'quite cheerfully' that Dixon indeed had to veto. *Ibid.*

[133] PREM 11/1100, Washington Embassy to Foreign Office, Telegrams 2205 and 2206, 30 October 1956.

[134] Clark, 'Whitehall Diary', entry 1 November 1956, p. 146.

[135] Cf. CM(56)70, 25 October 1956.

[136] Clark, 'Whitehall diary', entry 1 November 1956, p. 146. Clark's source was Monckton.

[137] CM(76)78, 2 November 1956.

[138] Reportedly, Lloyd told Dixon over the phone that 'we can accept anything from the UN so long as it doesn't stop our troops going in'. Clark, 'Whitehall diary', entry 3 November 1956, p. 149.

[139] It is not clear at which meeting. It could be the early Cabinet meeting of 2 November, the minutes of which are being withheld. On the other hand, the full Cabinet seldom discussed operational military plans. Indirect evidence of this crisis-like decision being taken on 2 November comes from Clark's remark that on 2 November Eden's temperature rose to 105 degrees. Clark, 'Whitehall diary', entry 4-5 November 1956, p. 158. Bourgès-Manoury's threat to have the French start the invasion unilaterally, may have added to the rise of temperature (Ely, 1969).

[140] CM(56)79, 4 November 1956.

[141] Three different accounts of Eden's disappointment and subsequent behaviour exist (see Carlton, 1986).

[142] Clark, 'Whitehall diary', entry 30 October 1956, p. 144.

[143] Clarissa Eden's diary, quoted by James (1986, p. 567).

[144] FO 800/717.

[145] PREM 11/1154, Home to Eden, 5 November 1956.

[146] Clark, 'Whitehall diary', entry 1 November 1956, p. 147.

[147] Minute from Monckton to the Cabinet, 7 November 1956, Monckton papers, 8(39-40).

[148] CM(56)79, 4 November 1956.

[149] Clarissa Eden's diary, quoted by James (1986, p. 567). Two other accounts exist, one from Butler, who claims Eden said he must go upstairs and reconsider his position (Butler, 1971,

p. 193). The second reports Eden to have broken down in tears, crying 'you are all deserting me', and going upstairs to compose himself. James Margach, *The Abuse of Power*, London, 1978, p. 113, quoted by Carlton (1986, p. 75).

[150] Clarissa Eden's diary, quoted by James (1986, p. 567).

# Chapter 6

# Resolving the Puzzle of Suez

## Introduction

Six decisional conflicts had British decision-makers entrapped in a legalistic pretext. This chapter will investigate to which extent the four explanatory factors account for their entrapment. This requires a more precise assessment of who belonged to the key policy-makers at various instances throughout the crisis and of the leadership exercised by Anthony Eden. It is argued that a small group of ministers, consisting of Eden, Macmillan, Lloyd, Salisbury, Kilmuir, Home, Monckton (up until a certain moment), and (in a more qualified manner) Butler, fell prey to Groupthink in preparing the major decisions in the Egypt Committee, or in informal meetings. Although the Cabinet also displayed an increasing number of Groupthink-symptoms, consensus at the Cabinet level should partly be explained in political terms, that is, by the importance of previous consensus among Senior Ministers. In that sense, the informal and formal rules of Cabinet decision-making in Great Britain played a crucial role. Second, in several instances Eden's worldview adds significantly to explaining the decision-making process. Finally, organizational and domestic political context affected the impact of the independent variables at specific instances considerably.

Next, this chapter will argue that leadership and group factors account for the puzzle of Suez, that is, the fundamental miscalculation of the attitude of the United States when the crisis culminated in the Anglo-French landings at Port Said. This chapter argues that Groupthink, combined with Eden's leadership, solicited the varying ways in which the small group rationalized the attitude of the United States. The contents of their rationalizations, however, should be explained in terms of the images widely shared by British policy-makers based on their perception of Anglo-American relations since 1945. Eden's individual worldview reinforced such rationalizations.

## The Structure of Decision-Making

The account of British decision-making in the previous chapter suggests that no single decision-making body dominated the process at all times. Rather the exact decision unit (Hermann and Hermann, 1989) varied throughout the crisis. Table 6.1 gives an overview of the frequency of meetings of three different decision-making bodies throughout the crisis: the full Cabinet, the Egypt Committee, and the informal small group of Senior Ministers. The last body was defined as any meeting referred to in primary or secondary sources at which three or more Senior Ministers are known to have been present.

### Table 6.1 Number of Meetings of Decision-Making Units per Decisional Conflict

|            | Informal | Egypt Committee | Cabinet |
|------------|----------|-----------------|---------|
| Decision 1 | 1        | 9               | 3       |
| Decision 2 | 2        | 9               | 3       |
| Decision 3 | 1        | 8               | 4       |
| Decision 4 | 4        | 4               | 1       |
| Decision 5 | 6        | 5               | 5       |
| Decision 6 | 4        | 5               | 5       |
| Total      | 18       | 40              | 21      |

*Source:* Author's calculation on the basis of available primary and secondary sources.

Table 6.1 shows an overall shift from decisions being taken in the context of frequent Egypt Committee meetings towards decisions taken in the context of regular Cabinet meetings that are surrounded by informal meetings of Senior Ministers. Remarkably, only one Egypt Committee meeting was held between 10 October and 1 November, the period in which Challe unfurls his plan, the Sèvres negotiations take place, and military operations start. Moreover, the sheer number of informal meetings surrounding Decisions 4 and 5 (the decision to refer the matter to the U.N.O. and the decision to adopt the Challe-plan) suggests that informal gathering became the dominant pattern of decision-making. A more precise description is needed, however, of the members of these three decision-making bodies. This will be followed by an assessment of the extent to which the four explanatory factors affected their policy-making.

Eighteen ministers belonged to the Cabinet: Sir Anthony Eden (Prime Minister), Lord Salisbury (Lord President of the Council), John Selwyn Lloyd (Foreign Secretary), Harold Macmillan (Chancellor of the Exchequer), R.A. Butler (Lord Privy Seal and Leader of the House of Commons), Lord Kilmuir (Lord Chancellor), Sir Walter Monckton (Minister of Defence, until 18 October 1956; from that date Paymaster-General), Anthony Head (Minister of Defence from 18 October 1956), Gwilym Lloyd-George (Home Secretary), Allan Lennox-Boyd (Colonial Secretary), Lord Home (Secretary for Commonwealth Relations), James Stuart (Secretary of State for Scotland), Peter Thorneycroft (President of the Board of Trade), Duncan Sandys (Minister of Housing and Local Government), Lord Woolton (Chancellor of the Duchy of Lancaster), Sir David Eccles (Minister of Education), Derick Heathcoat Amory (Minister of Agriculture), and Osbert Peake (Minister of Pensions). Most Ministers were present at the 21 Cabinet meetings that were held between 26 July and 6 November. Major absentees included Butler on 27 July (illness) and 21 August (holiday); Monckton on 1 and 2 August (illness); Lloyd on 3 and 9 October (United Nations), and Macmillan on 26 September (IMF meeting in Washington).

Membership of the Egypt Committee was not clearly defined. The committee was originally intended to include only some of the Ministers directly involved (Eden, Lloyd, Macmillan, Salisbury, and Monckton) (Butler, 1975). Over the months many others joined its deliberations, sometimes turning the Egypt Committee into another Cabinet. This was the case on 12, 14, and 17 September when 12 (out of 18) Cabinet members attended the Egypt Committee meetings (Verbeek, 1992, Appendix 3). Table 6.2 presents an overview of the frequency of participation by individual policy-makers between 27 July and 4 November (excluding one time-visitors).

**Table 6.2 Frequency of Attendance at 40 Egypt Committee Meetings**

| Policy-maker | Frequency |
|---|---|
| Eden* | 38 |
| Brook (Cabinet Secretary) | 37 |
| Home* | 36 |
| Macmillan* | 36 |
| Lloyd* | 32 |
| Head#* | 31 |
| Thorneycroft* | 31 |
| Salisbury* | 30 |
| Watkinson# (Minister of Transport) | 30 |
| Monckton* | 28 |
| Butler* | 27 |
| Lennox Boyd* | 21 |
| Dickson (Chairman Chiefs of Staff) | 19 |
| Kirkpatrick (Permanent Secretary FO) | 11 |
| Kilmuir* | 10 |
| Templer (Imperial General Staff) | 10 |
| Mountbatten (First Sea Lord) | 9 |
| Jones# (Minister of Fuel and Power) | 8 |
| Boyle (Chief of Staff Airforce) | 7 |
| Birch# (Secretary of State for Air) | 7 |
| Hailsham# (Secretary of State for Navy) | 7 |
| Heath (Chief Whip) | 6 |
| Keightley (Commander Musketeer) | 4 |
| Amory* | 3 |
| Nutting# (Under-Secretary at FO) | 2 |
| Ivelaw-Chapman (Air Force) | 2 |

* Member of the Cabinet
# Member of the Government

*Source:* Author's calculation based on CAB 134/1216.

Table 6.2 demonstrates that a group consisting of Eden, Home, Macmillan, Lloyd, Head, Thorneycroft, Salisbury, Watkinson, Monckton, and Butler usually attended the Egypt Committee. Lennox-Boyd and Dickson were regularly present as well.

Determining the membership of the inner circle of Senior Ministers is more difficult. First, undoubtedly, the number of informal meetings recorded here is incomplete. Second, many informal meetings between only two ministers took place. Sometimes the sources record a meeting but not the names of the participants. It proved possible to trace the attendance of twelve informal meetings with at least three Senior Ministers present (out of 18). Tables 6.3 and 6.4 present these data.

### Table 6.3 Participants at 18 Informal Meetings

|  | Participants known | Participants unknown | Total |
|---|---|---|---|
| Decision 1 | 1 | - | 1 |
| Decision 2 | - | 2 | 2 |
| Decision 3 | 1 | - | 1 |
| Decision 4 | 3 | 1 | 4 |
| Decision 5 | 4 | 2 | 6 |
| Decision 6 | 3 | 1 | 4 |
| Total | 12 | 6 | 18 |

*Source:* Author's calculation on the basis of primary and secondary sources.

### Table 6.4 Attendance of 12 Informal Meetings

| Policy-maker | Number of informal meetings attended |
|---|---|
| Eden | 10 |
| Lloyd | 9 |
| Macmillan | 8 |
| Kilmuir | 6 |
| Butler | 5 |
| Salisbury | 4 |
| Head | 4 |
| Home | 3 |
| Nutting | 1 |
| Lennox-Boyd | 1 |
| Thorneycroft | 1 |

*Source:* Author's calculation on the basis of primary and secondary sources.

Table 6.4 shows that those informal meetings of which participation is known, were dominated by Eden, Lloyd, and Macmillan, and to a lesser extent by Kilmuir, Butler, and Salisbury. The dynamics of participation of Egypt Committee (Verbeek, 1992, Appendix 3) and informal meetings (table 6.4) suggests that Kilmuir is involved with the Egypt Committee from 10 August onwards, which is reflected in his increasing attendance of informal meetings since September. Salisbury, on the contrary, is a frequent visitor of both decision-making bodies until the presentation of the Challe-plan on 16 October. Although he attended all Cabinet meetings, he no longer appeared in the Egypt Committee or at informal gatherings. This may indicate his growing apprehension about the use of force, and his eventual vote in favour of halting all operations on the crucial Cabinet meeting of 4 November.

Over all, tables 6.1, 6.2, and 6.3 justify the claim that an inner circle of Senior Ministers existed, consisting of Eden, Lloyd, Macmillan, Salisbury, Kilmuir (from mid-August), and Butler. Interestingly, apart from Butler and Kilmuir, these ministers kept in touch with representatives of the United States Government until mid-October. Moreover, the chronology of decision-making presented in the Appendix suggests that Eden, Lloyd, Macmillan, and Salisbury were the policy-makers who often met on a bilateral basis. These Senior Ministers were also the most regular visitors of the Egypt Committee. That committee was frequented also by two other Senior Ministers (Monckton and Home) by two other members of the Cabinet (Thorneycroft and Watkinson) and by one member of the wider Government (Head).

Now the principal policy-makers are known, it is important to bring back in the decision unit. Which small group (Cabinet, Egypt Committee, or inner circle) effectively determined which decision? The description of the decision-making process in chapter 6 allows for the following conclusions. Decision 1, the choice of diplomacy over force, was effectively taken by the Egypt Committee, but affected by an informal meeting on 26 July. Decision 2, sending off the Menzies mission to Egypt, was made by the Egypt Committee, but grounded in two informal meetings. The same can be said of Decision 3, the adoption of S.C.U.A. and the simultaneous withdrawal of the pilots. Decision 4, reference to the Security Council, was taken on a purely informal basis. The Cabinet effectively took Decision 5, accepting the Challe-plan, with an occasional role for the Egypt Committee (on 17 October). However, it was heavily dependent on consensus among Senior Ministers, previously reached on an informal basis. The last decision, to continue military operations, was contingent on the meetings of the Cabinet, but also on those of the Egypt Committee that surrounded them. However, the decision was seriously affected by an informal meeting on 1 November, outside the usual inner circle, in which the compromise of accepting a U.N.O. emergency force was prepared. To what extent have Groupthink, leadership, the organizational context, and domestic political institutions affected the choices of these decision units?

**Explanatory Factors**

*Groupthink*

*Was decision-making characterized by Groupthink?* Table 6.5 presents an overview of the occurrence of symptoms of Groupthink in three decision-making bodies (the Egypt Committee, the Cabinet, and the inner group) during the crisis. Three conclusions are warranted. First, overall, 29 instances of Groupthink could be traced.[1] Self-censorship appears the most frequent symptom, itself a clear expression of Groupthink's basic mechanism, the suppression of individual criticism in order to maintain group consensus (see Chapter 2). Second, Decisions 3, 5, and 6 display the largest number of symptoms of Groupthink. Third, the occurrence of Groupthink-symptoms runs parallel to the changes in *loci* of decision-making: towards the end of the crisis (Decisions 5 and 6) the Egypt Committee does not display Groupthink-symptoms in contrast with the inner group and especially the Cabinet. Until that time, apart from the first phase of the crisis, Groupthink-symptoms are absent at the Cabinet level, but surface in the Egypt Committee. The inner group regularly displays Groupthink-symptoms, most frequently during discussions of the London Conference (Decision 2). On the whole, it seems that during the first months of the crisis an inner group prepared decisions, which were effectively taken in the Egypt Committee, while towards the end of the crisis an inner group led the dance with the Cabinet rather than the Egypt Committee.

*Antecedent conditions* British policy-makers thus clearly displayed a tendency to premature consensus-seeking. Which factors contributed to their inclination? Groupthink-theory distinguishes between three major explanations: group cohesiveness, a provocative situational context, and the presence of structural organizational faults (cf. Chapter 2). With respect to cohesiveness, only the inner circle can be said to come close to a cohesive group. Yet, several relations within the inner group were affected by domestic politics. One indicator of cohesion is the type of education Cabinet members had enjoyed. All but two had been at Oxford and Cambridge, while nine came from Eton (Thomas, 1986). Although the socialization effect of a common educational background should not be underestimated, it would be equally hazardous to exaggerate its influence. Given the fact that, certainly in those days, Eton and Oxbridge furnished a large part of British Government officials, it does not prevent the regular occurrence of major policy divergences. A common wartime experience may be another factor of cohesion during the Suez crisis.[2] Similarly, it has been argued that the impact of Munich 1938 had a lasting impact on those Cabinet members who were in politics at the time. Eden, Salisbury, Macmillan, and Sandys had been opponents of appeasement in 1938, while Butler, Lennox-Boyd, Kilmuir, Stuart, and Home had been advocates. Although it is rather speculative to establish a direct link between group cohesion and an individual's attitude towards appeasement, it is the case that Salisbury, Macmillan, and Sandys were among the staunchest advocates of a tough policy over Suez. Munich may have been important to furthering a certain bond between Eden, Salisbury, and Macmillan.

**Table 6.5 Groupthink Symptoms in Three Groups during Six Decisional Conflicts**

| | II | IM | CR | SO | SC | IU | DP | SAM | Total |
|---|---|---|---|---|---|---|---|---|---|
| D 1 | | | | | | | | | 4 |
| EC | | | | | | | | 1 | |
| IG | | | | | | | | 1 | |
| Cab | 1 | 1 | | | | | | | |
| | | | | | | | | | |
| D 2 | | | | | | | | | 5 |
| EC | | | | | | 2 | | | |
| IG | 1 | | 1 | | 1 | | | | |
| Cab | | | | | | | | | |
| | | | | | | | | | |
| D 3 | | | | | | | | | 7 |
| EC | | | | 1 | 1 | 1 | 1 | | |
| IG | | | | 1 | 1 | | | | |
| Cab | | | | 1 | | | | | |
| | | | | | | | | | |
| D 4 | | | | | | | | | 1 |
| EC | | | | | | | | | |
| IG | | | 1 | | | | | | |
| Cab | | | | | | | | | |
| | | | | | | | | | |
| D 5 | | | | | | | | | 6 |
| EC | | | | | | | | | |
| IG | | | | | 2 | | | | |
| Cab | | | 1 | | 1 | 1 | | 1 | |
| | | | | | | | | | |
| D 6 | | | | | | | | | 6 |
| EC | | | | | | | | | |
| IG | 1 | | | | | | | | |
| Cab | 1 | 1 | 1 | | 1 | | 1 | | |
| | | | | | | | | | |
| Total | | | | | | | | | 29 |

D=Decisional Conflict; EC=Egypt Committee; IG=Inner Group; Cab=Cabinet. Symptoms of Groupthink: II=Illusion of Invulnerability; IM=Belief in Inherent Morality; CR=Collective Rationalizations; SO=Stereotypes of Outgroups; SC=Self-Censorship; IU=Illusion of Unanimity; DP=Direct Pressure on Dissenters; SAM=Self-Appointed Mindguards.

*Source:* Author's calculation.

On the whole, however, it is more likely that a variety of considerations explained the relative cohesion of the political elite. First of all, opposition to Chamberlain's appeasing of Mussolini had created strong personal ties between Eden and Salisbury. The latter, then known under the name Lord Cranborne, resigned with Eden from the Foreign Office, and is considered to have been one of Eden's few personal friends in politics. Second, internal party politics and personal ambitions should be taken into account. Two major sources of conflict come to mind: Eden's tendency to try to dominate foreign policy and the rivalry between Macmillan and Butler to become Eden's political heir. In April 1955 Eden appointed Macmillan as his Foreign Secretary, but replaced him with Lloyd in December, presumably because Macmillan proved to be too independent a Foreign Secretary. Although a standard interpretation of the dynamics within the Eden Government (Carlton, 1988; James, 1986; Horne, 1988), it does not account for Macmillan's pivotal aggressive role during Suez from the very start, notably his regular private meetings with Eden. No major differences occurred between Eden and Macmillan during the crisis. Butler's and Macmillan's jockeying for the position of heir apparent to Eden may have had an important effect on decision-making. Although Butler was critical with regard to the use of force, his outright opposition might have endangered his future career as long as his competitor, Macmillan, seemed close to the majority of the Cabinet and its leader. This may explain why Butler eventually went along with the majority throughout the crisis. Internal politics also affected Lloyd's position. He had been promoted to the Foreign Office after hardly eight months of cabinet experience. Indeed, his appointment allowed Eden more room to manoeuvre in foreign policy. Lloyd had accepted his subservient position: 'I know I have been over-promoted; there can be no question of my disloyalty'.[3] Lloyd's political career clearly depended on Eden. Therefore, consensus among British Senior Ministers may thus partly have been the product of different individual political calculations, in line with 't Hart's refinement of Janis's Groupthink-theory (cf. Chapter 2).

In conclusion, most members of the inner group around Eden (Macmillan, Salisbury, Kilmuir, and Home) formed a reasonably cohesive whole, despite the difficulties between Eden and Macmillan. Part of this cohesion is grounded in a common pre-war experience (Eden, Macmillan, and Salisbury). Other members of the inner group (Butler and Lloyd) were less motivated by cohesion than by political calculations.

In Groupthink-theory a provocative situational context is related to high levels of stress because of an external threat or temporary low self-esteem. An external threat is present in each of the six crucial decisions discussed in the previous chapter. They qualify as so-called decisional conflicts, or, situations in which every course of action available entails the risk of serious losses. This type of decision, presumably, raises the level of stress under which decision-makers operate. The fundamental conflict underlying all six decisions was the perceived choice between the immediate negative effects of a hard-line policy on the British position in the Middle East and the slow deterioration of the British Middle Eastern position of a soft-line policy. Such perceptions were held by such different individuals as Norman Brook, a civil servant central to decision-making, Harold Macmillan, a clear hawk, 'Bobbety'

Salisbury, a hawk with growing doubts, and Walter Monckton, an eventual opponent of force. Each crucial decision added to the high level of stress generated by this fundamental conflict, often because of specific deadlines. This was certainly the case regarding questions like how to respond to an equivocal outcome of the London Conference (Decision 2), what to do if Nasser gave no clear answer to Menzies, how to deal with new American proposals, such as the users' association (Decisions 3 and 4), and how to react to the likely introduction of the Winter-plan (Decision 5).

Evidence of low self-esteem is scarce. The Eden Government had not been a balanced, stable, and effective Government ever since the Cabinet reshuffle of December 1955. Kilmuir even speaks of 'a dramatic fall in the popularity of the Government and Sir Anthony Eden' (Kilmuir, 1964). It has been argued that during the first half of 1956 the Government deliberately looked for ways to improve its popularity by strong action in the field of foreign affairs, notably on Cyprus and in Buraimi (Carlton, 1988). Even though public approval of the Government and its leadership increased in the spring, it is conceivable that the label of weak Government had left its imprint on the Government when it had to face the nationalization of the Suez Canal Company. Indeed, evidence exists that, at least in the early stages of the crisis, the future of the Eden Government was considered closely tied to its handling of the crisis. Clark, Eden's press officer, repeatedly noted that the crisis was Eden's gravest moment: 'for if he does not act strongly and effectively, he will be out'.[4] Monckton as well thought not taking a tough line 'would be fatal for the Government'.[5] The political stakes were high, as one would reasonably expect in any major foreign policy crisis in which military action is contemplated. Yet, no evidence can be found that decision-makers suffered from low self-esteem due to the Government's low popularity.

The three decision-making bodies in Great Britain suffered from at least two structural organizational faults: British policy-makers remained relatively isolated from their political and bureaucratic environment. Second, the position of the British Prime Minister makes possible a directive leadership-style. British decision-makers operated in relative isolation from their environment in four respects. First, information on military planning was confined to a restricted group of Ministers, effectively the Egypt Committee. As a matter of fact, an entirely new procedure, named *Terrapin* was installed to this effect. Despite the obvious consideration that military plans should not come out in the open, the eventual consequence of adopting *Terrapin* was a lack of information about military planning at the level of the full Cabinet. In August Duncan Sandys expressed his worries about this matter to Eden in a letter. Eden's reply on August 22 underlined the role of the inner circle in military affairs.

> Knowledge of the details must, for obvious reasons of security, be confined within the narrowest possible circle. Such political guidance as the military authorities may need in the preparation of their plans must continue to be given by me, in consultation with a small number of my most senior Cabinet colleagues and, as necessary, such Departmental Ministers as may be directly concerned (quoted in James, 1986, p. 499).

The adoption of *Terrapin* had two important consequences. The Cabinet was unaware of any reservations the military might have about military operations. Second, the Cabinet had to discuss the Challe-plan without complete knowledge of the contingencies of military planning. By consequence, it had to make decisions about the feasibility of the plan without realizing that it would take the fleet about a week to arrive at Port Said.

Second, British decision-makers remained isolated from the civil service. Most civil servants were completely unaware of the considerations and decisions made by the Egypt Committee and Cabinet. Actually, only Sir Norman Brook (Secretary to the Cabinet), Sir Ivone Kirkpatrick (Permanent Under-Secretary at the Foreign Office), and Patrick Dean (Deputy Under-Secretary at the Foreign Office and Chairman of the Joint Intelligence Committee) were fully informed. Moreover, reports from civil servants on such vital matters as financial and economic consequences and international law reached decision-makers through their Ministers, Macmillan, Lloyd, and Kilmuir. The Egypt Committee had thus never been in a position to examine all positive and negative aspects of the objectives and alternative courses of action. Civil servants had to compile reports without full knowledge of political and military objectives. Moreover, their information had to pass several gatekeepers, such as Kilmuir, who sometimes decided to act as self-appointed mindguards, and not to pass on information to their colleagues (cf. Verbeek, 1992; Johnman, 2000).

Third, British policy-makers operated by and large without talking to the Opposition. Despite the fact that this crisis was defined as a threat to British national interests, British policy-makers did not put much effort in trying to solicit national support by keeping in touch with opposition parties. At the beginning of August Eden and Gaitskell corresponded by letter. Eden's aim had been to extract a confirmation that Gaitskell's rather belligerent speech in the Commons on 2 August still reflected his Party's mood. On 14 August Salisbury, Eden, and Lloyd met with a few representatives of Labour. After it had become clear that Labour was opposed to the use of force without United Nations approval, contacts were interrupted. Instead of trying to involve the opposition, even at an informative level, British decision-makers decided not to keep in touch.

Finally, British policy-makers increasingly isolated themselves from the Americans. After Challe and Gazier had visited Chequers to present their ingenious plan the United States Government was no longer informed, let alone consulted, about Anglo-French policies towards Egypt. This accounts for British surprise at American opposition to the Anglo-French policy from 30 October onwards. Moreover, the fact that Great Britain had no Ambassador available in Washington between 20 October and 8 November made it very difficult to explain this policy to the American Government.

A different issue is the effect of the position of the Prime Minister. The Prime Minister dominates the British Cabinet because of his or her prerogatives, such as setting its agenda and chairing its meetings. The particular leadership style that each Prime Minister develops will therefore strongly affect the quality of the decision-making process The style that Eden had developed as Prime Minister certainly did not contribute to methodical decision-making procedures. He introduced the habit of seeing his senior colleagues alone: 'I thought Baldwin's method of frequent consultation alone with each of his principal colleagues was good and I followed it. My colleagues knew that I was always available to each of them and we saved the Cabinet some extra stress of business that way' (Eden, 1960, pp. 269-70). Appendix 2 shows that Eden continued consulting the members of his inner circle individually in private meetings or over the telephone, especially Macmillan, Lloyd, Salisbury, and Kilmuir. As Foreign Secretary, Eden developed a habit of constantly phoning his collaborators about all aspects of policy. As Prime Minister Eden continued this habit, especially towards ministers involved in foreign policy, such as Macmillan and Lloyd, when they were Foreign Secretary, and Home, as Commonwealth Secretary (Reynolds, 1989). Eden displayed the same attitude towards his direct subordinates. Clark, Eden's press secretary, in reviewing his first six months at his job, noted in his diary that 'there never was a day when he didn't ring up one of the P[rivate] S[ecretaries] to worry about something'.[6]

This evidence of interference does not constitute sufficient ground for the claim that directive leadership characterized the Eden Government during the Suez crisis. As a matter of fact, in two decisions Eden did not display directive leadership at all. In four decisions, however, his handling situation affected the decision-making process, in two of which quite strongly. Eden's way of chairing meetings of the Egypt Committee and the Cabinet has been very important with respect to the simultaneous decision to accept S.C.U.A. and recall the pilots (Decision 3) as well as the decision to adopt the Challe-plan (Decision 5). In the former case, when it had to be decided how to respond to the results of the Menzies mission, Eden tried to rush things through. He wanted to refer the matter to the United Nations, so that military operations could start soon afterwards. Similarly, the adoption of S.C.U.A. was a result of the way Eden presented the likely American attitude to the Egypt Committee and Cabinet, and the personal judgement he added, first mistrusting Dulles's proposal, then going along with it. The adoption of the Challe-plan was strongly affected, first of all, by the way information about the American attitude was distributed. On the Cabinet of 3 October Eden passed the text of Dulles's anti-colonialist press conference around the table. Furthermore, the way he chaired those Cabinet meetings at which the Challe-plan was discussed shows that he did not shy away from soliciting his colleagues to agree, arguing that their senior colleagues had agreed upon the matter previously. Clearly then, Eden's directive leadership hindered the development of an open decision-making process regarding both Decisions 3 and 5. As a matter of fact, these decisions display a very high number of symptoms of Groupthink (7 and 6 respectively).

Directive leadership also affected Decisions 1 and 2. Eden's leadership style affected the definition of the issue at the very first Cabinet meeting on 27 July. Instead of assuming the role of an impartial chairman, who asks his colleagues after their definition of the problem, he chose to open the meeting by giving his own view. Later in August, when British decision-makers had to make up their minds about what should be done after the London Conference, Eden's reluctance to share the full contents of messages from the United States Government with the Cabinet inhibited a full and open Cabinet discussion. Had he done so, American hesitations about the use of force would have been more clearly known to the Cabinet.

Directive leadership less affected Decisions 4 and 6. This comes as no surprise with respect to the decision to refer the matter to the United Nations (Decision 4), as this decision has been taken informally by Eden, Lloyd, and probably, Macmillan. It is more puzzling in the case of the decision to continue operations despite growing international and domestic pressure (Decision 6), especially because this decision displays a rather high number of symptoms of Groupthink. As a matter of fact, the records of the Cabinet meetings in the relevant period reveal that the Cabinet held open and full discussions in which each member was explicitly invited to express his views, and which were characterized by a search for, and assessment of, alternative options.[7] The paradox is explained by entrapment: once the Cabinet had adopted the Challe-plan, and subsequent events had invited them to put the plan into action, all further discussion was held in terms of the agreed plan. Most symptoms of Groupthink thus reflect collective attempts to stress the positive aspects of the plan and to suppress possible negative consequences.

In sum, then, the inner group of British decision-makers was glued together in part by social ties, in part by political calculations based on functional interdependence, thus confirming 't Hart's refinements of Janis's theory (cf. pp. 21-2). Second, British policy-makers were constantly facing a situation of high stress, provoked by a situation that can be characterized as a choice between two evils. Third, they operated in isolation from their environment and were chaired by a leader who was not used to collective decision-making, but rather to meeting his colleagues individually. Low self-esteem, however, carried less weight. Eden's leadership style affected four decisions substantively.

### Eden's Worldview

Directive leadership is the link between Groupthink and the leader's worldview. A directive leader's worldview is like a window on the leader's substantive approach to the problem that he is facing together with the group. As a matter of fact, Eden's worldview can be said to have been relevant at three instances, all of which coincide with Eden displaying directive leadership. All three moments are related to two important elements of Eden's worldview. First, his vision that it is possible to reach agreements with every actor in international relations, as long as gentleman-like behaviour is observed, grounded in the recognition of one's respective national interest. Second, his conviction that the United Nations had been reduced to a Cold War and propaganda instrument, without much political influence.

From Eden's perspective, Nasser had passed a certain threshold with the nationalization of the Suez Canal Company. It was no longer possible to reach agreements with a man who defied the essential rules of international relations. Eden interpreted Dulles's anti-colonialist press conference in October in a similar fashion. Having faced an American Secretary of State who blew hot and cold without much apparent consistency, Eden (and his colleagues) decided to bother no longer about Dulles's misgivings about S.C.U.A. Instead, Eisenhower became the new focus of British expectations. In terms of Eden's worldview, Dulles had passed the same threshold and had become an unreliable actor in international affairs.

Eden's view of the nature of the United Nations explains why referring the matter to the Security Council was deemed unwise in July (Decision 1): no helpful situation was to be expected from a body where the Soviet Union would veto any Anglo-French-American resolution. Similarly, it explains why Eden thought that going to the United Nations would be helpful in September (Decision 3): because of the expected Russian veto any discussion would be quickly over with, and then military operations could start, unless Egypt would accept the 18 Powers' Proposals. Third, Eden's view of the United Nations contributes to our understanding of why British policy-makers did not consider the possibility that deliberations might be transferred to the General Assembly, with the Uniting for Peace Procedure, and might thus provoke strong pressure from international public opinion (Decision 5). An Anglo-French veto would paralyze the Security Council, and that would be the end of it.

## The Organizational Context

The considerations of British policy-makers have been influenced by the military organization at five instances. First, at the very beginning of the crisis, swift retaliation was impossible because the required number of troops and ships were not immediately available. Furthermore, a delay of a state of readiness was caused by fundamental changes of the military plan, first on 10 August, when the Chiefs of Staff decided to land near Alexandria instead of Port Said, and, again, on 7 September, when these plans were reversed to the original target. Fourth, the Chiefs' presentation of a Winter-plan made it clear to those British policy-makers who preferred a vigorous response to Egypt, that they would have to act soon, if measures that would give the impression of demobilization, were to be avoided. Finally, the time that elapsed between the sailing of the fleet and the disembarking of the troops was the product of organizational constraints. Although these were not directly relevant to the Cabinet's decision to continue the operation, they certainly enabled the mobilization of strong domestic and international pressure against Anglo-French policies. All in all, organizational constraints have seriously affected both Decisions 1, 2, and 5.

## Domestic Political Institutions

British policy-makers were permanently aware of the effect their policies would have on their support in Parliament and the country at large. Only in two instances, however, did domestic considerations influence decision-making substantively. One involved the decision to refer the matter to the Security Council; another the decision to continue operations as planned. When Parliament was to return from summer recess in mid-September, British policy-makers feared that they would be forced to give a pledge that no force would be used without permission from the United Nations. Eden succeeded in avoiding such a promise in the Commons on 12 September by offering the users' association. In the following days, however, Conservative opposition to the use of force without having sought recourse to the United Nations, was growing. The British decision to refer the matter to the Security

Council was partly taken in order to pacify dissenting members within the Conservative Party.

On 2 November, when handing over the 'policing task' to the United Nations seemed to offer a narrow escape from strong international pressure, the Cabinet faced a division within the Conservative Party because its hawks would consider that a pretext for aborting the invasion. In order not to offend the hard-liners, the Cabinet, although accepting U.N.O. interference, had had to insist on the inclusion of Anglo-French forces in a U.N.O. emergency force. Although these domestic considerations narrowed down the range of options available to the Cabinet, they did not affect the decision to continue military operations: no U.N.O. force had been formed, when Anglo-French forces landed in Port Said.

Domestic politics has not been a decisive factor during the Suez crisis. Interestingly, when it played a minor, yet substantive, role, British decision-makers were affected by tensions within the Conservative Party rather than by opposition from the Labour Party or from the public at large. In a different sense, however, domestic political institutions have affected decision-making in a very significant way. The informal hierarchy between Senior and Junior Ministers in the British Prime Ministerial system reinforces the Groupthink-danger in a very specific fashion. As long as Senior Ministers present a united front the full Cabinet is not likely to pay much attention to criticism raised by Junior Ministers.


**Resolving the Puzzle of Suez**

It was argued in Chapter 1 that British decision-making during the Suez crisis failed to meet at least three procedural criteria of high quality decision-making. This failure was intimately linked to confidence in the forthcoming of American diplomatic, economic, and logistical support. British decision-makers expected the faint legalistic justification provided by the Challe-plan to be sufficient to pacify the United States. Throughout the summer, however, the Eisenhower Administration had sent (albeit sometimes unclear) signals that the United States ruled out the use of force. The British Ambassador in Washington, Sir Roger Makins, had persistently warned against optimism regarding the American attitude. Clearly, a military intervention presented as a police operation was likely to raise many eyebrows in Washington. How to explain the common optimism among British policy-makers regarding the attitude of the United States? Two major rationalizations can be traced, at the level of mainly the inner group, but also of the Egypt Committee and the Cabinet, that served at explaining away American opposition to the use of force: the influence of the impending American Presidential elections and the selective interpretation of messages from Dulles and Eisenhower.[8] Both, however, underwent important changes in the period between the last week of September and the middle of October. Both shared the basic conviction that at least tacit American support would be forthcoming, sooner or later, and that diplomatic moves served at waiting for the right moment.[9]

*The American Presidential Elections*

Presidential Elections in the United States would be held on 6 November. Until mid-October, British policy-makers argued that the Americans were reluctant to support the use of force, because President Eisenhower was campaigning as the President of Peace. It would be unfortunate, they reasoned, if he had to associate himself with a major military intervention in the Middle East. American opposition indicated that the British and the French had to wait until after the elections. After the adoption of the Challe-plan, however, this way of reasoning changed completely. It was now argued that if the Eisenhower Administration were confronted with a swift military move in the last days of his election campaign, the President would be unable to take a stand against it. The argument that electoral motives might be behind American hesitations does not emerge until the beginning of September 1956. A shift in argumentation occurs during the first days of October 1956. Previously, British policy-makers considered Election Day as the date after which the Americans would be prepared to support Great Britain and France, at least on the diplomatic front. In the course of October, however, they interpreted American hints at Election Day as another tactic to refrain France and Great Britain from military action. This shift is connected to a shift in the image the British held of John Foster Dulles and is accompanied by a change of trust from Dulles to Eisenhower.

At the beginning of September 1956 the British and the French were contemplating referring the Suez dispute to the Security Council after a possible failure of the Menzies mission. The French and a large number of British decision-makers considered this step a prelude to military action. The British, notably Eden and Lloyd, had been in contact with the State Department about this move, but encountered strong opposition from Dulles. In fact, his idea of a Users' Association on 4 September was designed to prevent the British and the French from doing so. At that moment, however, the British wished to keep the French ignorant of that new development, and preferred to deal with Dulles's proposal in secret on their own for a few days until they would be sure that the Americans were committed to it. On 5 September Lloyd saw Pineau in Paris in order to discuss the issue of the Security Council, although he knew of Dulles's new proposal. Pineau emphasized that force should be employed as soon as possible. Lloyd answered that, according to him, Dulles wanted an eventual procedure at the Security Council to be an honest attempt to reach an agreement. Lloyd 'said that Mr. Dulles seemed reasonably determined to impose the will of the 18 nations on Egypt. But he wanted to stop us doing so by force, at all events before the U.S. elections. One could sympathize with his difficulties. He had said that it would be hard to get even subsidiary economic help to us through Congress before then. Until the elections, Mr. Dulles wanted no force used, unless there was a clear excuse'.[10] Lloyd was not alone in his impression. On 14 September Harold Macmillan wrote down in his diary, contemplating the likelihood of American assistance in putting stronger economic pressure on Egypt: 'but I cannot see that we can achieve much this side of 6 November [the American Presidential election]' (Macmillan, 1971, p. 127). Macmillan stuck to his analysis during his visit to Washington on the occasion of a

conference of the International Monetary Fund. He used his stay to meet with
Dulles, Eisenhower, and Deputy Under-Secretary Robert Murphy. In their
conversations he stressed Britain's firmness in its will to use force in the last resort.
In his messages to Eden, which were seen by Lloyd as well, Macmillan repeatedly
describes his impression that the United States would have backed Great Britain
100 percent, had there not been an upcoming election. 'I feel sure the President
understands our problems about Nasser, but he is, of course, in the same position
now as we were in May 1955 [British General election]'.[11] The private character of
Macmillan's talk with Eisenhower must have contributed to the idea that the
Americans could be frank in private, but not in public. Similarly, Macmillan saw
Dulles in private on 25 September, after a more formal meeting at which the
British ambassador Roger Makins had been present, and reports: 'some of the
things he [Dulles] said were very helpful, but might be dangerous to him if they got
about in the electioneering atmosphere'.[12]

This impression of being the confidant of Dulles and Eisenhower partly
explains why the regular warnings of Ambassador Roger Makins were ignored.
Already on 9 September Makins reminded London that the lack of public
American support was 'not due to the imminence of the elections, but a normal
manifestation of American public opinion'.[13] But even Makins's careful
observations allowed the British to stick to their convictions. Referring to
Eisenhower's re-election campaign Makins wrote to Lloyd on 17 September that 'it
remains true that the great Republican trump card is peace. So there is in my
judgement no prospect, as the international outlook appears today, that the U.S.
will themselves participate in military action before November 6'.[14] In fact, this
analysis allowed Lloyd to explain away Eisenhower's lack of support for Dulles's
tough speeches at the two London Conferences. '[Eisenhower] had made no effort
to make Nasser understand that he was in for trouble if he did not agree to a
reasonable settlement. Eisenhower's mind was concentrated on an election
campaign, appearing as the candidate who could preserve the peace of the world'
(Lloyd, 1978, p. 168).

In September British policy-makers expected to persuade the United States to
take a firm line with Nasser by supporting a strong S.C.U.A. They preferred to
ignore Pineau's warnings that the Americans could not be trusted at all and that
they would make the British and the French wait with the use of force until after
the election 'which could mean that we should never be able to take such action at
all'.[15] In the beginning of October, however, at a press conference Dulles declared
that S.C.U.A. was not supposed to have any real teeth, and described British and
French policies over Egypt as old fashioned colonialism. This urged a change of
perceptions at Whitehall. Dulles's suggestions were suddenly defined as opposite to
British interests. On 6 October Eden wrote to Lloyd, who was in New York in
order to defend the British case before the Security Council: 'I think we must never
forget that Dulles'[s] purpose is different from ours. The Canal is in no sense vital
to the U.S. and his game is to string us along at least until Polling Day'.[16]

Dulles's press conference is crucial to understanding the course British
decision-making was about to take. Eden seemed fed up with Dulles's ambiguity
and reluctance to commit the United States to a Users' Association that would be

able to put pressure on Egypt by withholding canal dues in case of alleged Egyptian misbehaviour. To Lloyd Eden expressed his fear that time was running out. 'It made me fear more than ever that our position is being eroded. We have been misled so often by Dulles's ideas that we cannot afford to risk another misunderstanding. Time is not on our side in this matter. I am glad you are standing firm with the French and so stiffening Dulles. That is the only way to a solution'.[17] Eden must have been worried that soon he would no longer be able to back this diplomatic effort by threatening with swift military action, as the British Chiefs of Staff had been working on the Winter-plan since 2 October. It is unlikely that Eden just wanted to go ahead with military action at that stage, as the meeting between Challe and Eden, the first step on the (British) path to collusion with Israel, did not take place until 14 October.

The election argument no longer surfaces after the adoption of the Challe-plan. Pineau recalls that on 16 October, when Eden and Lloyd flew to Paris, Eden showed Mollet and Pineau a message from Eisenhower stating that it would be better to wait with military action until after the elections. Pineau claims to have responded that the elections did not make a difference at all (Pineau, 1976). Indeed, when Pineau returned to London on 23 October the French Foreign Secretary, Eden, and Lloyd concluded that it would be best to act now because the Americans would be too busy because of the elections.[18]

By 25 October, when the Cabinet discussed the contingency of an Israeli invasion of Egypt, the argumentation of Eden and Lloyd had completely changed. When Ministers suggested that 'there was no prospect of securing the support or approval of the United States Government', Eden argued that the American government would support an Anglo-French operation to separate the fighting parties and secure the Canal, because it would be defensible under international law and because 'the United States had acted in conformity with these principles on many occasions in the last hundred years'.[19] The American Presidential elections were of no concern to the Cabinets held between 18 October and 6 November. This can be explained by the self-deceiving idea that a policing action in the Suez Canal area would be evidently defensible under international law.

The election argument thus mainly appears in the evaluations of those members of the inner circle who were in direct contact with leading American politicians: Lloyd with Dulles, Eden with Eisenhower, Macmillan with both of them. Despite evidence to the contrary, Eden, Lloyd, and Macmillan reassured each other in their belief that the Americans were willing to support them if only the elections would be out of the way. The misperception is corrected when Dulles's statements on S.C.U.A. and colonialism provoke a deep sentiment of disillusion among members of the inner circle. It did not lead, however, to a change of policy. On the contrary, it led to a further closing off of the minds of key British decision-makers. Election Day was now defined as a perfect moment to confront Eisenhower with a *fait accompli*.

*Selective Interpretation of Messages from Dulles and Eisenhower*

This form of rationalization came in two varieties: one was the tendency to tailor the interpretation of the messages from Eisenhower and Dulles to the belief that American support would be forthcoming. The second was the habit of distinguishing the messages that Dulles and Eisenhower communicated in public from those that were conveyed in private. Both varieties had a mutually reassuring effect on the members of the inner circle, and were not questioned in either the Egypt Committee or the Cabinet. A major change in this habit occurred towards the middle of October: after the adoption of the Challe-plan Dulles is completely ignored, while during the crisis itself British policy-makers prefer to rely on Eisenhower's tacit support, and tend to interpret his messages accordingly.

Throughout the crisis both Dulles and Eisenhower expressed their strong reluctance to the use of force. However, they never explicitly told the British that they would not approve of it, or even oppose it. Both had hoped to take the sting out of the wasp by exploiting every possible diplomatic means, thus postponing the decision to intervene until a satisfactory diplomatic settlement could be worked out. However, a confusing element appeared in their communications with British policy-makers: they persisted in approving of Anglo-French military precautions, first, because they genuinely thought this would pressurize Egypt into a satisfactory agreement, and, second, because they did not want to alienate their allies too much. This element offered British policy-makers ample room to misinterpret the messages from the Eisenhower Administration. Misconstruction came in three varieties: one was to engage in misreading, whenever an American message was received. The second was thinking that Dulles and Eisenhower could be considered apart. The third was to make a distinction between private and public utterances of Dulles and Eisenhower. The eventual consequence would be a tragic misinterpretation of the American attitude at the height of the crisis.

*Misreading messages*   Two important examples of misreading occurred during the crisis. When Dulles arrived in London on 1 August for trilateral discussions, he carried a letter from Eisenhower to Eden. Dulles had noticed himself that Eisenhower's letter contained an important ambiguity as to the purpose of holding an international conference. He therefore handed over his own interpretation of that passage, in order to avoid misunderstandings. As it happened, Eden preferred to believe Eisenhower's words and concluded: 'The President did not rule out the use of force' (Eden, 1960, p. 436). Similarly, when on 5 September Eisenhower made a statement to the American Press in which he declared to be committed to a peaceful settlement of the dispute, Macmillan made an effort to read into that statement the conclusion that Eisenhower still did not exclude military force, in the last resort.[20]

*Separating Dulles and Eisenhower*   In his letter of 3 September the American President had already told Eden that he thought military force would not be needed in order to make Nasser give way. In the margin on this letter, Eden scribbled 'Foster advocated going on' [taking military precautions and making military plans]'.[21] This reflects the tendency to explain away unwelcome news by relying on what Dulles had said.

*Separating public and private utterances*   British policy-makers, in particular Eden, Lloyd, Macmillan, and Salisbury, met with Dulles in private during the trilateral talks, the London Conference, and the S.C.U.A. conference. Moreover, Macmillan met both Dulles and Eisenhower in private when he travelled to Washington for a meeting of the I.M.F. Furthermore, Sir Roger Makins, British Ambassador to the United States, communicated the contents of several talks he had with Dulles, which left room for being misconstrued by British policy-makers. These were thus able to sustain the belief that private American statements were of more value than public utterances. For instance, Dulles handed over Eisenhower's letter of 8 September, which strongly discouraged the use of force, to Makins. In a subsequent telegram, Makins conveyed Dulles's accompanying words, which went much further than the contents of the President's letter. Dulles alluded to the possibility of occupying several key points along the Canal. Moreover, he added that the President did not rule out the use of force in the last resort. Eden immediately marked this phrase with his pencil.[22] Macmillan's meetings with Eisenhower at the White House and with Dulles have been especially crucial in this respect. Macmillan was convinced that the United States would tacitly support an Anglo-French move against Nasser. He told Eden so when he came back in early October. More than that, Macmillan's opinion carried much weight because in a meeting between Eden, Lloyd, and himself, he insisted, when Lloyd warned of Dulles's intransigence: 'I had a few words with Ike. Of course he's an ill man, but as brave as ever. I don't think there is going to be any trouble from Ike – he and I understand each other – he's not going to make any real trouble if we have to do something drastic'.[23]

The latter episode illustrates that a break occurred in the first two weeks of October. British policy-makers increasingly ignored the American Secretary of State and directed their attention to Eisenhower instead, relying on Macmillan's assurances that the President was with them. After the adoption of the Challe-plan, contacts with the United States were broken off, and the British continued planning on the assumption that tacit American approval was forthcoming. This would eventually lead to a fatal misinterpretation of Eisenhower's messages when France and Great Britain issued their ultimatum to Israel and Egypt. When the news broke of the Israeli invasion of Egypt, British policy-makers had to re-open the lines of communication with Washington that had been sealed off since mid-October. The exchange of letters between Eden and Eisenhower that followed is difficult to explain unless seen in the context of collective rationalization, which enabled Eden to think that limited American support would be forthcoming.

On 30 October Eisenhower felt offended by the fact that Eden sent him a message about the contents of his speech to the House of Commons only three hours beforehand. Eisenhower therefore had to learn of the French and British ultimatum to Egypt and Israel from press reports. Much has since been made of Eisenhower's 'stunningly cold and formal message which he went so far as to release to the press'. On top of that the letter was addressed to Dear Prime

Minister' instead of 'Dear Anthony' and was signed 'Sincerely, Dwight D. Eisenhower' and not with the usual 'warm regards, as ever, Ike E.' (James, 1986; Carlton, 1988). The common interpretation is that Eisenhower wanted to snub Eden in public and make him understand the American position once and for all (Neff, 1981). The interesting phenomenon, however, is that Eden did not feel humiliated at all, and, for a while, remained convinced of limited American support. In order to sustain his perception, he separated the private messages of the President from the public ones, and he was not alone in doing so. That Tuesday, 30 October 1956, several messages between Eden and Eisenhower crossed each other thus forming a source of misunderstanding.[24] It is important to realize that, when Eden sent his telegram in which he explained why he was 'asking for Port Said and Ismailia and Suez'[25] he had not yet received Eisenhower's second message of that day. When that telegram reached Eden, it spoke a rather cautious language. 'It seems obvious that your Government and ours hold somewhat different attitudes toward the Tripartite Declaration of 1950. In any event I shall earnestly and even anxiously watch the unfolding situation'.[26] Shortly afterwards, the American Ambassador Aldrich delivered Eisenhower's 'cold and formal' message to Eden over the phone, which clearly had been written without Eisenhower having read Eden's explanatory note. It is very likely that Eden understood that Eisenhower was angry by having had to learn the news from the press, but not necessarily that the President was completely opposed to his policy.

First, many authors have underlined that Eden, by issuing the ultimatum, had opted for a course of action that contradicted the 1950 Tripartite Declaration that was still fully supported by the United States (Carlton, 1981; Thomas, 1986). The declaration was, as a matter of fact, subject of Eisenhower's second letter to Eden on 30 October 1956. This Declaration, issued in 1950 by Great Britain, France and the United States, stated that they would try and balance the flow of arms to Israel and Arab countries and would seek each other's advice if either party crossed the 1948 armistice lines. As Aronson shows, however, this declaration had never been an instrument for the enforcement of the territorial status quo, but rather a justification for weapon delivery to all parties in the region (Aronson, 1986). When Eden visited Washington in January 1956, Dulles had told him that the declaration was in itself no assurance that the United States would honour its commitment to enforce the territorial status quo.[27] It is therefore not unlikely that Eden did not give that much weight to Eisenhower's request for respect for the Tripartite Declaration.

More importantly, Eden chose to separate Eisenhower's private messages from Ike's public statement that Tuesday. This is revealed by Eden's message of 31 October. It is instructive to quote it at full length.

I have received your formal message, and I see that its substance has already been published. I realise that you wrote in this way in order to avoid encroaching upon the confidential nature of our personal exchanges. But, in the view of the publicity given to it, I shall be obliged in our Parliamentary discussions, which are to be *resumed tomorrow*, to comment on some of the points made in your letter in order to justify British policy and action. For this purpose, I think I must be free to make public the substance, *though not, of course, the full text*, of the two messages which I sent to you in the course of today. *I am sure you will understand* (emphasis in the original).[28]

This letter shows that Eden thought Eisenhower's public statement was to be interpreted differently from their private correspondence. It suggests that he thought the American President somehow had to be critical for domestic purposes, but tacitly agreed with the British point of view, given his relatively accommodating earlier messages.[29] All the more because Eisenhower responded to Eden on the same day with a short note stating 'By all means, feel free to use any part of the exchanges between us that you see fit'.[30] From this perspective, Eden's later recollection that he 'had no reason at this moment [30 October 1956] to suppose that the United States would oppose us at the United Nations upon almost every point' is not as strange as it seems (Eden, 1960, p. 528). Eden was not alone in this misperception. The draft of Eden's message to Eisenhower reveals that the emphasized phrasings of the draft were added as 'amendments suggested by the Chancellor of the Exchequer'.[31] The interpretation of the American attitude to the British and French ultimatum was thus not as much a product of the obscure thinking of one individual, but the result of cognitive processes among more than one British decision-maker.[32]

**Conclusions**

British policy-makers were confident throughout the entire crisis that American support would be forthcoming. In the first stages of the crisis they thought that the Americans needed to be persuaded of how seriously Great Britain approached the situation. After the trilateral talks with Dulles, American hesitations about the use of force were explained away by various rationalizations, which were adapted to new circumstances once the Challe-plan was adopted. This misperception was predominantly present at the level of the inner group. Eden, Macmillan, Lloyd and Salisbury formed the narrow circle that stayed in touch with the United States Government. Nevertheless, their colleagues in both the Egypt Committee and the Cabinet shared the expectation of American support. Although the various types of collective rationalization mainly appeared within the inner circle, misreading the Americans was a product of Groupthink at all three levels of decision-making.

Eden's worldview accounts for two important attitude changes that occurred in the beginning of October. First, British policy-makers preferred to ignore Dulles and started relying completely on their conviction that Eisenhower in his public messages had shown to sympathize with the British position. Second, the argument of the American Presidential Election served as a pretext to proceed with the plan, rather than to wait until after the elections. Clearly then, the first two weeks of October 1956 hold the key to understanding the British decision to use force. Part of the explanation can be offered by Eden's worldview: it had become clear that Dulles was unwilling to use the users' association as a means to put pressure on Nasser. In Eden's eyes, the American Secretary of State had thus entered the category of actors in world politics that did not play the game according to the rules that Eden thought essential. These processes of misperception and the consequent process of defective decision-making can be understood as the product of the stress generated by the dilemmas of so-called decisional conflicts.

The British misperception of the American attitude is rooted in both the expectations and the experiences built up during Anglo-American relations between 1945 and 1956. British policy-makers remained convinced that the United States recognized the special interests of the United Kingdom in the Middle East. They remained unaware of a growing independent American policy towards the Middle East, and had actually considered American Middle Eastern policies as malleable to their own, such as in the case of the 1954 Suez Canal Treaty and the Baghdad Pact. The golden rule they had derived was that the United States would show hesitation, but would eventually follow the British lead. This pattern is repeated in the Suez crisis. High hopes of American support were grounded in the British conviction that the United States would recognize in Egypt's policies a threat to vital British interests in the area. When full American support did not come forward forthwith, British policy-makers adopted one of their familiar tactics to cajole the Americans to align with them. During the first weeks of the crisis until the end of the London Conference, they tried to exaggerate their case in order to make clear to the Americans that they meant serious business. They were convinced that the Americans needed a lead as usual in Middle Eastern affairs. The discussions around the proposal of a users' association display the same pattern. British policy-makers agreed to go along with Dulles's vague idea, because they were confident that they could persuade the United States Government into using the payment of shipping dues to the new association as a tool of leverage over Nasser. As a matter of fact, they used their proven post-war method of persuasion by incessantly imprinting on the Eisenhower Administration that Nasser was an instrument in the hands of Communism and a dictator comparable to Hitler or Mussolini. Eden's letters to the American President emphasized this aspect from the outset until the end of the crisis. When these policies did not bring immediate results, British policy-makers engaged in various different types of rationalization in order to maintain their cognitive balance. In order to obtain reassurance that American support was forthcoming, they had to explain away any signs of American opposition to the use of force.

## Notes

[1]   Collective efforts to rationalize American criticism were paramount throughout the Suez crisis (see pp. 146-53). Nevertheless, these were not counted as a symptom of Groupthink, because properly speaking they are part of the dependent variable, i.e., failure to assess correctly incoming information.
[2]   Six ministers had served in World War One (Eden, Macmillan, Lloyd George, Monckton, Salisbury, Stuart); four in World War Two (Lloyd, Sandys, MacLeod, Buchan-Hepburn) (Thomas, 1986).
[3]   Shuckburgh (1986), diary entry 28 January 1956, p. 327.
[4]   Clark, 'Whitehall diary', entry 29 July 1956, p. 102.
[5]   Monckton in a conversation with Clark over lunch, *ibid.*, entry 14 August 1956, p. 113.

6   Clark, 'Whitehall diary', entry 6 September 1955, p. 70.

7   Of course, Eden's threat to resign in a meeting of his most senior colleagues after a suspension of the cabinet meeting on 4 November clearly testifies to directive leadership.

8   To be correct, a third rationalization occurred, but had much less impact. American opposition to referring the matter to the United Nations or the International Court of Justice was explained by presumed American fears of the repercussions any such move would have on the international legal position of the Panama Canal. If an international body reconfirmed the Suez Canal to be Egyptian territory, Panama might claim that the territory of the international waterway of the Panama Canal belonged to Panama. Once the British and French Governments had decided on 23 September to refer the matter to the Security Council on, the parallel was no longer taken into consideration.

9   Richard Neustadt has explored this phenomenon, but limits his analysis to the elections argument (Neustadt, 1970, pp. 66-71).

10  FO 800/740.

11  FO 800/740, Macmillan to Eden, Telegram 2004, 25 September 1956.

12  FO 800/740, Macmillan to Eden, Telegram 2003, 25 September 1956.

13  FO 800/740, Makins to Lloyd, Telegram 1849, 9 September 1956.

14  FO 800/740, Makins to Lloyd, Telegram 1942, 17 September 1956.

15  PREM 11/1100, Jebb (British Ambassador to France) to Foreign Office, Telegram 295, 9 September 1956.

16  FO 800/740, Eden to Lloyd, Telegram 1063, 6 October 1956.

17  FO 800/741, Eden to Lloyd, Telegram 1078, 8 October 1956.

18  This can be concluded from Lloyd's minute to himself in which he summarizes the talks of 23 October, FO 800/725.

19  Quotations from CAB 128/30, CM(56)74, 25 October 1956.

20  Macmillan thought that 'read carefully, the last phrase could be interpreted to refer only to present undertakings' (1971, pp. 116-17).

21  PREM 11/1100, Eisenhower to Eden, 3 September 1956.

22  PREM 11/1100, Washington Embassy to Foreign Office, Telegram 1839, 8 September 1956.

23  Horne (1988, pp. 433-4). Horne quotes William Clark as his source and traces the conversation back to 24/25 October. Lloyd must have told Clark because Clark's diary indicates that Clark came back from a fortnight's leave on 29 October.

24  Most messages are printed in full length in Carlton (1986, pp. 125-9).

25  PREM 11/1100, Eden to Eisenhower, Telegram 491/56, 30 October 1956.

26  PREM 11/1100, Eisenhower to Eden, Telegram 487/56, 30 October 1956.

27  'Memo of Conversation: Eden Talks', p. 9, *Declassified Documents*, -78, Reference 283B, quoted in Aronson (1986, pp. 169-70).

28  PREM 11/1100, Eden to Eisenhower, Telegram 492/56, 31 October 1956.

29  Henri Azeau is one of the few authors referring to this episode. He stresses that Eisenhower's letter of 30 October 1956 did *not* ask the British not to pursue the military line. According to Azeau, Ike played 'bon prince', and tacitly accepted the announced occupation of Port Said. 'La tolérance est claire, précise. Et limitée' (Azeau, 1964, pp. 266, 303-4).

30  PREM 11/1100, Eisenhower to Eden, Telegram 494/56, 31 October 1956.

31  PREM 11/1100, Eden to Eisenhower, draft, 31 October 1956.

32  As a matter of fact, various officials at the Foreign Office shared these interpretations. On 1 November Evelyn Shuckburgh walked over to the Foreign Office 'to find out what there was to be said on the other side'. Dean told him that 'the world at large is

screaming blue murder but (a) *Eisenhower's statement was reasonably mild* and (b) Australia and New Zealand support us' (Shuckburgh, 1986, pp. 363-4, emphasis added).

# Chapter 7

# Conclusions

## Introduction

British decision-making during the Suez crisis was the product of deliberations within three small groups with overlapping membership headed by a persistent leader: the full Cabinet, the Egypt Committee and an inner circle of Senior Ministers. Each group was constrained by domestic politics and, especially, the context of planning by the military organization. This chapter puts this main conclusion in perspective by re-examining the theoretical expectations that were formulated in chapter 2. Next, an assessment will be made of the implications of this study for past and future analyses of Suez. This will be followed by the resolution of theoretical puzzle presented in chapter 1 and its ramifications for the (sub)disciplines of International Relations and Foreign Policy Analysis. After a discussion of several methodological aspects of this study the chapter concludes with a comparison between Suez and the war against Iraq in 2003.

## Re-Examining the Theoretical Expectations

### Centralization of Decision-Making

The advent of a foreign policy crisis, as perceived by the policy-makers involved, was expected to lead to centralization of decision-making. This study has demonstrated that during the period that was identified as the crisis phase, British decision-making was indeed centralized into the hands of a small number of key decision-makers. Between Egypt's nationalization of the Suez Canal Company on 26 July and the British decision to halt military operations on 6 November the Cabinet, the Egypt Committee or the inner circle effectively made the major decisions. Centralization even was a formal policy through the Cabinet's decision on 27 July to install the Egypt Committee. Even the co-ordination of all administrative implementations of decisions taken was formally centralized by awaking the dormant Defence (Transition) Committee.[1] This committee included the highest civil servants of the departments involved and operated on a need-to-know basis. It was headed by one of the few civil servants who remained fully informed throughout the crisis, Secretary to the Cabinet, Sir Norman Brook. The formal installation of the Egypt Committee and the re-activation of the Defence (Transition) Committee reinforced the policy-makers' isolation from regular departmental organizational expertise (cf. Kyle, 2000).

The exact nature of centralization of British decision-making during the Suez crisis has to be qualified, however. Chapter 5 demonstrated that the decision unit or the locus of decision varied considerably throughout the crisis. While one decision was effectively taken exclusively by the inner circle (Decision 4), others were made by the Egypt Committee (Decisions 1, 2, and 3) or the Cabinet (Decisions 5 and 6) but always heavily affected, sometimes even prepared, by meetings of the inner circle. Arguably, the reduced weight of the Egypt Committee was related to the gradual expansion of the numbers of participants making it sometimes even comparable to Cabinet meetings. Based on their participation at the Egypt Committee and at informal meetings, it seems safe to conclude that no decision could be made without the consent of the Prime Minister and a small group of Senior Ministers, including Butler, Home, Kilmuir, Macmillan, Monckton, Salisbury, and Lloyd.[2]

## *The Impact of Centralization Combined with Stress*

Centralization is likely to increase the weight of small groups and their leaders in decision-making. If a foreign policy crisis in addition increases levels of emotional stress, small group members are more likely to fall prey to Groupthink. If the premise is accepted that so-called decisional conflicts are likely to generate stress, then it is plausible to assume that British decision-makers suffered from increased levels of emotional stress between 26 July and 6 November 1956. As a matter of fact, British policy-makers displayed symptoms of Groupthink at least 29 times during that period.[3] On the other hand, the measurement of stress does not allow for the possibility that stress levels may have widely varied during the crisis. After all, policy-makers did go on holiday during the summer! An indication might be the small number of Groupthink-symptoms surrounding the decision to refer the matter to the Security Council. At the same time, the latter may be an indicator that Groupthink can be avoided despite high levels of emotional stress. Clearly, it remains uncertain whether a choice for decisional conflicts has solved in a satisfactory way the methodological problem of finding plausible indicators of stress.

## *Leadership*

It was expected that centralization of decision-making would increase the weight of leadership. It was demonstrated that four out of six decisions were affected by the way Prime Minister Eden handled the meetings of the Cabinet and the Egypt Committee. Cognitive consistency theory predicted that during crises and under stress, an individual is likely to rely on the most central beliefs of his worldview. As a matter of fact Eden's master belief regarding the appropriate way to conduct international affairs was important in defining the problem when the cabinet first met after Egypt's nationalization of the Canal. It was crucial in explaining the Cabinet approval of the Challe-plan: Eden had become severely disappointed by the policies of American Secretary of State John Foster Dulles who, in terms of Eden's worldview, had crossed the line between trustworthy and untrustworthy with his anti-colonialist speech on S.C.U.A. on 2 October. This study reinforces the recent findings in Groupthink-research that directive leadership (combined with the anticipatory compliance of the members of the group) is a major explanation of the occurrence of Groupthink. It also demonstrates that it can be useful to employ a leader's worldview in order to explain part of the contents of a small group's decisions.

## Political Institutions

Political institutions, both formal and informal, matter. Decision-making in the Cabinet, Egypt Committee, and the inner circles was constrained by domestic politics. Interestingly, during their meetings domestic public opinion hardly surfaces as a point of consideration. The same is true of the position of the Opposition in the House of Commons. British policy-makers were sensitive to maintaining unity within the Conservative Party. At two instances an apparent division among Tory MPs affected the substance of decision-making. The presentation of the users' association at the beginning of September helped to keep Tory doves on board without alienating Tory hawks. On 2 November insistence on Anglo-French participation in a U.N.O.-led intervention force served the same purpose. This study thus confirms the expectation that in the British political system backbenchers constitute the most important domestic audience.

Informal rules of the political system, however, have been a much more consequential factor than Tory backbenchers. In this study it has become clear that the inner circle who met before Cabinet or Egypt Committee meetings consisted of a small number of Senior Ministers. No decision could be taken without consensus among this selected group of politicians. In that sense Suez was much more a small group's war than Eden's war. Clearly, had Eden been opposed to the use of force, the situation would have been very different. Yet, the informal hierarchy between Senior Ministers and Junior Ministers in the Cabinet at the very least reinforced the Prime Minister's position, because consensus among Senior Ministers makes it very difficult for others in the Cabinet (or Egypt Committee) to be an effective critic. This informal hierarchy thus increased the risk that Groupthink would occur at the Cabinet level. However, Groupthink would then be rooted less in social psychology than in political dependencies.

## The Organizational Context

Centralization of decision-making was expected to reduce the impact of departmental organizations. It was suggested that departmental organizations would still be able to affect decision-making the more they possess expertise knowledge that policy-makers lack and cannot be obtained elsewhere. Under such circumstances departmental organizations are expected to affect the range of alternative options as well as the timing of decision-making and its subsequent implementation. On the whole, British decision-makers took their decisions in isolation from their civil servants. As suggested above, this was reinforced by the re-activation of the Defence (Transition) Committee. Nevertheless, at least three times their decisions were heavily constrained by military planning. The impossibility to mobilize and transport sufficient military personnel instantly ruled out an immediate forceful reaction to Egypt's nationalization of the Suez Canal Company. Similarly, the changes in operational plans induced by military (and partly political) considerations occurred at unfortunate moments from the British point of view. When the Chiefs of Staff recommend Port Said instead of Alexandria as the target of the assault, British policy-makers had wanted to have the possibility to react forcefully to Egypt's expected flat rejection of the 18 Powers' proposals in early September. About a month later the military caught their political superiors again by surprise when they issued the Winter-plan which implied a relaxation of the state of readiness of the forces and which risked a postponement of military intervention until the spring of 1957. In both instances shrewd solutions had to be found in order to maintain the momentum. In September Dulles's users' association seemed a welcome means to put pressure on Egypt. In October Challe's plan to intervene in the case of a war between Egypt and Israel saved the day.

All in all, therefore, British decision-makers gradually were entrapped in a plan that seemed to make them have their cake and eat it. The Challe-plan offered the possibility to occupy the Suez Canal without alienating international public opinion too much, especially the United States. With a little luck, it would produce the downfall of Nasser. However, the long path to entrapment implied that British policy-makers had to explain away every sign that the United States might not support the use of force or even actively oppose it. This constitutes the first piece of the empirical puzzle of Suez. Chapter 6 has demonstrated to what lengths British decision-makers went in their efforts to rationalize signs of American resistance. Two major mechanisms could be observed. First, their focus on the weight of the impending presidential elections in the United States. Second, the specific manners in which they tailored messages from Dulles and Eisenhower to their own convictions. The way British policy-makers approached the United States comes as no surprise, however. The British political elite shared the same image of Anglo-American relations. This centred around the belief that the United States considered Great Britain to be the dominant power in the Middle East and that American policy-makers would eventually follow a British lead in Middle East policy as long as Great Britain persisted in its endeavours. In this sense, the contents of deliberations in all three small groups that were distinguished (Cabinet, Egypt Committee, and inner circle) can be partly accounted for by this common image. This was especially true for the small group of decision-makers that communicated with the United States during the crisis (Eden, Lloyd, Macmillan, and Salisbury).

## Past and Future Studies of Suez

*Past Studies*

In some respects the findings of this study differ from previous analyses of British decision-making during the Suez crisis. First, its main claim that British decision-making has been the product of three small groups and a persistent leader qualifies those studies that emphasize the predominance of the British Prime Minister. There can be no doubt that Anthony Eden's impact has been significant through his leadership style and worldview. At the same time, as any leader, he could not simply impose his will, but was constrained by the need for consensus among his immediate followers, the Senior Ministers.

Second, this study argues that domestic politics during the Suez crisis had relatively little impact on British decision-making. Its effect was primarily felt through the formal and informal institutions at the level of the House of Commons and the Cabinet rather than through public opinion in the wider sense. Although most studies of Suez point to the crucial role of backbenchers in maintaining Parliamentary support for the Government, they rarely point to the informal hierarchy between Senior Ministers and Junior Ministers which seems to have increased the chances that Groupthink would occur.

Third, this study found little support for the popular claim (e.g., Thomas, 1986) that British policy-makers suffered from myopia because they approached the Suez crisis as if Nasser were comparable to Hitler and Egypt's nationalization of the Suez Canal Company were identical to Germany's re-occupation of the Rhineland in 1936. Indeed, such historical analogies surface regularly among British policy-makers. The evidence presented in Chapter 5, however, suggests that these parallels were used to convince the United States of the British point of view or to mobilize Tory support for the Government's policies. Only seldom was there evidence that British policy-makers were themselves defining the situation in terms of these parallels. It is important to keep in mind that historical analogies can be used as an analytical as well as mobilizing device (Shimko, 1995). The available evidence points into the direction of the latter rather than the former.

*Future Studies*

This study resolved one empirical puzzle, but has created another: decision-making within the military. Three times political decision-making has been considerably affected by military planning. The military's considerations affected both the timing and the contents of political decision-making. Two fundamental changes in operational plans prevented British policy-makers from having the possibility to use force. The military's decision to develop an operational plan directed at Port Said rather than Alexandria implied that the political objective of toppling Nasser was much more difficult to attain. It would be interesting if future studies of Suez focused on an explanation of military decision-making. This study suggests at least two possible inroads. On the one hand military planning seems to have been guided, at least in part, by standard operation procedures. The lack of speed in military preparations is accounted for by a tradition of meticulously planning large-scale operations comparable to those against Germany during World War Two. Similarly, hesitation as to the use of airborne troops seems rooted in lessons drawn from the disaster of Operation Market Garden in 1944. On the other hand, such a study could focus on intra-organizational conflict regarding the political objectives of British policies and its impact on military planning. Elements of such a conflict transpire in the differences between Mountbatten (against the use of force) and Templer (strongly in favour) (cf. Gorst, 2000; Grove and Rohan, 2000). The principal problem of investigation should be the question to what extent the military contributed in postponing the use of force because they wanted to or as a consequence of the standard ways in which they plan and prepare.

## Resolving the Theoretical Puzzle of Suez

### The Theoretical Puzzle

The theoretical puzzle of Suez refers to the relative weight of explanatory factors in accounting for British foreign policy during the Suez crisis (cf. Chapter 1). Systemic theories are able to explain the outcome, but are incapable of explaining the British decision to resort to the use of force knowing that full American support was highly unlikely. Systemic theories agree that states misperceive and miscalculate. Indeed, the anarchical nature of the international political system implies that uncertainty is one of its permanent features. However, systemic theories do not want to account for misperceptions and miscalculations. This requires a theory of foreign policy (Waltz, 1979).

This study demonstrates that in the advent of a foreign policy crisis misperception and miscalculation are likely to occur at the level of key decision-makers, because centralization of decision-making will enlarge their grip on policy-making. Groupthink and directive leadership are likely to steer their decision-making and make them more prone to misperception and miscalculation. The explanation of the specific contents of their misperceptions and miscalculations, however, requires insight in the images shared by most key decision-makers as well as in the specific worldview of their leader. Moreover, these policy-makers operate in an organizational context that will affect the timing and substance of their policies, the more they are dependent on these organizations for expert knowledge and services. In addition, individual political calculations and the formal and informal rules of the political system in which they operate also guide these policy-makers. A combination of these factors is needed in order to account for British decision-making during the Suez crisis.

### Implications for Foreign Policy Analysis

The findings of this study have several implications for the subdiscipline of Foreign Policy Analysis. First, it has been demonstrated that cognitive beliefs matter, not only as a property of an individual, but also as the images of a wider group of policy-makers. This implies that studies of cognitive belief systems of individuals who can be expected to have a significant impact on a state's foreign policy should be geared more often to assessing that expected impact. Furthermore, studies directed at small group dynamics should not only focus on their consequences for the decision-making *process*, but also on its outcome. Second, this study has shown that political institutions matter. The specific features of political systems, both formal and informal, have a clear impact on decision-making, both in substance and in process. Recent research on foreign policy has taken up this issue. Studies of how American Presidents structure their advisory process suggest that variation in advisory systems may produce differences in foreign policy (Haney, 1997; Preston, 2001). Third, with respect to Groupthink-research this book confirms the view that structural faults in the organization are likely to be the main cause of Groupthink. Eden's leadership style in combination with the informal hierarchy between Senior and Junior Ministers contributed to the small groups' falling prey to Groupthink. Furthermore, it appeared that premature consensus in the inner circle and Egypt Committee was not simply the product of cohesion but in part also of individual political calculations. The latter was the case for Butler, who probably did not want to ruin his chances to become Eden's successor, and possibly Lloyd, whose political career depended on Eden. This study thus strengthens 't Hart's (1990/1994) claim that the functional interdependence of actors within political and administrative systems may carry more weight than Janis's original notion of group cohesion. Given the differences between British Prime Ministers in their use of their formal position,[4] a further analysis of the relationship between prime ministerial leadership styles and institutional constraints is needed (e.g., Kaarbo, 1997). This may help clarify its impact on small group behaviour in prime ministerial (and parliamentary) political systems.

**Methodological Issues**

This study also gives rise to two methodological considerations. First, it testifies to the theoretical and methodological problem in Groupthink-research that it is not self-evident what constitutes the small group. In the case of Suez it seemed plausible at face value to study the Egypt Committee. Yet, the application of the method of process tracing, which implied a reconstruction of the decision-making process (Appendix 2), made it clear that what constituted the relevant small group differed from time to time.

Second, this study has applied the method of structured-focused comparison. It structured British decision-making by distinguishing between six so-called decisional conflicts, which followed on from each other chronologically. It thus became possible to identify the slow path to entrapment followed by British policy-makers. Its focus on four explanatory factors made it possible to identify a shift in decision units or locus of decision and to determine the extent to which each decisional conflict was affected by these factors. Moreover, its formulation of the puzzle of Suez provided a clear sharpening of its research subject. This will enable other scholars in future to accumulate knowledge on the basis of comparative case studies (cf. Kaarbo and Beasley, 1999).

## Suez and the 2003 War Against Iraq: Parallels and Differences

In the early hours of 20 March 2003, a coalition of several countries, led by the United States, started a war against Iraq. Great Britain supplied the second largest military force. To what extent could the present study contribute to analyzing the war against Iraq? The British press did not fail to draw parallels to the Suez crisis. Like in 1956, Great Britain was part of a hasty coalition eager to topple a dictator in the Middle East. It claimed not to fight the people of a Middle Eastern country, but its dictator, who had persistently shown disrespect for international rules and whose policies constituted a major threat. In addition, Great Britain seemed prepared to go to war against large segments of (international) public opinion. Furthermore, the coalition that Great Britain joined gave many the impression that international law could be tailored to the coalition's own needs. Yet, as a Foreign Official pointed out, despite the face value parallels, this time France, unlike the United States in 1956, would be unable to 'to pull the plug on us' (quoted in *The Economist*, 22 March 2003, p. 36). As a matter of fact, at the time of writing (Spring 2003) it seemed unlikely that the British Government decided to go to war whereas a proper assessment of the available information would have made a different choice more likely.[5] The puzzle of Suez thus differs from the puzzle of Iraq in a significant way.

At the same time, several interesting parallels occur in the decision-making processes leading to the decision to intervene militarily in both crises.[6] First of all, late in 2002 the Anglo-American coalition seemed confident that the inspections by UNMOVIC led by Hans Blix would produce a clear-cut legitimisation for military intervention. Yet Iraq's equivocal reactions, such as slowly dismantling missiles with a reach beyond the permitted range of 150 kilometres, split the original consensus within the Security Council. This invokes the frustration of France and Great Britain in 1956 at Nasser's equivocal responses to the Menzies mission. Interestingly, the Iraqi crisis points to the possible unanticipated room for manoeuvre for an international civil servant such as Blix, whose assessments were an important factor in allowing members of the Security Council to take a different position from the United States and Great Britain. Secondly, policy-makers in Great Britain and the United States seemed to have considered it a real possibility that Iraq would have created a *casus belli* by disrespecting the UNMOVIC mission, especially by forbidding its members to enter certain inspection sites. Likewise, in 1956 France and Great Britain expected Egypt to create a *casus belli* by refusing a British warship passage through the Suez Canal or by mismanaging traffic through the Canal after the withdrawal of the pilots. Thirdly, the Anglo-American coalition seemed to count on a swift downfall of the regime of Saddam Hussein after the start of the campaign, because of its presumably weak popular support. The unexpectedly tough resistance of the Iraqi forces and the lukewarm reception of the coalition troops in the first weeks proved this optimism wrong. Similarly, in 1956 Anglo-French policymakers expected the immediate collapse of Nasser's government even without their troops marching towards Cairo. If correct, these three parallels testify to important collective rationalizations by the major decision-makers. The tools of analysis employed in this book will serve a future detailed analysis of their occurrence in, and impact on, 21st Century British foreign policy.

## Notes

[1] Appendix 2 indicates that the Defence (Transition) Committee met 17 times during the crisis phase. No meetings were held between 28 August and 7 September and between 18 September and 30 October. The former period indicates that the military were ready to launch *Musketeer*. The latter points to their readiness for *Musketeer Revise*.

[2] Although Lloyd probably did not qualify as a 'true' Senior Minister because of his overpromotion.

[3] Quite a few more could have been observed if the analysis had not been confined to the empirical puzzle of Suez formulated in Chapter 1. British policy-makers displayed Groupthink-symptoms also regarding their detailed deliberations regarding the withdrawal of the pilots from the Canal and their discussions regarding the justifiability of the Challe-plan under international law (Verbeek, 1992, pp. 341-53).

[4] For instance, Clement Attlee, James Callaghan, and Harold Wilson in his second Government did not develop directive leadership styles (Rose, 2001).

[5] Although rumours that intelligence reports on Iraq's weapons of mass destruction may have been doctored could indicate the British Cabinet did not meet all procedural criteria of high quality decision-making.

[6] The postponed resignation of the Minister for International Development, Clare Short, in May 2003, and its effect on Labour support for Blair's policy towards Iraq, provides an interesting parallel to Walter Monckton's postponed resignation from Eden's Cabinet (cf. pp. 118, 140).

# Appendix 1

# Who is Who?

| | |
|---|---|
| Aldrich, Winthrop | United States Ambassador London |
| Ben Gurion, David | Prime Minister of Israel |
| Birch, Nigel | Secretary of State for Air |
| Bourgès-Manoury, Maurice | Minister of Defence of France |
| Boyle, Sir Edward | Permanent Secretary to the Treasury |
| Brook, Sir Norman | Secretary to the Cabinet |
| Butler, R.A. ('Rab') | Lord Privy Seal, Leader of the House of Commons |
| Caccia, Sir Harold | Deputy Under-Secretary of State at the Foreign Office |
| Challe, Maurice | Deputy to the French Chief of General Staff |
| Chauvel, Jean | French Ambassador London |
| Clark, William D. | Press Secretary to Eden |
| Dean, Sir Patrick | Chairman of Joint Intelligence Committee |
| Dixon, Sir Pierson | British Permanent Representative to the United Nations |
| Dulles, John Foster | United States Secretary of State |
| Eden, Sir Anthony | Prime Minister of Great Britain |
| Eisenhower, Dwight D. | President of the United States |
| Ely, Paul | French Chief of Staff |
| Fitzmaurice, Sir Gerald | Foreign Office legal adviser |
| Gaitskell, Hugh | Leader of the Opposition |
| Gazier, Albert | French Minister for Social Affairs |
| Glubb, Sir John | Chief of Staff Arab Legion |
| Head, Anthony | Secretary of State for War; Minister of Defence (from 18 October 1956) |
| Heath, Edward | Government Chief Whip |
| Home, Lord (Alec Douglas-Home) | Commonwealth Secretary |
| Keightley, Sir Charles | Anglo-French Commander in Chief |
| Kilmuir, Viscount | Lord Chancellor |
| Kirkpatrick, Sir Ivone | Permanent Secretary to the Foreign Office |
| Lloyd, John Selwyn | Foreign Secretary |
| Macleod, Iain | Minister of Labour |
| Macmillan, Harold | Chancellor of the Exchequer |

| | |
|---|---|
| Makins, Sir Roger | British Ambassador Washington |
| Menzies, Sir Robert | Prime Minister of Australia |
| Mollet, Guy | Prime Minister of France |
| Monckton, Sir Walter | Minister of Defence; Paymaster-General (from 18 October 1956) |
| Mountbatten of Burma, Earl | First Sea Lord |
| Murphy, Robert | US Deputy Under-Secretary of State |
| Nasser, Gamal Abdul | Prime Minister of Egypt |
| Nutting, Anthony | Minister of State at the Foreign Office |
| Pineau, Christian | French Foreign Minister |
| Salisbury, Marquess of | Lord President of the Council |
| Sandys, Duncan | Minister of Housing and Local Government |
| Shuckburgh, Sir Evelyn | Assistant Under-Secretary at the Foreign Office |
| Templer, Sir Gerald | Chief of the Imperial General Staff |
| Thorneycroft, Peter | President of the Board of Trade |
| Watkinson, Herald | Minister of Transport |

# Appendix 2

# Who Met Whom at Whitehall?

## Introduction

This book's main claim holds that British decision-making during the Suez crisis was dominated by a small group of so-called Senior Ministers who participated in various small group settings, informal as well as formal ones, such as the Cabinet and the Egypt Committee. This appendix gives a chronological overview of all meetings of two or more policymakers that could be deduced from the so-called hard and soft primary sources. The enumeration will allow the reader to check the calculations regarding the number of formal and informal meetings of policymakers in Great Britain during the crisis.

## Decision 1

| | | |
|---|---|---|
| 26 July | 10.30 p.m.-4 a.m. | Informal meeting (Eden, Salisbury, Home, Lloyd, Kilmuir, Caccia, Chauvel, Piquot, Foster, Mountbatten, Templer) |
| 27 July | before 11 a.m. | Eden telephones Macmillan |
| | 11 a.m. | House of Commons statement |
| | 11.10 a.m. | Cabinet (Cab) |
| | 5 p.m. | Defence (Transition) Committee (DTC) |
| | 6.30 p.m. | Eden and Lloyd meet Commonwealth ministers |
| | 7 p.m. | Egypt Committee (EC) |
| 28 July | 10.30 a.m.-lunch | EC |
| 30 July | 10.30 a.m. | EC |
| | lunch | Lunch Eden, Lloyd, Macmillan, Pineau, Murphy |
| | 17.45 p.m. | EC |
| | dinner | Dinner Murphy, Macmillan, Foster, Lord Alexander |
| 31 July | 9.45 a.m | Meeting Eden, Watkinson, Head, Brook, CIGS, QMG |
| | 'morning' | Lloyd meets the 1922 Committee of Backbenchers of Conservative Party |

|         | 'lunch'      | Lunch with Eden, Murphy, Lloyd, Salisbury, Macmillan, 'and three Americans' |
|---------|--------------|---------------------------|
|         | 3.30 p.m.    | EC                        |
|         | 5.30 p.m.    | DTC                       |
|         | 10.00 p.m.   | EC                        |
| 1 Aug   | 'morning'    | Home meets Commonwealth ministers |
|         | 12 noon      | EC                        |
|         | 'afternoon'  | Macmillan, Dulles, Murphy, Aldrich |
|         | 7.20 p.m.    | Cabinet                   |

## Decision 2

| 2 Aug   | 10 a.m.      | Cabinet                   |
|---------|--------------|---------------------------|
|         | ?            | Eden meets Gaitskell      |
|         | 6 p.m.       | EC                        |
| 3 Aug   | 10 a.m.      | Defence (Transition) Committee |
|         | 11 a.m.      | Cabinet                   |
|         | noon         | EC                        |
|         | x            | Exchange of letters between Eden and Gaitskell |
| 5 Aug   |              | Macmillan dines with Churchill |
| 6 Aug   |              | Churchill meets Eden at Chequers |
| 7 Aug   | noon         | D(T)C                     |
|         | 3 p.m.       | Ministerial meeting       |
|         | 3.15 p.m.    | EC                        |
| 9 Aug   | 11.15 a.m.   | EC                        |
|         | 10.00 p.m.   | EC                        |
| 10 Aug  | 10.30 a.m.   | EC                        |
|         | 3.30 p.m.    | D(T)C                     |
| 11 Aug  | ???          | Staff Conference: Chiefs of Staff, Anthony Head, Eden, Monckton |
| 14 Aug  | 10.00 a.m.   | D(T)C                     |
|         | 10.45 a.m.   | Lloyd, Eden, and Salisbury meet Labour delegation |
|         | 5.15 p.m.    | EC                        |
| 16 Aug  | 11.45 a.m.   | EC                        |
| 17 Aug  | 10.00 a.m.   | D(T)C                     |
|         | 11.00 a.m.   | EC                        |
| 19 Aug  | ???          | Macmillan and Salisbury meet Aldrich |
| 20 Aug  | 11.30 a.m.   | EC                        |
| 21 Aug  | 10.00 a.m.   | D(T)C                     |
|         | 11.15 a.m.   | Ministerial meeting       |
|         | noon         | Cabinet                   |
| 22 Aug  | 2.30 a.m.    | Eden, Dulles, and Lloyd meet Menzies |

**Decision 3**

| | | |
|---|---|---|
| 22 Aug | 11.00 a.m. | Tripartite consultations: Dulles, Lloyd, Pineau |
| | 11.30 a.m. | EC |
| 23 Aug | morning | London Conference ends |
| | 11.00 a.m. | Tripartite consultations |
| | 11.30 a.m. | EC |
| | 12.15 p.m. | Cabinet |
| | 3.00 p.m. | Informal meeting of Eden, Salisbury, Macmillan, Butler, Head, Heath |
| 24 Aug | 10.00 a.m. | D(T)C |
| | noon | EC |
| | ??? | Eden and Lloyd (together with Beeley from the Foreign Office) meet Dulles |
| | ??? | Macmillan meets Dulles |
| 26 Aug | ??? | Macmillan meets Monckton |
| 27 Aug | 6.00 p.m. | EC |
| 28 Aug | 10.00 a.m. | D(T)C |
| | 11.00 a.m. | Cabinet |
| | 3.30 p.m. | EC |
| 29 Aug | 3.30 p.m. | Eden and Lloyd meet at 10 Downing St. |
| | evening | Eden telephones Macmillan |
| 4 Sep | 1.00 p.m. | Lloyd lunches with Macmillan |
| | 6.00 p.m. | EC |
| 5 Sep | afternoon | Kirkpatrick meets Eden |
| 6 Sep | 11.00 a.m. | Cabinet |
| 7 Sep | morning | Eden and Monckton meet Chiefs of Staff |
| | 10.00 a.m. | D(T)C |
| | 'later' | Keightley meets Eden |
| | 2.45 p.m. | EC |
| | 6.15 p.m. | Eden and Lloyd meet at 10 Downing St. |
| 10 Sep | 12.30 p.m. | Lloyd meets Macmillan |
| | 1.15 p.m. | Lloyd lunches with Eden |
| | 3.00 p.m. | EC |
| | 6.15 p.m. | Lloyd and Eden meet Mollet and Pineau at 10 Downing St. |
| | 8.15 p.m. | Dinner at 10 Downing St. Eden, Lloyd, Mollet, Pineau, and Menzies |
| 11 Sep | 10.00 a.m. | D(T)C |
| | 3.00 p.m. | Cabinet |

**Decision 4**

| 11 Sep | after Cabinet | Informal meeting of Salisbury, Kilmuir, Butler, and Macmillan |
| 12 Sep | 10.45 a.m. | Egypt Committee |
|        | afterwards | House of Commons debate |
| 13 Sep | 2.30 p.m. | House of Commons: vote of confidence |
|        | 6.00 p.m. | Informal meeting of at least Eden, Macmillan, and Butler, Salisbury, and Kilmuir |
| 14 Sep | 10.00 a.m. | D(T)C |
|        | 11.00 a.m. | Cabinet |
|        | 4.15 p.m. | EC |
| 15 Sep | ??? | Eden phones Macmillan |
| 16 Sep | ??? | Eden phones Macmillan |
| 17 Sep | 5 p.m. | EC |
|        | 9 p.m. | Ministerial meeting at 10 Downing Street |
| 18 Sep | 10.00 a.m. | D(T)C |
|        | after dinner | Macmillan and Salisbury meet Dulles and Aldrich at the American Embassy |
| 19 Sep | morning | Staff conference, Chiefs of Staff, Monckton, Eden, Kirkpatrick |
|        | ??? | Opening S.C.U.A. Conference |
|        | 3.15 p.m. | EC |
|        | after EC | Macmillan meets Eden |
| 20 Sep | ??? | Eden meets William Clark to discuss Clark's paper on public opinion |
|        | dinner | Eden and Lloyd meet Dulles |
| 21 Sep | lunch | Eden and Lloyd |
|        | 2.30 p.m. | End of S.C.U.A. Conference |
|        | afterwards | Lloyd meets Dulles |
| 23 Sep | ??? | Dispute referred to the Security Council |

**Decision 5**

| 24 Sep | ??? | Letter Monckton to Eden announcing probable resignation |
| 25 Sep | morning | Eden meets the Chiefs of Staff |
|        | 11.00 a.m. | EC |
|        | 3.00 p.m. | Eden meets Lloyd |
| 26 Sep | ??? | Eden meets Lloyd |
|        | 10.30 a.m. | Cabinet |

| 27 Sep | | Monckton drafts resignation letter |
|---|---|---|
| 1 Oct | ??? | Admiral Barjot meets Dickson |
| | 12.15 p.m. | Meeting Eden, Monckton, and Dickson |
| | 2.30 p.m. | EC |
| 2 Oct | until lunch | Eden meets Macmillan |
| 3 Oct | ??? | Monckton resigns formally |
| | 10.45 a.m. | Cabinet |
| 8 Oct | 7.00 p.m. | EC |
| 9 Oct | 11.00 a.m. | Cabinet |
| 10 Oct | ??? | Informal meeting with Monckton |
| | noon | EC |
| 11 Oct | ??? | Staff conference Monckton, Head, Eden, and Kirkpatrick |
| | ??? | Meeting Eden, Monckton, and Watkinson |
| 13 Oct | | Conservative Party Conference at Llandudno |
| 14 Oct | ??? | Challe and Gazier meet Eden and Nutting at Chequers |
| 16 Oct | 11.15 a.m. | Lloyd meets Nutting |
| | 12.15 p.m. | Ministerial meeting with at least Kilmuir, Thorneycroft, Head, Monckton, Lloyd, Nutting, and Eden |
| | 4.00 p.m. | Eden and Lloyd take off for Paris |
| 17 Oct | ??? | Eden meets several ministers individually |
| | 2.30 p.m. | Eden and Lloyd at 10 Downing Street |
| | 4.00 p.m.[1] | Egypt Committee |
| 18 Oct | 11.30 a.m. | Cabinet |
| | ??? | Lloyd lunches with Monckton |
| 19 Oct | 11.30 a.m. | Lloyd and Eden at 10 Downing Street |
| | ??? | Lloyd lunches at Buckingham Palace |
| | 2.45 p.m. | Lloyd at 10 Downing Street |
| 21 Oct | ??? | Meeting at Chequers: Butler, Macmillan, Head, Kilmuir, Brook, Lloyd, Eden, Powell, and Keightley Afterwards Lloyd leaves for Paris |
| 22 Oct | | Secret Anglo-French-Israeli talks at Sèvres near Paris |
| 23 Oct | morning | Lloyd meets Nutting |
| | 10.00 a.m. | Meeting of Senior Ministers |
| | 11.00 a.m. | Cabinet |
| | 7.30 p.m. | Pineau arrives in London |
| | 8.30 p.m. | Pineau, Lloyd, and Eden (after dinner) at 1 Downing Street (Foreign Office) |
| 24 Oct | 10.00 a.m. | Lloyd meets Patrick Dean |

|         | 11.00 a.m.[2]  | Cabinet                                          |
|         | 4.00 p.m.      | Meeting in the Prime Minister's room             |
|         | 10.30 p.m.     | Dean and Logan return from Sèvres                |
|         | 11.00 p.m.     | Meeting of Senior Ministers at 10                |
|         |                | Downing Street, includes at least Eden,          |
|         |                | Butler, Macmillan, Head as well as               |
|         |                | Mountbatten                                      |
| 25 Oct  | 10.00 a.m.     | Cabinet                                          |
|         | 5.45 p.m.      | Meeting at 10 Downing Street                     |
|         | 6.15 p.m.      | Meeting at 10 Downing Street                     |
|         | 8.15 p.m.      | Lloyd (at dinner) called upon by Dean            |
|         |                | and Logan                                        |

**Decision 6**

| 26 Oct  | 10.30 a.m.     | Lloyd has meeting at 10 Downing                  |
|         |                | Street                                           |
|         | 6.45 p.m.      | Lloyd has meeting at 10 Downing                  |
|         |                | Street                                           |
| 29 Oct  | 2.30 p.m.      | Meeting at 10 Downing Street: at least           |
|         |                | Lloyd, Eden, Keightley, Dickson,                 |
|         |                | Templer, and Mountbatten                         |
| 30 Oct  | 10.15 a.m.     | Cabinet                                          |
|         | afterwards     | Pineau and Mollet meet Lloyd and                 |
|         |                | Eden at 10 Downing Street                        |
|         | 3.30 p.m.      | D (T)C                                           |
|         | 10.00 p.m.     | Meeting at 10 Downing Street with at             |
|         |                | least Kilmuir and Eden present, as well          |
|         |                | as Lloyd; probably Macmillan                     |
| 31 Oct  | 9.45 a.m.      | D(T)C                                            |
|         | noon           | Lloyd meets Monckton                             |
|         | 12.30 p.m.     | Cabinet                                          |
| 1 Nov   | 9.45 a.m.      | D(T)C                                            |
|         | 10.00 a.m.     | Ministerial meeting in Lloyd's room at           |
|         |                | the House of Commons: Lloyd, Home,               |
|         |                | Lennox Boyd, Monckton, Kirkpatrick,              |
|         |                | Burke Trend,[3] Service ministers, and           |
|         |                | (can be deduced from notes) Head                 |
|         | 2.35 p.m.      | Egypt Committee                                  |
|         | 3.30 p.m.      | Censure motion House of Commons                  |
|         | 4.00 p.m.      | 'Suez meeting' (Kilmuir [1964: 275])             |
|         | 10.00 p.m.     | 3-line whip                                      |
|         | 10.45 p.m.     | EC (lasts until 1.30 a.m.)                       |
| 2 Nov   | 9.45 a.m.      | D(T)C                                            |
|         | 4.30 p.m.      | Cabinet                                          |

|         |            |                                                                                 |
|---------|------------|---------------------------------------------------------------------------------|
|         | 6.00 p.m.  | Pineau meets Lloyd                                                              |
|         | 9.30 p.m.  | Cabinet (lasts until 2 a.m.)                                                     |
| 3 Nov   | 2.00 p.m.  | EC (lasts 1 hour)                                                               |
|         | 10.30 p.m. | Meetings at 10 Downing Street, at least Kilmuir is present (lasts until 2.30 a.m.) |
| 4 Nov   | before     | Lloyd and Eden at 10 Downing Street                                             |
|         | 12.30 p.m. | EC (lasts until 1.30 p.m.)                                                      |
|         | 3.30 p.m.  | EC                                                                              |
|         | 6.30 p.m.  | Cabinet (lasts until 9.30 p.m.)                                                 |

## Notes

[1]   Lloyd's diary of engagements reads: Egypt Committee at 3 p.m., Defence Committee at 4 p.m.

[2]   CAB 128/30 says 10.00 a.m.

[3]   The future Baron Trend (Deputy Secretary to the Cabinet).

# Appendix 3

# The Impact of Sir Anthony Eden's Health

The available records suggest that Eden suffered from weak physical health at three instances during the crisis. A first moment occurred on Tuesday 21 August 1956, when Eden noted 'physical pain' in his diary (James, 1986, p. 523). Next day, however, his physician, Dr. Kling, declared him to be in good health: 'it was really all a matter of nerves'.[1] On the day of Eden's pains a small group of ministers thought it a good thing to take some provocative action against Egypt.[2] The third week of August was a critical week indeed, because the London conference was about to come to an end, and it was unclear what the British attitude should be if the Conference were to reach a conclusion that would not satisfy British demands. This is therefore a situation in which the point could be made that Eden's physical suffering may have influenced his stand at the Ministerial meeting at 11.15 a.m., just before the Cabinet meeting of 11.30, although it is unclear when his pains actually set in.

At the beginning of October 1956 Eden wrote to Lloyd that he had 'been struck down by a tiresome virus with a high temperature, [that he] hope[d] to be about again in a day or two', and let him know the next day that the temperature had turned normal again.[3] Actually, that very day, when visiting his hospitalized wife, Eden fell ill again and had to stay at the hospital. On 9 October 1956 Eden told Lloyd that the temperature had been 105 degrees Fahrenheit at its height.[4] This date of physical weakness cannot be connected to any crucial decision. It occurred after the crucial day that Dulles made his notorious anti-colonialist speech (2 October 1956), which was the definitive incident that persuaded the British to go it alone without consulting the Americans. Eden was back in good shape by 13 October 1956 when he met General Challe.

Another case of 105 degrees Fahrenheit occurred on 4 November 1956, when the United Nations General Assembly condemned the Anglo-French ultimatums to Egypt and Israel and when Israel seemed willing to agree to a cease-fire. The fever coincided, it seems with the vote at the U.N.O. and possible with the Cabinet meeting that day.[5] On the one hand during that Cabinet meeting Eden displayed no directive leadership and rather stimulated open discussion. On the other hand, when the Cabinet proved divided Eden allegedly suspended the meeting and threatened his senior colleagues with resignation (see chapter 5). Although a clear example of directive leadership this does not look like a foolish act of a physically and mentally broken man, but a normal, albeit extreme, move of a Prime Minister in danger of losing his majority among Senior Ministers. Moreover, the overall elation at the news that Israel had decided not to comply with a cease-fire suggests that the overwhelming majority of Cabinet believed in the pretext the Challe-plan offered.

This makes it unlikely that their decision to continue was imposition of a will of a madman.

Clearly, it remains difficult to establish a connection between Eden's physical health, emotional stability, and decision-making on the basis of the available primary sources. It seems, however, that the occasions at which such a relationship could have been possible do not prove a strong nexus. First of all, most crucial decisions were taken without such circumstances. Second, at no stage did an ill Eden take action on his own. On every occasion, his colleagues contributed to the decisions made.

## Notes

1    Clark, 'Whitehall diary', entry 22 August 1956, p. 117.
2    WO 32/16709 DUS(A)/BM/425, Key to Head, 21 August 1956.
3    FO 800/741, Eden to Lloyd (at UN), Telegram 1063, 6 October 1956; Telegram 1070, 7 October 1956.
4    FO 800/741, Eden to Lloyd (at UN), Telegram 1086, 9 October 1956.
5    Clark, 'Whitehall diary', entry 4/5 November 1956, p. 158.

# References

## Primary Sources

Public Record Office, Kew:

| | |
|---|---|
| AIR | Air Ministry |
| ADM | Admiralty |
| CAB | Cabinet Office |
| DEFE | Ministry of Defence |
| DO | Commonwealth Office |
| FO | Foreign Office |
| LCO | Lord Chancellor's Office |
| PREM | Prime Minister's Office |
| T | Treasury |
| WO | War Office |

Bodleian Library, Oxford:
Clark, W., 'Whitehall Diary'
Monckton Papers

Collected Governmental Documents:
*British Documents on Foreign Policy*
*Foreign Relations of the United States*

## Secondary Sources

Adamthwaite, A. (1988), 'Overstretched and Overstrung. Eden, the Foreign Office and the Making of Policy, 1951-1955', *International Affairs*, Vol. 64, pp. 241-59.

Adamthwaite, A. (1989), 'La France Pendant la Crise de Suez Vue Par la Grande Bretagne', *Relations Internationales*, Vol. 58, pp. 187-94.

Aldrich, W.W. (1967), 'The Suez Crisis. A Footnote to History', *Foreign Affairs*, Vol. 44, pp. 541-52.

Allison, G.T. (1971), *Essence of Decision: Explaining the Cuban Missile Crisis*, Little Brown, Boston.

Allison, G.T. and P. Zelikow (1999), *Essence of Decision: Explaining the Cuban Missile Crisis*, 2nd revised edition, Longman, London.

Anstey, C. (1984), 'The Projection of British Socialism: Foreign Office Publicity and American Opinion, 1945-50', *Journal of Contemporary History*, Vol. 19, pp. 417-51.

Aronson, G. (1986), *From Sideshow to Center Stage. US Policy Toward Egypt, 1946-1956*, Lynne Rienner, Boulder.

Astorino-Courtois, A. (2000), 'The Effects of Stakes and Threats on Foreign Policy Decision-Making', *Political Psychology*, Vol. 21, pp. 489-510.

Axelrod, R. (ed.) (1976), *The Structure of Decision. The Cognitive Maps of Political Elites*, Princeton University Press, Princeton.

Azar, E.E. (1972), 'Conflict Escalation and Conflict Reduction in an International Crisis: Suez, 1956', *Journal of Conflict Resolution*, Vol. 16, pp. 183-201.

Azeau, H. (1964), *Le Piège de Suez. 5 Novembre 1956*, Robert Laffont, Paris.

Bar-On, M. (1989), 'David Ben-Gurion and the Sèvres Collusion', in W.R. Louis and R. Owen (eds.), *Suez 1956. The Crisis and its Consequences*, Oxford University Press, Oxford, pp. 145-60.

Beaufre, A. (1969), *The Suez Expedition 1956*, Faber and Faber, London (1st. French edition, 1967).

Bettenhausen, K. and Murnighan, J.K., 'The Emergence of Norms in Competitive Decision-Making Groups', *Administrative Science Quarterly*, Vol. 30, pp. 350-72.

Billings, R.S. and Hermann, C.F. (1998), 'Problem Identification in Sequential Policy Decision Making', in D.A. Sylvan and J.F. Voss (eds.), *Problem Representation in Foreign Policy Decision Making*, Cambridge University Press, Cambridge, pp. 53-79.

Blondel, J. (1987), *Political Leadership. Towards a General Analysis*, SAGE, London.

Boulding, K.E. (1965), *The Image: Knowledge in Life and Society*, University of Michigan Press, Ann Arbor.

Bovens, M. and Hart, P. 't (1996), *Understanding Policy Fiascoes*, Transaction, New Brunswick.

Boyle, P.G. (1979), 'The British Foreign Office View of Soviet-American Relations, 1945-1946', *Diplomatic History*, Vol. 3, pp. 307-20.

Boyle, P.G. (1988), 'The "Special Relationship" with Washington', in J.W. Young (ed.), *The Foreign Policy of Churchill's Peacetime Administration 1951-1955*, Leicester University Press, pp. 29-54.

Brecher, M., Steinberg, B. and Stein, J.G. (1969), 'A Framework for Research on Foreign Policy Behavior', *Journal of Conflict Resolution*, Vol. 13, pp. 75-101.

Brecher, M. and Wilkenfeld, J. (2000), *A Study of Crisis*, University of Michigan Press, Ann Arbor.

Bromberger, S. and Bromberger, M. (1957), *Les Secrets de l'Expédition d'Egypte*, Les 4 Fils Aymon, Paris.

Burnstein, E. and Berbaum, M.L. (1983), 'Stages in /Group Decision Making: The Decomposition of Historical Narratives', *Political Psychology*, Vol. 4, pp. 531-61.

Butler, Lord (1975), interviewed by N. Hunt, 'Reflections on Cabinet Government', in V. Herman and J.A. Alt (eds.), *Cabinet Studies: A Reader*, Macmillan, London, pp. 193-209.

Butler, R.A. (1979), *The Art of the Possible. The Memoirs of Lord Butler K.G.C.H.*, Hamish Hamilton, London.

Carlton, D. (1981), *Anthony Eden. A Biography*, Allen and Unwin, London (paperback edition, 1986).

Carlton, D. (1986), *Britain and the Suez Crisis*, Basil Blackwell, Oxford.

Challe, M., *Notre Révolte*, Paris, 1968.

Cohen, R. (1979), *Threat Perception in International Crisis*, The University of Wisconsin Press. Madison.

Colville, J. (1987), *The Fringes of Power. Downing Street Diaries, 1939-1955. Volume Two: 1941-April 1955*, Sceptre, Sevenoaks.

Cottam, R.W. (1988), *The United States and Iran. A Cold War Case Study*, University of Pittsburgh Press, Pittsburgh.

Crozier, W.P. (1973), *Off the Record. Political Interviews 1933-1943*, edited with an introduction by A.J.P. Taylor, Hutchinson of London, London.

Eden, A. (1939), *Foreign Affairs*, Faber and Faber, London, (Kraus Reprint, New York, 1971).

Eden, A. (1948), *Freedom and Order. Selected Speeches 1939-1946*, Houghton Mifflin, Boston.

Eden, A. (1949), *Days for Decision*, Faber and Faber, London.

Eden, A. (1960), *Full Circle*, Cassell, London.

Edmonds, R. (1986), *Setting the Mould. The United States and Britain, 1945-1950*, Clarendon, Oxford.

Ely, P. (1969), *Mémoires. ii. Suez...le 13 Mai*, Plon, Paris.

Epstein, L. (1960), 'Partisan Foreign Policy. Britain in the Suez Crisis', *World Politics*, Vol. 12, pp. 201-24.

Epstein, L. (1964), *British Politics in the Suez Crisis*, University of Illinois Press, Urbana.

Fennema, M. (1994), 'Dutch Policy Networks and Discourses in the Decolonization of Indonesia', *Acta Politica*, Vol. 29, pp. 147-71.

Ferro, M. (1982), *Suez. Naissance d'un Tiers Monde, 1956, Mémoire de Siècle*, Editions Complexe, Bruxelles.

Festinger, L. (1957), *A Theory of Cognitive Dissonance*, Stanford University Press, Stanford.

Fish, M.S. (1986), 'After Stalin's Death: The Anglo-American Debate Over a New Cold War', *Diplomatic History*, Vol. 10, pp. 333-55.

Flowers, M. (1977), 'A Laboratory Test of Some Implications of Janis's Groupthink Hypothesis', *Journal of Personality and Social Psychology*, Vol. 35, pp. 888-96.

Folly, M.H. (1988), 'Breaking the Vicious Circle: Britain, the United States, and the Genesis of the North Atlantic Treaty', *Diplomatic History*, Vol. 12, pp. 59-77.

Foot, R.J. (1986), 'Anglo-American Relations in the Korean Crisis: the British Effort to Avert an Expanded War. December 1950-January 1951', *Diplomatic History*, Vol. 10, pp. 43-58.

Foot, R.J. (1988/1989), 'Nuclear Coercion and the Ending of the Korean Conflict', *International Security*, Vol. 13, pp. 92-112.

Fuller, S.R. and Aldag, R.J. (1997), 'Challenging the Mindguards: Moving Small Group Analysis Beyond Groupthink', in P. 't Hart, E.K. Stern and B. Sundelius (eds.), *Beyond Groupthink. Political Group Dynamics and Foreign Policy-Making*, University of Michigan Press, Ann Arbor, pp. 55-93.

Fullick, R. and Powell, G. (1979), *Suez: the Double War*, Hamish Hamilton, London.

George, A.L. (1969), 'The "Operational Code": A Neglected Approach to the Study of Political Leaders and Decision Making', *International Studies Quarterly*, Vol. 13, pp. 190-222.

George, A.L. (1979a), 'The Causal Nexus between Cognitive Beliefs and Decision Making Behavior. The "Operational Code" Construct', in L. Falkowski (ed.), *Psychological Models in International Politics*, Westview, Boulder, pp. 95-124.

George, A.L. (1979b), 'Case Studies and Theory Development: the Method of Structured, Focused Comparison', in P. Lauren (ed.), *Diplomacy. New Approaches in History, Theory and Policy*, The Free Press, New York, pp. 43-69.

George, A.L. (1980), *Presidential Decisionmaking in Foreign Policy. The Effective Use of Information and Advice*, Westview, Boulder.

George, A.L. (1997), 'From Groupthink to Contextual Analysis of Policy-Making Groups', in P. 't Hart, E.K. Stern, and B. Sundelius (eds.), *Beyond Groupthink. Political Group Dynamics and Foreign Policy-Making*, University of Michigan Press, Ann Arbor, pp. 35-53.

George, A.L. and Holsti, O.R. (1975), 'The Effects of Stress on the Performance of Foreign Policy-Makers', in C.P. Cotter (ed.), *Political Science Annual. Volume 6*, Bobbs-Merrill, Indianapolis, pp. 255-319.

Gorst, A. (2000), '"A Modern Major General": General Sir Gerald Templer, Chief of the Imperial General Staff', in S. Kelly and A. Ghost (eds.), *Whitehall and the Suez Crisis*, Frank Cass, London, pp. 29-45.

Grove, E., and Rohan, S. (2000), 'The Limits of Opposition: Admiral Earl Mountbatten of Burma, First Sea Lord and Chief of Naval Staff', in S. Kelly and A. Ghost (eds.), *Whitehall and the Suez Crisis*, Frank Cass, London, pp. 98-116.

Halperin, M.H., with the assistance of P. Clapp and A. Kanter (1974), *Bureaucratic Politics and Foreign Policy*, Brookings, Washington.

Hamwee, J., Miall, H. and Elworthy, S. (1990), 'The Assumptions of British Nuclear Weapons Decision-makers', *Journal of Peace Research*, Vol. 27, pp. 359-72.

Haney, P.J. (1997), *Organizing for Foreign Policy Crises. Presidents, Advisers, and the Management of Decision Making*, University of Michigan Press, Ann Arbor.

Hart, J.A. (1977), 'Cognitive Maps of Three Latin American Policy Makers', *World Politics*, Vol. 30, pp. 115-40.

Hart, P. 't (1990/1994), *Groupthink in Government. A Study of Small Groups and Policy Failure*, Swets and Zeitlinger, Amsterdam, The Johns Hopkins University Press, Baltimore.

Hart, P. 't, Rosenthal, U. and Kouzmin, A. (1993), 'Crisis Decision Making. The Centralization Thesis Revisited', *Administration & Society*, Vol. 25, pp. 12-45.

Hart, P. 't, Stern, E.K. and Sundelius, B. (eds.) (1997), *Beyond Groupthink. Political Group Dynamics and Foreign Policy-Making*, University of Michigan Press, Ann Arbor.

Heikal, M.H. (1986), *Cutting the Lion's Tail. Suez Through Egyptian Eyes*, André Deutsch, London.

Heller, J. (1983), 'The Dangers of Groupthink', *The Guardian*, 31 January, p. 13.

Heradstveit, D. (1981), *The Arab-Israeli Conflict. Psychological Obstacles to Peace*, Universitetsverlaget, Oslo, Bergen, Tromsø.

Herek, G.M., Janis, I.L. and Huth P. (1987), 'Decision Making During International Crises. Is Quality of Process Related to Outcome?', *Journal of Conflict Resolution*, Vol. 31, pp. 203-26.

Hermann, C.F. (1969), 'International Crisis as a Situational Variable', in J.N. Rosenau (ed.), *International Relations and Foreign Policy*, The Free Press, New York, pp. 409-21.

Hermann, C.F., and Mason, R.E. (1980), 'Identifying Behavioral Attributes of Events that Trigger International Crises', in O.R. Holsti et al. (eds.), *Change in the International System*, Westview, Boulder, pp. 189-210.

Hermann, M.G. (1979), 'Indications of Stress in Policymakers During Foreign Policy Crises', *Political Psychology*, Vol. 1, pp. 27-46.

Hermann, M.G. and Hermann, C.F. (1989), 'Who Makes Foreign Policy Decisions and How: An Empirical Enquiry', *International Studies Quarterly*, Vol. 33, pp. 361-87.

Hermann, M.G. and Preston, T. (1994), 'Presidents, Advisers, and Foreign Policy: The Effect of Leadership Style on Executive Arrangements', *Political Psychology*, Vol. 15, pp. 75-96.

Herring Jr., G.A. (1965), *Experiment in Foreign Aid: Lend-Lease, 1941-1945*, Dissertation University of Virginia, University Microfilms, Ann Arbor.

Holsti, O.R. (1970) 'The "Operational Code" Approach to the Study of Political Leaders: John Foster Dulles' Philosophical and Instrumental Beliefs', *Canadian Journal of Political Science*, Vol. 3, pp. 123-57.

Holsti, O.R. (1972), *Crisis, Escalation, War*, McGill Queens University Press, Montreal and London.

Holsti, O.R. (1976a), 'Foreign Policy Decision Makers Viewed Psychologically: "Cognitive Process" Approaches', in J.N. Rosenau (ed.), *In Search of Global Patterns*, The Free Press, New York, pp. 120-44.

Holsti, O.R. (1976b), '"Operational Code" Belief Systems: A Code-Book', Final Report to the National Science Foundation.

Holsti, O.R. (1977), 'A Typology of "Operational Code" Belief Systems', paper presented to the Conference on Approaches to Decision Making, Oslo.

Holsti, O.R. (1979), 'Theories of Crisis Decision Making', in P.G. Lauren (ed.), *Diplomacy. New Approaches in History, Theory, and Policy*, The Free Press, New York, pp. 99-136.

Horne, A. (1988), *Macmillan 1894-1956. Volume 1 of the Official Biography*, Macmillan, London.

Ikenberry, G.J. (1989), 'Rethinking the Origins of American Hegemony', *Political Science Quarterly*, Vol. 104, pp. 375-400.

James, R.R. (1986), *Anthony Eden*, Weidenfeld and Nicolson, London.

Janis, I.L. (1959), 'Decisional Conflicts: A Theoretical Analysis', *Journal of Conflict Resolution*, Vol. 3, pp. 6-27.

Janis, I.L. (1982), *Groupthink. Psychological Studies of Policy Decisions and Fiascoes*, (revised second edition), Houghton Mifflin, Boston.

Janis, I.L. (1985), 'Sources of Error in Strategic Decision Making', in J.M. Pennings (ed.), *Organizational Strategy and Change. New Views on Formulating and Implementing Strategic Decisions*, Jossey-Bass, San Francisco, pp. 157-97.

Janis, I.L. (1989), *Crucial Decisions. Leadership in Policymaking and Crisis Management*, The Free Press, New York.

Janis, I.L. and Mann, L. (1977), *Decision Making. A Psychological Analysis of Conflict, Choice, and Commitment*, The Free Press, New York.

Jervis, R. (1976), *Perception and Misperception in International Politics*, Princeton University Press, Princeton.

Jervis, R. (1985), 'Perceiving and Coping with Threat', in R. Jervis, R.N. Lebow and J.G. Stein, *Psychology and Deterrence*, The Johns Hopkins University Press, Baltimore, pp. 13-33.

Johnman, L. (2000), 'Playing the Role of Cassandra: Sir Gerald Fitzmaurice, Senior Legal Advisor to the Foreign Office', in S. Kelly and A. Ghost (eds.), *Whitehall and the Suez Crisis*, Frank Cass, London, pp. 46-63.

Johnston, L.K. (1977), 'Operational Codes and the Prediction of Leadership Behavior: Senator Frank Church at Midcareer', in M.G. Hermann and T.W. Milburn (eds.), *A Psychological Examination of Political Leaders*, The Free Press, New York, pp. 80-119.

Jönsson, C. (1987), *International Aviation and the Politics of Regime Change*, Frances Pinter, London.

Jönsson, C. (1990), *Communication in International Bargaining*, Pinter, London.

Kaarbo, J. (1997), 'Prime Minister Leadership Styles in Foreign Policy Decision Making: A Framework for Research', *Political Psychology*, Vol. 18, pp. 553-81.

Kaarbo, J. and Beasley, R. (1999), 'A Practical Guide to the Comparative Case Study Method in Political Psychology', *Political Psychology*, Vol. 20, pp. 369-91.

Kameda, T. and Sugimori, S. (1993), 'Psychological Entrapment in Group Decision Making: An Assigned Decision Rule and a Groupthink Phenomenon', *Journal of Personality and Social Psychology*, Vol. 65, pp. 282-92.

Kelly, S. (2000), 'Transatlantic Diplomat: Sir Roger Makins, Ambassador to Washington and Joint Permanent Secretary to the Treasury', in S. Kelly and A. Gorst (eds.), *Whitehall and the Suez Crisis*, Frank Cass, London, pp. 157-77.

Keohane, R.O. (1984), *After Hegemony. Cooperation and Discord in the World Political Economy*, Princeton University Press, Princeton.

Kilmuir, Earl of (1964), *Political Adventure. The Memoirs of the Earl of Kilmuir*, Weidenfeld and Nicolson, London.

King, A. (1994), 'Ministerial Autonomy in Britain', in M. Laver and K.A. Shepsle (eds.), *Cabinet Ministers and Parliamentary Government*, Cambridge University Press, Cambridge, pp. 203-25.

Klotz, A. (1995), *Norms in International Relations*, Cornell University Press, Ithaca.

Kowert, P.A. (2002), *Groupthink or Deadlock. When Do Leaders Learn from Their Advisors?*, State University of New York Press, Albany.

Krasner, S. (1972), 'Are Bureaucracies Important? (Or Allison Wonderland)', *Foreign Policy*, Vol. 7, pp. 159-79.

Kunz, D. (1989), 'The Importance of Having Money: The Economic Diplomacy of the Suez Crisis', in W.R. Louis and R. Owen (eds.), *Suez 1956. The Crisis and its Consequences*, Oxford University Press, Oxford, pp. 215-32.

Kyle, K. (1989), 'Britain and the Crisis, 1955-1956', in W.R. Louis and R. Owen (eds.), *Suez 1956. The Crisis and its Consequences*, Oxford University Press, Oxford, pp. 103-30.

Kyle, K. (1991), *Suez*, Weidenfeld and Nicolson, London.

Kyle, K. (2000), 'The Mandarins' Mandarin: Sir Norman Brook, Secretary of the Cabinet', in S. Kelly and A. Ghost (eds.), *Whitehall and the Suez Crisis*, Frank Cass, London, pp. 64-78.

Lamb, R. (1987), *The Failure of the Eden Government*, Sidgwick and Jackson, London.

Larson, D.W. (1985), *Origins of Containment. A Psychological Explanation*, Princeton University Press, Princeton.

Leitner, M. (1985), 'Iran's Attempt at Oil Nationalization, 1951-1953: Causes and Consequences', in Eylah Kadjar et al., *Moyen-Orient. Perspectives Regionales et Internationales, Cahiers d'Histoire et de Politique Internationale, no. 5*, Institut Universitaire de Hautes Etudes Internationales, Geneva, pp. 34-69.

Levi, A. and Tetlock, P.E. (1980), 'A Cognitive Analysis of Japan's 1941 Decision for War', *Journal of Conflict Resolution*, Vol. 24, pp. 195-211.

Little, R. and Smith, S. (eds.) (1988), *Belief Systems and International Relations*, Basil Blackwell, Oxford.

Lloyd, J.S. (1978), *Suez 1956. A Personal Account*, Jonathan Cape, London.

Longley, J. and Pruitt, D.G. (1980), 'Groupthink. A Critique of Janis's Theory', in L. Wheeler (ed.), *Review of Personality and Social Psychology. Volume 1*, SAGE, Beverly Hills, pp. 74-93.

Louis, W.R. (1984), *The British Empire and the Middle East, 1945-1951. Arab Nationalism, the United States and Postwar Imperialism*, Oxford University Press, Oxford.

Louis, W.R. (1985), 'American Anti-Colonialism and the Dissolution of the British Empire', *International Affairs*, Vol. 61, pp. 395-420.

Louis, W.R. (1986), 'A Prima Donna with Honour', *Times Literary Supplement*, 31 October 1986, pp. 1207-09.

Love, K. (1969), *Suez: the Twice-Fought War*, McGraw Hill, New York.

Lundestad, G. (1998), *'Empire' by Integration. The United States and European Integration, 1945-1997*, Oxford University Press, Oxford.

McDermott, G. (1969), *The Eden Legacy and the Decline of British Diplomacy*, Leslie Frewin, London.

McLellan, D.S. (1971), 'The "Operational Code" Approach to the Study of Political Leaders: Dean Acheson's Philosophical and Instrumental Beliefs', *Canadian Journal of Political Science*, Vol. 4, pp. 52-75.

Macmillan, H.(1969), *Tides of Fortune, 1945-1955*, Macmillan, London.

Macmillan, H. (1971), *Riding the Storm, 1956-1959*, Macmillan, London.

March, J.G. and J.P. Olsen (1989), *Rediscovering Institutions*, The Free Press, New York.

Marston, G. (1988), 'Armed Intervention in the 1956 Suez Canal Crisis: the Legal Advice Tendered to the British Government', *International and Comparative Law Quarterly*, Vol. 37, pp. 773-817.

Mastanduno, M. (1988), 'Trade as Strategic Weapon: American and Alliance Export Control Policy in the Early Postwar Period', *International Organization*, Vol. 42, pp. 121-50.

Menzies, R. (1967), *Afternoon Light. Some Memoirs of Men and Events*, Cassell, London.

Metselaar, M.V. and Verbeek, B. (1997), 'Beyond Decision Making in Formal and Informal Groups: The Dutch cabinet and the West New Guinea Conflict', in P. 't Hart, E.K. Stern and B. Sundelius (eds.), *Beyond Groupthink. Political Group Dynamics and Foreign Policy-Making*, University of Michigan Press, Ann Arbor, pp. 95-122.

Murphy, R. (1964), *Diplomat Among Warriors*, Doubleday and Company, Garden City.

Neff, D. (1981), *Warriors at Suez. Eisenhower takes the United States into the Middle East*, the Linden Press, Simon and Schuster, New York.

Negrine, R. (1982), 'The Press and the Suez Crisis: A Myth Re-Examined', *The Historical Journal*, Vol. 25, pp. 975-83.

Neustadt, R.E. (1970), *Alliance Politics*, Columbia University Press, New York.

Neustadt, R.E. and May, E.R. (1986), *Thinking in Time. The Uses of History for Decisionmakers*, The Free Press, New York.

Nutting, A. (1967), *No End of a Lesson. The Story of Suez*, Clarkson N. Potter, New York.

Parmentier, G. (1980), 'The British Press in the Suez Crisis', *The Historical Journal*, Vol. 23, pp. 435-48.

Peters, A.R. (1986), *Anthony Eden at the Foreign Office 1931-1938*, St. Martin's Press, New York.

Peters, B.G. (1998), *Institutional Theory in Political Science. The 'New Institutionalism'*, Pinter, London.

Pineau, C. (1976), *1956, Suez*, Robert Laffont, Paris.

Post, J.M. and Robins, R.S. (1993), *When Illness Strikes the Leader*, Yale University Press, New Haven.

Preston, T. (2001), *The President and His Inner Circle. Leadership Style and the Advisory Process in Foreign Affairs*, University of Columbia Press, New York.

Preston, T. and Hart, P. 't (1999), 'Understanding and Evaluating Bureaucratic Politics: The Nexus Between Political Leaders and Advisory Systems', *Political Psychology*, Vol. 20, pp. 49-98.

Putnam, R.D. (1988), 'Diplomacy and Domestic Politics: The Logic of Two-Level Games', *International Organization*, Vol. 42, pp. 427-69.

Reid, B.H. (1988), 'The "Northern Tier" and "Baghdad Pact"', in J.W. Young (ed.), *The Foreign Policy of Churchill's Peacetime Administration 1951-1955*, Leicester University Press, Worcester, pp. 159-80.

Reynolds, D. (1989), 'Eden the Diplomatist, 1931-56: Suezside of a Statesman?', *History*, No. 289, pp. 64-84.

Risse, T. (1995), *Cooperation among Democracies*, Princeton University Press, Princeton.

Roberts, J.N. (1988), *Decision-Making during International Crises*, Macmillan, Houndmills.

Robertson, T. (1964), *Crisis. The Inside Story of the Suez Conspiracy*, Hutchinson, London.

Rosati, J.A. (1995), 'A Cognitive Approach to the Study of Foreign Policy', in L. Neack, J.A.K. Hey and P.J. Haney (eds.), *Foreign Policy Analysis. Continuity and Change in Its Second Generation*, Prentice Hall, Englewood Cliffs, pp. 49-70.

Rose, R. (2001), *The Prime Minister in a Shrinking World*, Polity, Cambridge.

Rubin, B. (1982), 'America and the Egyptian Revolution 1950-1957', *Political Science Quarterly*, Vol. 96, pp. 73-90.

Ryan, H.B. (1987), *The Vision of Anglo-America. The US/UK Alliance and the Emerging Cold War, 1943-1946*, Cambridge University Press, Cambridge.

Sbrega, J.J. (1983), *Anglo-American Relations and Colonialism in East Asia, 1941-1945*, Garland Publishing, New York.

Schafer, M. and Crichlow, S. (1996), 'Antecedents of Groupthink', *Journal of Conflict Resolution*, Vol. 40, pp. 415-35.

Schafer, M. and Crichlow, S. (2000), 'Bill Clinton's Operational Code: Assessing Source Material Bias', *Political Psychology*, Vol. 21, pp. 559-71.

Schafer, M. and Crichlow, S. (2002), 'The *Process-Outcome* Connection in Foreign Policy Decision Making: A Quantitative Study Building on Groupthink', *International Studies Quarterly*, Vol. 46, pp. 45-68.

Schelling, T.C. (1966), *Arms and Influence*, Yale University Press, New Haven.

Seymour-Ure, C. (1984), 'British "War Cabinets" in Limited Wars: Korea, Suez and the Falklands', *Public Administration*, Vol. 62, pp. 181-200.

Shimko, K. (1995), 'Foreign Policy Metaphors: Falling "Dominoes" and Drug "Wars"', in L. Neck, J.A.K. Hey and P.J. Haney (eds.), *Foreign Policy Analysis. Conituity and Change in Its Second Generation*, Englewood Cliffs, Prentice Hall, pp. 71-84.

Shlaim, A. (1983), *The United States and the Berlin Blockade, 1948-1949. A Study in Crisis Decision Making*, University of California Press, Berkeley.

Shuckburgh, E. (1986), *Descent to Suez. Diaries 1951-1956*, Weidenfeld and Nicolson, London.

Sjöblom, G. (1982), 'Some Problems of the Operational Code Approach', in C. Jönsson (ed.), *Cognitive Dynamics and International Politics*, Frances Pinter, London, pp. 37-74.

Smith, Steve, 'Groupthink and the Hostage Rescue Mission', *British Journal of Political Science*, (15), 1, 1984, pp. 117-23.

Sørensen, V. (1989), 'Economic Recovery versus Containment: the Anglo-American Controversy over East-West Trade, 1947-1951', *Cooperation and Conflict*, Vol. 24, pp. 69-97.

Spaak, P.-H. (1969), *Combats Inachevés I. De l'Indédependence à l'Alliance*, Fayard, Paris.

Starr, H. (1984), *Henry Kissinger. Perceptions of International Politics*, University of Kentucky Press, Lexington.

Steiner, Z. (1987), 'Decision Making in American and British Foreign Policy: an Open and Shut Case', *Review of International Studies*, Vol. 13, pp. 1-18.

Stern, E.K. and Verbeek, B. (eds.) (1998), 'Whither the Study of Governmental Politics in Foreign Policymaking? A Symposium', *Mershon International Studies Review*, Vol. 42, pp. 205-55.

Strange, S. (1988), *States and Markets. An Introduction to International Political Economy*, Pinter, London.

Stuart, D.T. and Starr, H. (1981/1982) 'The "Inherent Bad Faith Model" Revisited: Dulles, Kennedy, and Kissinger', *Political Psychology*, Vol. 3, pp. 1-33.

Sylvan, D.A. and Voss, J.F. (eds.), *Problem Representation in Foreign Policy Decision Making*, Cambridge University Press, Cambridge.

Tetlock, P.E., Peterson R.S., McGuire, C., Chang, S. and Feld, P. (1992), 'Assessing Political Group Dynamics: A Test of the Groupthink Model', *Journal of Personality and Social Psyhology*, Vol. 63, pp. 403-25.

Thomas, H. (1986), *The Suez Affair*, Weidenfeld and Nicolson, London (1st. edition 1967).

Thomas, H. (1987), *Armed Truce. The Beginnings of the Cold War*, Atheneum, New York.

Vaisse, M. (1989), 'France and the Suez Crisis', in W.R. Louis and R. Owen (eds.), *Suez 1956. The Crisis and its Consequences*, Oxford University Press, Oxford, pp. 131-45.

Verbeek, B. (1992), *Anglo-American Relations, 1945-1956. A Comparison of Neorealist and Cognitive Psychological Approaches to the Study of International Relations*, Ph.D dissertation, European University Institute, Florence.

Verbeek, B. (1994), 'Do Individual and Group Beliefs Matter? British Decision-Making during the 1956 Suez Crisis', *Cooperation and Conflict*, Vol. 29, pp. 307-32.

Vertzberger, Y. (1990), *The Worlds in Their Minds. Information Processing, Cognition, and Perception in Foreign Policy Decisionmaking*, Stanford University Press, Stanford.

Walker, S.G. (1977), 'The Interface Between Beliefs and Behavior. Henry Kissinger's Operational Code and the Vietnam War', *Journal of Conflict Resolution*, Vol. 21, pp. 129-68.

Walker, S.G. (ed.) (1987), *Role Theory and Foreign Policy Analysis*, Duke University Press, Durham.

Walker, S.G. (1990), 'The Evolution of Operational Code Analysis', *Political Psychology*, Vol. 11, pp. 403-17.

Walker, S.G. and Falkowski, L.S. (1984), 'The Operational Codes of U.S. Presidents and Secretaries of State: Motivational Foundations and Behavioral Consequences', *Political Psychology*, Vol. 5, pp. 237-66.

Walker, S.G. and Murphy, T.G. (1981/1982), 'The Utility of the Operational Code in Political Forecasting', *Political Psychology*, Vol. 3, pp. 24-60.

Walker, S.G., Schafer, M. and Young, M.D. (1998), 'Systematic Procedures for Operational Code Analysis: Measuring and Modeling Jimmy Carter's Operational Code', *International Studies Quarterly*, Vol. 42, pp. 175-89.

Walker, S.G. and Watson, G.L. (1992), 'The Cognitive Maps of British Leaders, 1938-1939', in E. Singer and V. Hudson (eds.), *Political Psychology and Foreign Policy*, Westview, Boulder, pp. 31-58.

Waltz, K.N. (1979), *Theory of International Politics*, Addison Wesley, Reading.

Waltz, K.N. (1988), 'The Origins of War in Neorealist Theory', *Journal of Interdisciplinary History*, Vol. 18, pp. 615-28.

Warner, G. (1979), '"Collusion" and the Suez Crisis of 1956', *International Affairs*, Vol. 32, pp. 226-39.

Watt, D.C. (1965), *Personalities and Policies. Studies in the Formulation of British Foreign Policy in the Twentieth Century*, Greenwood Press, Westport.

Watt, D.C. (1984), *Succeeding John Bull. America in Britain's Place*, Cambridge University Press, Cambridge.

Weiler, P. (1987), 'British Labour and the Cold War: the Foreign Policy of the Labour Governments, 1945-1951', *Journal of British Studies*, Vol. 26, pp. 54-82.

Welch, D. (1992), 'The Organizational Process and Bureaucratic Politics Paradigms: Retrospect and Prospect', *International Security*, Vol. 17, pp. 112-46.

Wilkie, J.H. (1984), *The Influence of British Arms. An Analysis of British Military Intervention Since 1956*, Allen and Unwin, London.

# Index